Tanglewood

The
Clash
between
Tradition
and Change

Northeastern University ⌒ 1898–1998

Tanglewood

The
Clash
between
Tradition
and Change

ANDREW L. PINCUS

Northeastern University Press
Boston

Northeastern University Press

Copyright 1998 by Andrew L. Pincus

Library of Congress Cataloging-in-Publication Data

Pincus, Andrew L., 1930–

Tanglewood : the clash between tradition and change / Andrew L. Pincus.

    p.   cm.

Includes index.

ISBN 1-55553-346-9 (cloth : alk. paper)

I. Title.   1. Tanglewood (Music festival). 2. Boston Symphony Orchestra.

ML38.L393T362 1998

780'.79'7441—dc21   98-9605

                        MN

Designed by Diane Levy

Composed in Simoncini Garamond by Graphic Composition, Athens, Georgia. Printed and bound by Thomson-Shore, Inc., Dexter, Michigan. The paper is Glatfelter Supple Opaque Recycled, an acid-free sheet.

MANUFACTURED IN THE UNITED STATES OF AMERICA

02 01 00 99 98   5 4 3 2 1

Dedicated to the memory of Louis Krasner

"All great masters, each in the language of his own time, address themselves innerly to man and his universe."

—Tanglewood, July 11, 1985

Contents

Illustrations

Foreword

Perhaps fifteen years into my performance life I decided it was certainly time I sang a recital of songs all in English, my mother tongue and that of the great majority of my audiences in the United States. After all, recitals at which American audiences may hear the standard German lieder are not infrequent. My manager strongly disapproved of my plan but I held firm. He politely did not say "I told you so" when the presenter of the concert called immediately to say that he did not want a "radical" program like that, but a "regular" song recital. That means one in which songs are in two or three languages almost no one understands, and perhaps an encore or so in English.

On another occasion, as I was getting into a cab after singing Carlisle Floyd's *Susannah*, the driver asked which opera had been performed. I replied, "A new American opera, *Susannah*." He turned to me and said, "An American opera? What language can you sing it in?"

With such prejudices abroad, one can appreciate the enormous problems in programming for today's audiences, getting new music before the public, and keeping the musical arts alive and growing and the audiences coming. The variety of music in the United States has never before been so great. Jazz, pop, rock, country, country western, salsa, light classical, early music, nineteenth-century romantic, atonal, aleatory: one could easily expand the list. Expectations as to the nature of "good" music depend on nearly limitless factors: experience, taste, education, family, emotion, reaction to sound, standards of the society one keeps, and so on. The effect on recital hall, symphony hall, and opera house is of deep concern to institutions, managements, boards, and audiences of markedly varied interests. A particular concern is the conflict in programming beloved classics and contemporary music and how that conflict affects attendance, funding, and commitment to the finest in music, old and new. Our great performing institutions must not be museums but educate as well as entertain, must celebrate creativity of our own time, and must somehow keep and build audiences.

Using his twenty-three years of close attention to the great Tanglewood music festival of the Boston Symphony, Andrew Pincus, experienced as a musician, avid listener, scholar, and critic, vividly and thoroughly observes these struggles between tradition and change. He shows us how excruciatingly difficult it is to balance standard masterpieces and their devotees with unusual and contemporary repertory and its enthusiasts, to schedule superstars and present brilliant new artists, all the while maintaining full houses. Pincus delves into these thickets in hopes of clearing a way out. The Tanglewood Music Center, which has played such a vital role in American musical life, as well as the symphony, chamber music, recital, and contemporary series come under his scrutiny. This is a valuable book for music lovers, patrons, concert producers, and musicians.

—Phyllis Curtin

Author's Note

In one sense this book is a sequel to my *Scenes from Tanglewood* (1989), a look at the personalities and dynamics in the making of a major music festival. In a broader sense the new book stands by itself. *Scenes from Tanglewood* examined developments from 1975 through 1988, ending with the seventieth-birthday celebration for Leonard Bernstein. *Tanglewood: The Clash between Tradition and Change* picks up at that point and carries the story to the present. But now I attempt to place Tanglewood within the larger context of American musical life during the period, a time when popular culture and commercial forces are transforming the face of serious music and high art in general.

Tanglewood provides a unique laboratory for a study of this kind. Although it offers a smattering of popular events, it is primarily a classical music festival and the summer home of the Boston Symphony Orchestra. Yet by design it attracts a large audience with many listeners who are not regular concertgoers or operagoers. If high art is to survive in an age dominated by television, film, rock, and other aspects of popular culture, it is uninitiated listeners like these whom it must reach. The problem becomes how to reach them without compromising the nature of an art. Already the temptations facing symphony orchestras—and arts institutions generally—are evident in programming, marketing, and fund-raising techniques in widespread use to sell music. At Tanglewood, with its expanse of lawn to accommodate audiences in the thousands, these techniques come into play on a wide vista. The opportunities for good and ill are writ large.

This book is based on my twenty-three years of covering Tanglewood as a music critic, primarily for the *Berkshire Eagle.* I have drawn on my own writings for the *Eagle* along with other work I have done for the *New York Times* and the *Boston Globe.* Except where otherwise indicated, all quotations are from my own interviews and reporting. Notes on other sources appear at the end.

Many people have helped, directly or indirectly, with the preparation of the book. I particularly want to acknowledge the assistance of Daniel R. Gustin, Anthony Fogg, Sarah J. Harrington, Susanna Bonta, and Caleb Cochran of the Boston Symphony staff. Jeremy Yudkin offered encouragement during the early stages of the writing, and my editor at Northeastern

University Press, William A. Frohlich, was a constant goad to get me to dig deeper. I am also indebted to the musicians whom I have quoted by name and to others who spoke to me in confidence. Without all of them I could not have put together this mosaic and its picture of an art whose importance to America remains greater than its troubles, numerous as they are.

Lenox, Massachusetts
July 1997

Tanglewood

The

Clash

between

Tradition

and Change

Prologue

The House That Koussevitzky Built

A Short History of Tanglewood

SET ON FIVE HUNDRED ACRES overlooking a picturesque lake and the Berkshire Hills of western Massachusetts, Tanglewood is known around the world as the summer home of the Boston Symphony Orchestra. But the BSO's eight weekends of concerts, which attract thousands of picnickers and other listeners to the spacious lawn outside the Koussevitzky Music Shed, are only the most visible side of this beehive of music.

Just as importantly, there is the Tanglewood Music Center, one of the world's leading academies for advanced studies in classical music, providing 150 students with full-tuition fellowships each year. These students give orchestral, chamber, and vocal concerts of their own, often combining the virtues of youthful zest and professional polish. Other major events take place in the weeklong Festival of Contemporary Music, the East Coast's premiere new-music festival and one of the most important in the country. The Boston University Tanglewood Institute offers a separate training program for high school–age musicians, who present their own concert series. Leading professional artists from the United States and abroad appear in a midweek recital and chamber series as well as in the BSO's concerts. Many of these programs present important debuts or premieres.

Serge Koussevitzky, the BSO's music director from 1924 until 1949, is known as Tanglewood's founding father. While it is true that the imperious Russian conductor brought the BSO to the Berkshires, it was actually a group of Berkshire socialites—mostly women—who conceived the idea of music under the summer stars. This committee, headed by Gertrude Robinson Smith, a New Yorker and summer Berkshire resident, decided in the early 1930s to create an American version of Austria's Salzburg Festival, the summer home of the Vienna Philharmonic. Although the United States was mired in the Great Depression, she had reason to believe the idea would take root in the Berkshires. Since the nineteenth century the region had been a watering place for wealthy New Yorkers and others—Vanderbilts, Westinghouses, and Carnegies among them. The "cottagers," as these residents modestly referred to themselves, answered the musical call to arms, even if the year-round citizenry was less enthusiastic. Tanglewood thus followed in a literary and artistic tradition that had attracted such figures as Melville, Hawthorne, Edith Wharton, and Fanny Kemble to the Berkshires in an earlier time.

The committee first engaged members of the New York Philharmonic, under Henry Hadley, to give two weekends of concerts in a riding ring during the summers of 1934 and 1935. The Philharmonic, however, chose to concentrate on its own summer concert series in New York, and when the committee in 1936 turned to Koussevitzky for a replacement, he jumped at the opportunity. Despite some reluctance by the orchestra's trustees, he and the BSO made their Berkshire debut on an estate about three miles east of the present Tanglewood. The three concerts, performed in a single weekend in 1936, took place under a tent.

Not content with the makeshift setting, Koussevitzky quickly began pressing for a permanent site with a concert pavilion. But where? And how would the BSO find the money? Enter a deus ex machina: in the winter of 1936–37 Mrs. Gorham Brooks, a Boston resident and BSO patron, and Miss Mary Aspinwall Tappan, her elderly aunt, offered their unoccupied estate in Lenox and Stockbridge as a home for the festival. The 210-acre property was called Tanglewood, a name that Hawthorne had bestowed upon it while living there as a guest of the Tappan family in 1850–51. (A replica of his cottage provides teaching studios today.) The BSO trustees accepted the descendants' offer, and on this site, under the aegis of the Berkshire committee, Koussevitzky founded his festival. On August 5, 1937, he conducted the BSO in an all-Beethoven program, the first of six concerts spread over two weekends, that launched the Tanglewood of today.

The first year's concerts, which attracted widespread attention in the press, still took place in a tent. Planning began for a permanent pavilion, but money was hard to come by and the construction faced delays. Enter a deus ex machina of another kind: a whopping thunderstorm during an all-Wagner program on the opening night of the second weekend in 1937. As concertgoers in all their finery (people dressed for concerts then) became mired in rain and mud under the dripping tent, Gertrude Robinson Smith took the stage during intermission to appeal for money, on the spot, to build the pavilion. By the end of the quagmire evening, $30,000 of the necessary $100,000 had been subscribed. The rest quickly followed, and the Music Shed—today's open-sided five-thousand-seat pavilion—opened with the 1938 season.

In 1940 Koussevitzky realized a vision he had cherished ever since his days in Russia, which he had left in 1920: an "academy of music and art" where "the greatest living composers would teach the art of composition, the greatest virtuosi, the art of perfect performance, the greatest conductors, the mystery of conducting orchestras and choruses." Thus was born the Berkshire (now Tanglewood) Music Center, which still functions on the principles that Koussevitzky laid down.

The greatest composers were embodied in Aaron Copland, the faculty chairman for the first quarter-century; the greatest virtuosi, in cellist Gregor Piatigorsky, who headed the chamber music program; the greatest conductors, in Koussevitzky himself and his young protégé Leonard Bernstein, who remained a Tanglewood fixture until his final concert, which took place at Tanglewood fifty years later, just a few weeks before his death. A grand total of 312 young musicians pursued six weeks of studies in opera as well as chamber music, conducting, and choral and orchestral work. The emphasis, which continues today, was on ensemble performance and collegiality rather than instrumental studies or solo careers. Meanwhile, the BSO season was extended to three weeks.

The next step was the opening of the twelve-hundred-seat Theater–Concert Hall in 1941. Facing the Shed across the lawn, it served as the home of the Music Center's concerts and operas until its replacement in 1994 by Seiji Ozawa Hall. Such noted conductors as Bernstein, Ozawa, Zubin Mehta, and Claudio Abbado led some of their earliest performances in this barnlike venue. There, too, such leading singers as Phyllis Curtin, Leontyne Price, and Sherrill Milnes got their grounding in a pioneering opera program run by Boris Goldovsky until 1962, and leading professional soloists and chamber ensembles appeared.

The war years slowed but did not stop Koussevitzky. After Pearl Harbor he kept the Music Center going, partly at his own expense, for a six-week session in 1942, but gas rationing put an end to the BSO's season in the country. In 1943 Koussevitzky had to content himself with chamber concerts in the Lenox Library as a Red Cross benefit. In 1944 and 1945, however, he was able to muster a chamber-sized BSO to present two weekends of Bach-Mozart concerts in the Theater–Concert Hall.

The festival and school reopened in full force in 1946, with the BSO again

Layout of the original and new Tanglewood campuses and their principal buildings. (Boston Symphony Orchestra)

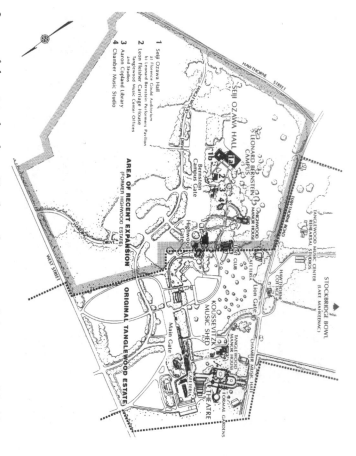

1 Seiji Ozawa Hall
  a) Florence Gould Auditorium
  b) Leonard Bernstein Performers' Pavilion
2 Leon Fleisher Carriage House and Studios
  Tanglewood Music Center Offices
3 Aaron Copland Library
4 Chamber Music Studio

playing three weeks of concerts in the Shed. Bernstein was back, now as Koussevitzky's assistant, and Goldovsky's opera department presented the American premiere of Benjamin Britten's *Peter Grimes*—one of Koussevitzky's many coups—with Bernstein in the pit and Britten in attendance. In 1948 Koussevitzky announced his intention to retire as BSO director the following year, when he would be seventy-five. He hoped to force the appointment of Bernstein as his successor, but the trustees, wary of hiring a jazz-playing, Broadway-wise young American, turned instead to a veteran Frenchman, Charles Munch. Koussevitzky remained active in Tanglewood performance and planning as an emeritus figure until his death, just before the 1951 season.

Tanglewood both prospered and languished during Munch's tenure, which lasted from 1949 until his retirement in 1962. The BSO season grew to the present eight weeks, and Munch became a mentor to Seiji Ozawa, who won the esteemed Koussevitzky Prize as a conducting student from Japan in 1960 and became the BSO's director thirteen years later. In 1956 the Fromm Music Foundation, created by Paul Fromm, a Chicago wine importer, began its support for a series of new music concerts. They were formalized eight years later as the Festival of Contemporary Music, today's weeklong orgy of twentieth-century classics, discoveries, and premieres. But Munch took a laissez-faire attitude toward the Music Center (and toward BSO rehearsals as well). Though such future luminaries as Abbado and Mehta, both members of the class of 1958, came for study, Munch's casual approach created a leadership vacuum. Bernstein became de facto head of the student conducting program, but over the succeeding years he faded from the scene as his celebrity and career blossomed.

Erich Leinsdorf, a stronger leader with an active interest in the Music Center, succeeded Munch in 1962. In one of his reforms he abolished the opera department, although he conducted sporadic operatic performances with both students and the BSO. He also instituted today's program of tuition-free fellowships, worked closely with the student conductors and orchestra, initiated the Festival of Contemporary Music, brought the Boston University Tanglewood Institute into the fold, and began a series of Friday evening prelude concerts of chamber music before the main BSO event. Those preludes, employing both BSO members and guest artists, continue to this day.

The Austrian-born Leinsdorf was a disciplinarian out of the old school, one of the last of the breed in an age of union contracts and democratic procedures. While the orchestra respected his musicianship, his tenure was marked by bad blood between him and both the players and the administration. He departed in 1969, to be succeeded for three years by the German-born William Steinberg. Ailing, and still director of the Pittsburgh Symphony, Steinberg gave notice that he could not be responsible for Tanglewood beyond conducting a few concerts.

To prevent another vacuum at the top, the BSO trustees named a triumvirate of Ozawa, Bernstein, and Gunther Schuller to run the summer activities in 1970, with Ozawa as the festival director. Returning to the fold, Bernstein assumed the title of adviser and began his acclaimed series of two-week residencies to conduct and teach. Schuller, a composer, conductor, educator, and author who had been head of contemporary music at the Music Center during Leinsdorf's last years, became the school's artistic director. He remained until 1984, when he resigned in a dispute with the BSO leadership, which he accused of pandering to commercial interests. Leon Fleisher, the gifted pianist who in the 1960s had lost the use of his right hand at the keyboard through overexertion at practice, succeeded him.

The 1970 appointment as festival director, which followed a series of well-received guest-conducting appearances with the BSO, was the first step in

Ozawa's ascent to the command of Koussevitzky's and Munch's orchestra. In 1972, when Steinberg retired, Ozawa became the BSO's music adviser, a polite title in this case for an interim director. He moved up to the directorship the following year.

Under Ozawa Tanglewood continued to expand. In 1978 chamber music took on heightened importance with the resumption of a midweek recital and chamber series, absent since 1968, and the inauguration of an opening weekend of concerts presented by the Boston Symphony Chamber Players. Made up of the BSO's first-chair members, the Chamber Players extended the season to nine weeks with their pre–July Fourth programs. Their concerts and the midweek series, both given in the Theater-Concert Hall, featured guest artists of international caliber—singers, pianists, other instrumentalists, trios, and quartets. In time, the midweek series grew to include chamber orchestras as well.

The next year Tanglewood hosted its first visiting orchestra, the New York Philharmonic. As its conductor, Zubin Mehta returned for the first time since his student summer to preside over the final weekend of concerts while the BSO embarked on a European festival tour. A precedent was set. In succeeding years one or more guest orchestras played Shed concerts while the BSO took a night off or traveled to Europe on other tours. In some years, too, celebrity soloists such as Itzhak Perlman, Yo-Yo Ma, or Leontyne Price gave Shed recitals, creating the odd spectacle of chamber music performed in a vast, open-sided pavilion for audiences numbering in the thousands.

In 1980 Ozawa was back with another innovation: opera. This was neither student opera nor opera in concert form such as Leinsdorf had espoused. With the BSO in the Shed, Ozawa began conducting a series of semistaged productions with international casts of singers. Because of the size and inflexibility of the Shed's stage, the annual presentations were limited to basic sets, costumes, lighting, and movement. But Ozawa insisted that Tanglewood would not be a complete festival, nor he a complete conductor, until both regularly performed opera. The series lasted through 1991, when a combination of financial and logistical problems forced its suspension. By then planning was under way for revival of a student opera program.

The next major step toward expansion involved real estate. In 1979 Tanglewood had acquired Seranak, Koussevitzky's former mansion and 170-acre hillside estate, as an off-campus teaching and social center. In 1986 acquisition of the 120-acre Highwood estate followed. Situated on the eastern flank of the original 210-acre festival grounds, Highwood offered the opportunity to build a new concert hall and other modern amenities. In 1994 eight years of planning and construction were crowned with the opening of Seiji Ozawa Hall, a $9.7 million, 1,180-seat building modeled on the great concert halls of Europe. Highwood was designated the Leonard Bernstein Campus; the Music Center offices, studios, and concerts were moved to the new site; and the barriers between the old and new properties were removed. Then in 1996, with Ozawa in the pit, the refurbished Theater–Concert Hall was returned to use as an opera house with another student production of *Peter Grimes*, marking the fiftieth anniversary of the opera's American premiere. The two performances also served as a trial run for a return of opera to Tanglewood's menu of orchestral, instrumental, vocal, conducting, and composition studies.

Although Tanglewood presents occasional Popular Artists concerts, it is, preeminently, a center for classical music performance and study. Attendance has steadily risen over the years, reaching as high as 18,700 for a single concert and 5/6,500 for a season. About 20 percent of the members of the country's principal symphony orchestras, according to BSO records, are alumni of the Music Center. The list of conductors, singers, and ensemble players who have made careers is endless. In addition to the twenty-four Shed concerts by the BSO and guest artists, Tanglewood each year presents about twenty professional recitals and chamber concerts, the Boston Pops, the Festival of Contemporary Music, a Labor Day weekend jazz festival, and almost daily programs by student ensembles, including the professional-level Tanglewood Music Center Orchestra.

No longer a musical oasis, Tanglewood is an international festival on a par with those in Europe. And unlike those festivals or any other in the world, Tanglewood runs an internationally renowned school in conjunction with a major symphony orchestra's concerts. The elegance of ambiance and dress in the early years has been replaced by a democracy of listeners in many states of dress (and sometimes near-undress). Little did that band of socialites in the 1930s realize how their Salzburg would be transformed by larger developments in American life.

1

A Shot Fired across the Bow

As a HEAT WAVE smothered the Northeast on July 7, 1994, an international press corps of about 120 music and architecture critics, lifestyle writers, reporters, and cameramen—representing news media from the *New York Times* and CNN to the BBC and Japanese newspapers—gathered on the lawn at Tanglewood. Under a sodden sky the assemblage feasted on box lunches, courtesy of the festival's press office, while waiting for an orchestral rehearsal to end. After half an hour of overtime, conductor Seiji Ozawa emerged with cellist Yo-Yo Ma and Norio Ohga, president and CEO of the Sony Corporation, to face the battery of cameras, microphones, pads, and pencils.

The press conference proved anticlimactic. The perspiring speakers' banter and pleasantries turned up nothing more newsworthy than Ozawa's admission that the whole affair of the new concert hall left him slightly embarrassed. After fifteen minutes everyone gladly adjourned to seek cooler haunts and await the evening's concert.

At six o'clock the musicians and press corps reassembled, now in the black-tie company of nearly twelve hundred patrons who had paid $250 to $1,000 each for admission. As the audience gathered, a thundershower added its drumbeat to a brass ensemble's opening fanfares. On the lawn, in a scene reminiscent of the storm in Beethoven's *Pastoral* Symphony, casually dressed listeners who had paid a more modest $25 to attend scurried to shelter under eaves, umbrellas, and a few hastily erected tents. Inside the hall the atmosphere was thick with humidity and mosquitoes but electric with anticipation. Amid congratulatory speeches John Williams, Leon Fleisher, Ozawa, and Ohga took turns conducting the Boston Symphony

11

Orchestra and Tanglewood Music Center Orchestra in music that ranged from a commissioned cello concerto by Williams, in its world premiere, to Beethoven's celebratory Choral Fantasy. The program lasted three hours. Across the rain-dampened grass afterward a Japanese-style dinner awaited patrons under three mammoth tents.

The gala occasion was the opening of Seiji Ozawa Hall, the first new concert hall at Tanglewood—the first significant change of any kind on the stately grounds of the Boston Symphony Orchestra's summer home in Massachusetts' Berkshire Hills—in fifty-three years. Ozawa, Williams, and Fleisher, each a major national as well as Tanglewood figure, were familiar to the media and the audience. So were Ma and pianist Peter Serkin, the principal soloists. But Ohga? What was this publicity-shy captain of a Japanese electronics and entertainment conglomerate doing in the glory circle?

A former baritone and a conductor by avocation, Norio Ohga had made the climactic gift that allowed him to name the $9.7 million concert hall after anyone he chose, including himself. (Though never officially disclosed, the amount of his gift was reliably said to be $2 million.) After much thought, and much suspense in musical circles, he designated his fellow Japanese, Ozawa, for the honor. Unusual as it was for a concert hall to be named after an active musician, the BSO's music director overcame his em-

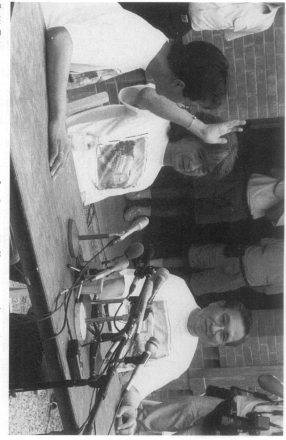

Seiji Ozawa answers a question at the Ozawa Hall press conference as Yo-Yo Ma (left) and Norio Ohga listen. The T-shirts portray the exterior of the hall. (Walter H. Scott)

barrassment and accepted the honor for the sake of the gift. Tanglewood thanked the giver by inviting him to indulge his conducting hobby with the BSO in Viennese bonbons by Franz von Suppé and Josef Strauss. Ohga-san, Ozawa cheerfully called him at the press conference. As multicultur alism and multinational corporations more and more took the stage in American life, Ohga-san demonstrated benefits of both for an American or chestra.

Seiji Ozawa Hall gave Tanglewood a world-class concert and recording facility to replace the Theater–Concert Hall, which had served honorably since its opening in 1941 but was now antiquated and dilapidated. The BSO would continue to perform in the Koussevitzky Music Shed, the hangarlike pavilion that opened in 1938 and seats five thousand. Ozawa Hall would provide a modern, 1,180-seat home, with refined acoustics, for student pro grams and professional recitals and chamber concerts.

Tanglewood knows how to create an occasion, and the inaugural concert was laden with symbolism. Works by Aaron Copland, Leonard Bernstein, Lukas Foss, and Oliver Knussen—each a composer, conductor, and teacher with a Tanglewood history as long as twilight shadows stealing across the festival's lawns—were on the program. To end the musical part of the eve ning, Ozawa led the audience and the Tanglewood Festival Chorus in sing ing Randall Thompson's *Alleluia*, the a cappella work that has opened the Music Center every summer since its founding in 1940. Ozawa Hall, more over, anchored the new Leonard Bernstein Campus. Named for Tangle wood's most illustrious son, the recently acquired estate increased the festi val's land area by 40 percent and provided a new home for the Music Center, its school for advanced studies in composition and performance. In time Ozawa Hall would also make possible the restoration of the Theater– Concert Hall and its return to service as an opera theater; this, in turn, would lead to a return of an opera training program. Meanwhile, new com posers were coming along, and most of them, including some who had been unwelcome at Tanglewood in the Theater–Concert Hall years, would be heard in Ozawa Hall. In more than the obvious sense of inaugurating a new building, Tanglewood was entering a new era.

As it happened, Tanglewood's new era coincided with a new era in Ameri can music. Just the year before, a shot had been fired across the bow. The American Symphony Orchestra League issued a report, *Americanizing the Symphony Orchestra*, warning that orchestras must adapt to an increasingly multicultural society or die. The adaptations were to include new program ming—often of a popular or ethnic nature—and social events to make mi nority groups and the young feel welcome. Symphony orchestras had to shed their staid, elitist image.

The study was roundly attacked by many critics and musicians as a summons to dilution of a great musical heritage. Yet the danger of a changing audience was real. A decline in musical literacy, through abandonment of art music in the home and the school, heightened the threat.

In its own way Tanglewood had addressed the problem well before the league discovered it. From its founding in 1937 by Serge Koussevitzky, Tanglewood has been dedicated to presenting the symphonic repertory for a popular audience. These largely untutored listeners can be seen any weekend in the summer, lounging on the greensward with picnic hampers, bottles of wine, and newspapers while Mozart, Beethoven, Brahms, and an occasional modern waft over them like soothing breezes. Over the years, moreover, the size of this legion has grown steadily, seeking the very repertory that the league's report found in need of reform. Yet the deeper question raised by the report and the dilemma faced by Tanglewood were the same: how far should a music festival—how far should *any* serious arts organization—go in making its art accessible to a broad audience bred to expectations raised by movies, records, radio, commercial pop, and television?

As it entered its seventh decade, Tanglewood combined the appeal of a Macy's and a Tiffany's in the packaging and marketing of classical music as a desirable commodity. Audiences in the thousands flocked to the orchestral concerts, even in inhospitable weather and at ever-escalating ticket prices. Thanks to media attention fed by celebrity events and galas like the Ozawa Hall opening, the festival was more and more in the public eye, and the Berkshires increasingly became—especially among residents of the New York metropolitan area—the summer place to be.

Except for an occasional gala such as a "brass bash" featuring the Canadian Brass, Tanglewood did not cross the line into outright commercialism. The festival's popularity and built-in audience, moreover, allowed it freedom to experiment gingerly with new music, lesser-known works from the past, new artists, and thematic programming, whether a summer of Copland (1989) or a summer of Mozart (1991). But in the 1990s serious music, and the arts generally, were under stress from powerful cultural forces ranging from the entertainment industry to successive Congresses bent on dismantling the National Endowment for the Arts. Like the orchestra league study, these forces assumed that high art—the tradition that had nurtured Western civilization whether as Renaissance frescoes or Mahler symphonies—had no relevance to modern American society. Or if it had relevance, it was as a private playground for the elite, as if art were no more than a game of croquet. As costs mounted, government support dwindled, and competing attractions siphoned off audiences, pressures built to make art pay, or at least attract more corporate money. A provident arts institution had to fight back with the most powerful weapons at its disposal. At Tanglewood these took the form of galas, telecasts, media hype, warhorse programming, and celebrity artists that acted as magnets for the crowd. The stakes and strategies were the same for museums, theaters, and libraries across the land.

If Tanglewood, with its combination of great music and great scenic beauty reinforcing each other, represented some of the best aspects of American musical life, it also flirted with some of the worst. Amid these opposing pulls Seiji Ozawa Hall, a superbly executed concert facility whose publicity blitz turned it overnight into a tourist shrine, came along as a symbol of the march toward the twenty-first century. Was great music to be only another stop on the tourist circuit, a kind of putty to be molded to suit the whims of the day? Or did it have enduring values that spoke to all people in all ages? On Tanglewood's tranquil lawns would be fought some of the most momentous cultural battles of the day.

ARCHITECT WILLIAM RAWN calls it "a room for music."

A short walk from the Shed, yet isolated from it by welcoming groves of trees, Seiji Ozawa Hall rises in unadorned timber-and-brick splendor like an overgrown New England barn. It has also been compared on the outside to a Shaker meetinghouse and on the inside to a Japanese teahouse. What the interior most resembles is some of the great concert halls of Europe. But unlike those halls it is simply an auditorium—spectacularly beautiful, spectacularly clear and warm in sound—without elaborate lobbies, restaurants, or bars. That is what makes it "a room for music."

Seiji Ozawa Hall changed the face and sound of Tanglewood. Beyond providing a modern setting for student and chamber concerts, it became the centerpiece and showplace of the new Leonard Bernstein Campus, as the 120-acre former Highwood property was named. The Tanglewood Music Center moved from the original grounds to the new campus, setting up studios and offices in renovated outbuildings from the old estate. The old manor house provided more studios and offices upstairs and became the site of a ground-floor dinner club. It also set a new tone for social life. On concert afternoons and evenings signs went up on the manicured lawn outside the club, warning that the grass, chairs, and tables, with their commanding view of the lake and hills, were for the use of club members only. Tanglewood had never seen anything like that before. Nor had it seen anything like the mammoth, UFO-like white tent, capable of sheltering one thousand guests, that went up on a far corner of the new campus. It was for dinners and receptions to accommodate corporate supporters and repay generous BSO patrons. Money consciousness, never entirely absent but kept discreetly out of sight before, as befits a Boston brahmin institution, was a new adornment at Tanglewood.

Seiji Ozawa Hall represents a collaborative effort by hundreds of people: BSO officials, architects, landscape designers, bricklayers, carpenters, roofers, chair makers. But two men, both Bostonians of brahmin persuasions, embody the values and vision that brought the project to completion: George H. Kidder, the BSO president at the time, and William Rawn, the architect. Kidder persuaded a reluctant board of trustees to go ahead with the project and spend the $9.7 million it required. Rawn, a novice at concert hall work, came up with the unconventional design.

A Boston native and Tufts University graduate, Kidder had worked for the same Boston law firm for forty-two years—virtually his entire career since completing his World War II military service and graduating from Harvard Law School—when Ozawa Hall opened. He first entered BSO service in 1969 as an overseer, or member of the trustees' fund-raising and advisory board. He moved up to trustee status in 1977 and became president in 1987, just as planning for Ozawa Hall was beginning. In September 1994, having seen the hall through its first summer of use, he retired from the presidency and the board. His wife of thirty-five years, Priscilla, had died of melanoma the November before, and with her no longer there to attend BSO concerts and go on BSO tours with him, he felt "a real change in a pattern of life which had been built largely on sharing." Sixty-nine, lanky, and white-haired, he decided that "it's time to let somebody else have some of the fun that this job represents. It's the best volunteer job in Boston."

When Kidder says fun, Kidder isn't kidding. A volunteer leader at one time or another for a host of other blue-ribbon Boston institutions, ranging from Children's Hospital to the Episcopal Church, he considers the endless meetings, fund raising, labor negotiations, budgeting issues, construction and maintenance needs, planning, phone calls, and trips—the kind of thing that got Ozawa Hall built—a pleasure and privilege. Public service: it's a Boston tradition.

"You guys are the best therapy I have," a bereaved Kidder told BSO members in 1993 when they clustered around him in the lobby of Vienna's Hotel Intercontinental, where he had just joined them on a European tour the month after Priscilla's death. Players and trustees aren't supposed to be on friendly terms; it's a case of labor versus management. But Kidder earned the respect of his employees by traveling with them and sticking up for music, if not always for their demands. He disclaimed credit for pushing through plans for Ozawa Hall, listing the acquisition of Seranak, Koussevitzky's old estate, and Highwood as the principal Tanglewood accomplishments of his board service. Colleagues on the board and in BSO management said otherwise. Without a George Kidder as president, they said, Seiji Ozawa Hall might well have existed only on paper.

Looking ahead to his new life after the 1994 Tanglewood season, Kidder said, "I'm a strong believer that when you finish up in a job like this, you ought to get out of the way of your successor. You ought not to be hanging around making him or anybody else feel like you're looking over his shoulder. He should find his own style and set his own pace." The BSO saluted the departing leader by dedicating the final day's performance of Beethoven's Ninth Symphony to him and bringing him onstage for a bow.

Seid umschlungen, Millionen! the chorus exults in the symphony's climactic "Ode to Joy": Be embraced, ye millions! It could be Tanglewood's theme music, welcoming the multitudes to brotherhood through music. Even with keep-off signs on the lawn, that is the heritage left by Koussevitzky and carried on by followers like Kidder.

Unlike Kidder, who blends in amid a crowd, Bill Rawn stands out—literally. Six feet eight, he is, in the words of the *Boston Globe Magazine*, "a likable, doorframe-tall, rather serious man who gets teased for his earnestness, an inevitability that he takes in stride."[1] A Californian by birth, he came to Boston to study at Harvard Law School. Until Tanglewood entered his life, he and his eleven-year-old firm were best known for their award-winning affordable-housing developments at the former Charlestown Navy Yard and in the Mission Hill section of Boston. There was also the matter of Tracy Kidder's 1985 best-seller, *House.* Rawn was the young architect-hero of that tale of the creation of a home in the country, far from the urban milieu where he did most of his work.

William Rawn Associates was one of a few dark-horse candidates that the BSO invited, along with about thirty-five of the country's most prestigious architectural firms—some with extensive concert hall credentials—to submit proposals for a new hall at Tanglewood. The nearest thing to a concert hall that Rawn Associates had designed before was an open-air performance pavilion in Lowell, Massachusetts. But Rawn's unconventional career had prepared him for finding an unconventional solution to the assignment that Tanglewood presented.

After getting his Harvard law degree, Rawn practiced law for two years

The interior of Seiji Ozawa Hall. The Tanglewood Music Center Orchestra performs. (Steve Rosenthal)

in a Washington firm. A stint as assistant chancellor for physical planning at the University of Massachusetts introduced him to the problems of student housing—and to their flip side, the problems of families that might get pushed aside by student housing. The experience taught him to deal with not only construction issues but also communities and their goals. So the road led to the Massachusetts Institute of Technology, where in 1979, at the age of thirty-five, Rawn received a master's degree in architecture. On founding his firm in Boston, he continued to be concerned with people within their environments. For faculty housing at Dartmouth College, his plans included fifteen-foot-high bookshelves. For a parking garage in Rochester, New York, he evoked the locks and iron construction he discovered along the nearby Genesee River.

Tanglewood would get the same consideration. Tanglewood manager Daniel R. Gustin told Katharine Whittemore of the *Globe* that the most impressive thing about Rawn was the way he anonymously talked to patrons, watched rehearsals, and got to know the flavor of Tanglewood. "We were more concerned about creating a place where we wanted to listen to music, not about building an architectural monument per se," Gustin said. After looking at the Charlestown Navy Yard housing project and the Lowell performance pavilion, the search committee decided, "Yes, this is our man." [2]

Ⲛ OT ALL THE CHOICES were so clear. When a BSO emissary showed Norio Ohga a proposed logo for the hall he would be naming, his face registered displeasure. Politeness forbade him to say why. His secretary later explained: although the logo design, four squares enclosed within a larger square, echoed the design of the hall's clerestory windows, it was the Japanese ideogram for a rice paddy. It was modified to preserve the window idea without the muddy association.

Seiji Ozawa Hall is not in a rice paddy, and neither is the Theater–Concert Hall. But the Theater–Concert Hall, whose roof leaked, flooded during heavy rains. Opened in 1941 for student performances, the humpbacked structure across the lawn from the Shed showed the effects of hard use and hard winters. The orchestra pit had been filled in. The flies for scenery were no longer usable. Backstage dressing and warm-up areas were primitive at best. Out front, the acoustics were harsh, the seats an invitation to sciatica. One winter during a heavy snow, the roof had caved in. With its rough wooden beams and walls, the building, though designed by the celebrated Eliel Saarinen and his son Eero, looked like a relic of a 1940s music camp. [3]

Yet the Theater–Concert Hall had been the scene of some of Tanglewood's grandest and most historic occasions. For two decades ending in 1962, a student opera program directed by Boris Goldovsky had flourished there, presenting such notable events as the American premieres of Benjamin Britten's *Peter Grimes* and Mozart's *Idomeneo*. Leonard Bernstein, Seiji Ozawa, Zubin Mehta, Claudio Abbado, Lorin Maazel, and Michael Tilson Thomas—to name only a few—had cut their teeth as conductors there, Bernstein and Ozawa returning as teachers and mentors in their own right. Until 1960 a chamber-sized BSO had presented two opening weekends of Bach-Mozart concerts there. Aaron Copland had presided there as a composition teacher and chairman of the faculty during the Music Center's first quarter-century. The East Coast's most important contemporary-music festival had taken place there, regularly presenting works by such established masters as Copland, Bartók, and Schoenberg and by newer figures, often in premieres. Since 1978 a midweek chamber and recital series there had attracted such internationally known artists as soprano Jessye Norman and pianist Alfred Brendel. Generations of singers and instrumentalists, many of whom had gone on to prominence and fame, had plied their trade on this splintered stage and under this leaking roof.

History was one thing, adequate musical facilities another. In the mid-1980s the BSO's trustees reluctantly faced up to the reality that the Theater-Concert Hall was aging, and not aging well. Their initial idea was to tear down the old building and replace it with a combined opera and concert facility (as the original had been) on the same site. But in a modern building the two uses were not compatible in terms of either acoustics or stage requirements. The site, moreover, was not large enough for the bigger building that would be needed, and with the flat lawn in front, there was no way of letting the outdoor audience—always a Tanglewood consideration—see clearly to the stage. Then an architects' study suggested a new concert hall on a new site, leaving opera for a renovated Theater-Concert Hall later.

It was obviously the right solution. But without cluttering the idyllic grounds, Tanglewood had no site for a sizable new building. To create would be to destroy.

At that point, in December 1986, the gods took a hand. The next-door neighbors, John Mason Harding and his wife, Margaret, informed the BSO that they planned to sell their 120-acre Highwood estate. A few years before, the BSO had signed an agreement giving it the right of first refusal on the property. Now, preparing to move, the Hardings set only one condition: because of changes in the capital gains tax, they wanted to sell by the end of the year. On the last day of 1986 the orchestra took title, getting the property at less than market value.

Highwood was prime residential property, and the BSO's clear interest in acquiring it was protection against developers, who were buying up choice Berkshire acreage—even some that was less than choice—amid a second-home and condominium boom. In the rush to buy, there was no time to draw up a plan for the manor house, caretaker's cottage, other outbuildings, and land. But it wasn't long till the realization dawned that Tanglewood had a site for its new concert hall.

Still, some trustees remained skeptical about putting money into a building that would be in use only two months of the year. They were also uncertain whether enough money could be raised, although an initial $3 million had come in as part of a Music Center fund drive. And they saw a need for such additional facilities as new gates, parking lots, ticket booths, and toilets if another hall was built.

Kidder and a cadre of other BSO leaders, including Gustin, fought hard for the project.[4] Highwood, Kidder told the board, provided a protected environment with an opportunity to create not just a new concert hall but a new home for the Music Center and other amenities that a late-twentieth-century festival required. He set a "break point" of $7 million in gifts and pledges toward the eventual $9.7 million cost before he would ask the board to approve construction. When the $7 million had been raised, Kidder said, the last objections melted away, and the board "caught the vision of the whole thing and what it was going to be like when we were done." In the end, $10.7 million was needed and raised, the extra $1 million providing an endowment for maintenance of the building.

THE NEXT STEP was preparation of a master plan for both Highwood and its integration with the original campus. The job fell to Catherine Verhulst, an associate in the Cambridge planning and design firm Carr, Lynch, Hack, & Sandell, and William Porter, former dean of the MIT School of Architecture (and son of composer Quincy Porter). Porter went back to Koussevitzky's original design, which combined classically inspired buildings with naturalistic landscapes. He sought to further the sense of Tanglewood as "a wonderful, removed, idealized place" offering respite from the shocks of the outside world.

At Highwood, Verhulst and Porter found a concert hall site that, unlike those of the Shed and Theater–Concert Hall, sloped to give the lawn audience a clear view inside to the stage. (Rawn would later say that the slope was just enough to let listeners see over the next person's head yet leave a wineglass standing upright.) The two lawns would be joined to provide a single expanse about a half-mile long, with a common view of the lake. The parking lot for Shed box holders, a symbol of privilege, would be filled in (with earth from the Ozawa Hall excavation) to remove a lawn obstruction. The other new construction—gates, ticket booths, studios, cafeteria, and the like—would subtly repeat the design styles of the older ones. New parking lots at Highwood would provide improved access to both the Shed and the new campus.

With the master plan drawn and applications for the architect's job in hand, a fifteen-member BSO committee convened for two days in 1989 in the Highwood manor house to interview the six applicant-finalists. On the first ballot Rawn Associates was the first or second choice of all fifteen voting members. (Rawn remembers the exact date well; it was July 7, five years to the day before the inaugural concert.) Dean Freed, chairman of the trustees' building committee, said:

Rawn had expressed great sensitivity for the new building to look like and feel like it belonged at Tanglewood and great necessity to work with the symphony people at Tanglewood—and that means students, orchestra, management. There were other architects who said, in effect, "Give me the contract, go away, and in a year I'll give you a pile of drawings." Rawn said all along, "You've got to work with me so that we'll achieve what you want at Tanglewood."

Rawn virtually camped at Tanglewood that summer, spending five weeks on the grounds with a team of five from his office. They talked to Seiji Ozawa, Leon Fleisher (the Music Center's artistic director), and other key figures about their needs, sat in on rehearsals and concerts, and, Rawn said, "just tried to soak up what Tanglewood's all about."

Rawn was "dumbstruck by the sense of openness and democratic spirit" on the lawn, where he found Fortune 500 CEOs in the crowd. He also found "a place of remarkable New England self-restraint." But the surprising thing to him was "the intensity of the musical experience" for the Music Center's 150 fellowship students. They were absorbed virtually from dawn till midnight in classes, practice, rehearsals, discussions, and performances. For the man concerned with people in their environments, the nature and extent of the activity in this central aspect of Tanglewood life became a consideration in the planning.

In December that year, carrying letters of introduction from Gustin, Rawn went on a working tour of Europe. Photographing, measuring, and sketching, he studied eleven concert halls known for their acoustical excellence. These included the two that, by general consent, rank with Boston's Symphony Hall as the world's finest: Amsterdam's Concertgebouw and Vienna's Musikvereinssaal, the so-called Golden Room. R. Lawrence Kirkegaard, a leading concert hall acoustician (and trained architect) whom the BSO had hired for the Tanglewood project, met him in Amsterdam and Vienna to coach him on what made those cities' nineteenth-century halls acoustical marvels. By coincidence, Ozawa was conducting the Vienna Philharmonic in the Musikvereinssaal while Rawn and Kirkegaard were there. He spent an hour after a concert showing them around the stage and explaining why the sound and ambience were so beloved by musicians.

Rawn had spent fifteen years attending the BSO's Thursday night concerts in Boston and had come to think of Symphony Hall as all a concert venue should be. Now his eyes were opened to other possibilities. Out of his studies came Ozawa Hall's loges and balconies, which are modeled on the Golden Room's. Ozawa Hall also has the rectangular "shoebox" shape that helps to give the Musikvereinssaal, Concertgebouw, Symphony Hall, and other important halls from the nineteenth century their acoustical warmth. Seating for listeners behind the stage is also a European idea. It and the absence of a proscenium arch would create a "community of sound" for the orchestra and audience, Rawn believed.

By now the nationwide boom in concert hall and arts center building, which in the 1960s, 1970s, and 1980s had given birth to such showplaces as New York's Lincoln Center and Washington's Kennedy Center, was over, and the recession of the early 1990s was forcing arts organizations to cut back or, in some cases, go out of business altogether. Yet on September 12, 1992, just after the Tanglewood season ended, the BSO broke ground for Seiji Ozawa Hall.

The next two winters were among the coldest and snowiest in Berkshire history. But for twenty-two months, through both heat and ice, construction went on at Highwood. During the winter the site looked like a modern Valley Forge, with men and equipment moving across snowfields and work taking place inside propane-heated plastic "tents" that sheathed the unfinished outer walls. Job superintendent Greg Hescock remembered the difficulties of having to pour the foundation section by section on arctic days and then cover the concrete with insulated tarpaulins overnight to let it cure: "You dig. And you pour. And you cover. In good weather you could just dig the whole wall and walk away from it."

Crews of up to seventy-five men worked continuously—and into the nights and weekends during the last rush to make up for cold-weather delays—to have the building ready for the opening night in 1994. Modifications and finishing touches were taking place up till the moment when the musicians walked onstage. During rehearsals Ozawa had found that two cloth scrims behind the stage were absorbing too much sound; in the afternoon before the concert, one of them had to come down. Floor lamps provided lighting at the front corners of the stage, behind the violins and double basses, until additional permanent fixtures could be installed.

The finished building has a rather plain brick exterior softened by wooden arcades on either side and a curved roof covered with lead-coated copper. The first impression, which troubled some early critics, is of a massive barn looming up in the midst of a park. The height was a given: anything less than a fifty-foot ceiling—the standard for a concert hall—would not have provided enough reverberation. The height, in turn, dictated the brick finish, unlike anything else at Tanglewood: under state building codes a structure as high as Ozawa Hall had to be was required to have a fire-resistant exterior. Rawn cushioned the effect with bricks of different reddish shades, the arched roof, and the two cedar arcades, which provide stairways

WHATEVER THE CRITICISMS of the big brick barn, the interior won instant acclaim. The Ozawa Hall auditorium is rich in Douglas fir and teak detailing and in cream tones trimmed with red. The seating in the round, with loges and balconies, draws audiences and musicians together in the "community" that Rawn sought. The overall impression, heightened by the ergonomically designed, green-upholstered chairs (movable, and with footrests, in the loges and balconies), is of airiness, light, and comfort: something like a concert hall as a large drawing room.

Ozawa Hall is 140 feet long, 70 feet wide, and 66 feet high and has 1,180 seats, about the same as the Theater-Concert Hall. A large, barn-style door at the back of the auditorium folds open to the lawn, which can accommodate up to two thousand more concertgoers. A state-of-the-art amplification system carries music outdoors. The building was also designed to be a recording studio, partly to spare the BSO the trouble and expense of a trip back to Symphony Hall when it had a summer performance ready for the microphones. Although the orchestra did not immediately take advantage of the opportunity, other musicians—among them Yo-Yo Ma and soprano Sylvia McNair—did. The side doors and barn door can be sealed to shield the interior from birdsong, human conversation, and the occasional hum of distant traffic; the $9.7 million construction cost included $1.3 million for soundproofing. A propane-fired heating system makes the hall comfortable on nippy August evenings and available for recording and community concerts during the spring and autumn. Never before had Koussevitzky's festival had a heated public building (and only in a few places, such as green rooms, does it have air conditioning).

Kirkegaard also adopted the Musikvereinssaal as his model in the acoustical design, using curved or recessed surfaces and grillwork to break up sound waves that would cause harsh echoes. The thick masonry walls are canted slightly outward for the same reason. Low-frequency sound that would "make the dishes rattle" with thinner walls, Kirkegaard said, is re-

to the balconies and shelter from the elements. To the *Boston Globe* architecture critic Robert Campbell, who served as an Ozawa Hall consultant, the wooden galleries suggest "the long, lazy porches of resorts and summer camps, and the big brick shape suggests the great rural mills of New England." Rawn, Campbell wrote in the opening-night souvenir book, "has little patience with passing fads or styles, but he does possess a strong urge to accommodate new buildings within the traditions of the past."5

Architect William Rawn in Ozawa Hall. At the back the barn-style door that opens to the lawn is closed for a rehearsal. (Walter H. Scott)

flected back into the room to give the "rich, strong, undergirding bass response that is part of what we know and love about old spaces."

As in other new concert halls, the acoustics required a bit of tinkering after musicians actually tried them. Upper string tone proved especially troublesome at first. It tended to turn thin and interfere with ensemble balances, particularly in chamber music. Performers, moreover, had to use trial and error (as they will in any unfamiliar hall) to find the best stage positions for their instruments. But, returning repeatedly for concerts, rehearsals, and consultations, Kirkegaard modified first one detail and then another until he achieved a three-dimensional richness and transparency. Most importantly, he had an excess of a sound-absorbent coating scraped off the ceiling, where it was causing the problem with strings. Acoustical panels above the stage and acoustical curtains, or "banners," near the ceiling permit concert-by-concert adjustments according to the kind of ensemble and its disposition onstage. Especially in the light of the acoustical failures of other post–World War II halls, such as Lincoln Center's Avery Fisher Hall, which had to be gutted, redesigned, and rebuilt in 1972 at an additional cost of $6.4 million, the BSO's success on first try was remarkable.

Reviewing the inaugural concert in the *New York Times*, Edward Rothstein wrote that the new hall "is precisely what a concert hall should be: a resonant, warm space that comes to life with sound. There are refinements to be made, but it is rare for a new hall to begin its career with such a mature, seasoned character and such respect for the tasks of the musicians and the privileges of the audience."[6] In *New York* magazine, Peter G. Davis offered a similar reaction: "I have seldom sat in a new concert space more sensitive to so many different needs, nor one that accommodates them all so successfully and comfortably."[7]

There is more than New England plain speaking in Rawn's description of Ozawa Hall as "a room for music." To keep costs down, the building has a conspicuous lack of the backstage and audience amenities found in year-round concert halls. Most of Ozawa Hall's support facilities—dressing areas, library, audio booth, storage areas—are in the connecting Leonard Bernstein Performers Pavilion, a low wooden building that centers like a cloister on a courtyard. (Campbell likens the musicians' pavilion to "a tugboat pushing the liner of Ozawa Hall.") The nearest toilets and refreshments are in buildings about three hundred feet away, a hardship journey on rainy nights.

The fundamental design question, Rawn wrote in the opening-night program book, was, "How do you build a structure with thick walls, as you must for optimal acoustics, and yet open the building to the landscape? Or, put more broadly: how do you retain Tanglewood's feeling of intimacy and informality and yet respond to the intensity of the music?"

Ozawa Hall's 1,180 seats are fewer than the Musikvereinssaal's 1,600 or Symphony Hall's 2,600. In its seating capacity, rustic setting, brick-and-timber exterior, and quietly elegant interior, the building is, in fact, kin to Snape Maltings, the quaintly named principal hall of the Aldeburgh Festival in England, which Rawn also visited, and to the new theater—also opened in 1994—at England's Glyndebourne opera festival. Ozawa Hall opens onto the landscape with long views of the lawn and sky from the windows, glass doors on the sides, and big barn door at the back. Evergreen bowers shade the approaches from the Shed and the Highwood manor house. On pleasant evenings the arcades and lawn invite preconcert and intermission mingling with friends. The light of the setting sun enters through the doors and windows. Few Tanglewood sights are more memorable than late sunlight bathing the audience and stage in a mellow glow as musicians bend to their task in some Mozart or Beethoven during a Friday Prelude concert.

Existing buildings on the Highwood estate found new uses when it became the Bernstein Campus. An old carriage house was converted into the Music Center's new headquarters and named after Leon Fleisher. (The naming was done privately at the request of a Berkshire couple, John and Jane Fitzpatrick, whose donations for the hall exceeded Ohga's but who wanted no recognition for themselves.) A large caretaker's cottage was relocated and also renovated for school use. It houses the Aaron Copland Library.

The 120 additional acres connect with the original 210-acre Tanglewood grounds to offer an unbroken expanse of lawn with distant views. There are new gates, ticket booths, and practice rooms, and a new cafeteria, bookstore, and gift shop. The elderly and infirm are chauffeured along the paths on electric "jitneys" that brush past promenaders much as they do in an airport terminal. In addition to the Ozawa Hall expense, $2.5 million was spent in creating the new campus. More conspicuously than ever, a corporation rather than a band of musicians was running the show.

Like the Theater–Concert Hall before it, Ozawa Hall is booked with rehearsals and performances straight through the day and long into the night. So crowded is the schedule that when soprano Sylvia McNair and composer-pianist André Previn went to record some songs during a concert visit, they had to do it between 11 P.M. and 2 A.M. and again between 5 and 8 A.M. The two-day project was an insomniac's paradise.

Students perform an average of six vocal, chamber, and orchestral concerts—each with its own rehearsals—a week in Ozawa Hall. The stage has also hosted such ensembles and recitalists as the Juilliard, Emerson, and Vermeer string quartets, the King's Singers, Yo-Yo Ma, pianists Emanuel Ax and Richard Goode, baritone Hermann Prey, and sopranos Renée Fleming and Barbara Bonney. The Festival of Contemporary Music takes place there, presenting student ensembles (the principal performers) and visiting groups like the Bang on a Can All-Stars and Steve Reich and Musicians. Both of these New York ensembles brought "cutting-edge" and pop-driven works to the once-staid festival-within-a-festival. The Dmitri Pokrovsky Ensemble, a folk troupe from Russia, and the Japanese gagaku ensemble Reigakusha have also appeared, the former doing a staged version of Stravinsky's *Les*

Noces, the latter performing Japanese classical and contemporary pieces on traditional instruments. Most of the Labor Day weekend jazz festival and all of the twilight Prelude concerts on Friday nights have been shifted to the new venue. The Preludes' hourlong chamber programs especially benefited from the move out of the cavernous Shed.

Seiji Ozawa Hall quickly reaped many design honors, the most prestigious of which were the New England and national honors awards of the American Institute of Architects. The national award, given for buildings up to ten years old, was especially noteworthy, coming as it did in Ozawa Hall's first year of eligibility. Recognition also came from ordinary visitors who, even when there were no concerts, made pilgrimages to see in person the building they had read about or seen on television. When the glass doors were locked for a rehearsal or because the building was closed for the season, the visitors stood singly or in groups with noses pressed to the panes, peering inside in a candy-store-window effect. Some, Tanglewood hoped, would return for concerts.

Ozawa Hall made a difference not only in the acoustics and logistics of concert giving but in the tone of the festival as well. A degree of efficiency—even elegance—crept into what had seemingly been, for musicians and audiences alike, a holiday in the country. The two primary activities, BSO and school, were now on separate campuses instead of one. Indeed, where once it had been possible to hear the two orchestras—BSO and Music Center—going at it in a grand, Charles Ives–like cacophony across the lawn when they rehearsed simultaneously, now everything was organized to avoid overlap or competition. Instead of a common meeting place for musicians at the old cafeteria between the Shed and the Theater-Concert Hall, now there were two cafeterias, each with its own menu (upscale at the new facility) and clientele. There were more tour buses, more tourists, more refreshment stands, more sales of T-shirts and bumper insignia, more Frisbees on the lawn during concerts. Then there were those keep-off signs, and that UFO-like tent, on the lawn of the new campus. They were a constant reminder of a class distinction that had been kept invisible before. Not only were the concert hall and campus new; the audience was taking on a different complexion.

The Theater-Concert Hall had history saturated in its timbers and chairs, but the timbers were aging and the chairs were hard. Ozawa Hall was at once as timeless as the great concert halls it was modeled on and as contemporary as the shopping malls springing up nearby in the Berkshire Hills. Leonard Bernstein, to whom the Music Center had been dear, was dead, but the campus bearing his name would provide a training ground for future composers, conductors, singers, and instrumentalists. Yet in the number and kinds of concerts, Tanglewood remained as it was before.

On the original campus Serge Koussevitzky, the sainted founder, would have discovered hardly a blade of grass unchanged. A few steps to the east, he wouldn't have recognized his festival. As the American Symphony Orchestra League study suggested, America was on the march toward a society in which the arts were no longer considered a necessity but had become a social adornment, a pastime no more consequential than watching television. Seiji Ozawa Hall embodied Tanglewood's response.

2

The
Complete
Music
Director

$\mathcal{F}$OR A CONCERT billed as "The Three Birthdays," an army of 18,709, by Tanglewood's official count, encamped on the grounds on the Sunday afternoon of July 23, 1995. Given the star caliber of the guests of honor, the title's echo of the "Three Tenors" concerts then trooping Luciano Pavarotti, Placido Domingo, and José Carreras through the world's stadiums, television sets, VCRs, and compact-disc players could hardly have been accidental. For the first time in the memory of those who keep track of such things, the Shed was sold out for a concert before the season began. The adoring crowd, in fact, set a Tanglewood attendance record for a classical music event.[1]

The year after the hall named in his honor opened, Seiji Ozawa turned sixty. His fellow celebrants on the warm, hazy afternoon of the birthday concert were Itzhak Perlman, who was turning fifty, and Yo-Yo Ma, the youngster of the group at forty. The three-hour program, which ended with a fifty-inch-high cake (made of steel) being wheeled onto the stage and four thousand colored balloons dropping and popping from the rafters, featured the three musicians first as principal performers and then as guests of honor while a parade of other musicians paid tribute to them. About the only things missing from the party were a real cake and funny T-shirts. But they came afterward at a benefactors' reception at Highwood.

Two weeks later Ozawa was back on the podium in a pair of programs commemorating the fiftieth anniversary of the Hiroshima bombing and the end of World War II. On Saturday night he led the BSO and Tanglewood Festival Chorus in the Berlioz *Requiem*. The next afternoon, August 6, the Hiroshima anniversary, he did Mahler's *Resurrection* Symphony.

The two works made a giant diptych honoring the dead and affirming the promise of eternal life. It was Ozawa's tribute to the war dead—all dead in all wars, he insisted, despite the historic date. With the Smithsonian Institution still smarting from the cancelation of a Hiroshima exhibition heavily criticized as too sympathetic to the Japanese, Ozawa wanted to make his statement in a way that was not "too raw" politically. In his piquant English he explained: "I didn't want to focus on Second World War. If people in Japan look at this program, they say, 'Oh, Seiji did it for Hiroshima.' I didn't want it to be that way. I think that's not right. Especially, I'm Japanese but I feel like I'm American. This is for anybody who died in war."

The two mega-events—birthday bash, war memorial—showed two faces of Ozawa in the sixtieth year of his life and twenty-second of his BSO reign. Impish and serious by turns, Japanese in habits and thought but Western in his art, guarded in private life yet seemingly incapable of refusing a television camera, superficial or rushed in one performance yet able to move Tanglewood's pines to tears in the next, loyal to Tanglewood yet also to his Saito Kinen Orchestra and Festival in Japan, which call him away from Tanglewood for part of each summer: more than most, this conductor was a man of paradox. Contradictions also characterized Tanglewood during his stewardship; it seemed, in fact, that his fortunes and Tanglewood's had waxed—and sometimes waned—together. Tanglewood was at once one of the most ambitious music festivals in the United States and one of the most staid. It was the home of the East Coast's most important contemporary-music festival and the purveyor of stars and easy-listening fare for tourists. It was a highly pressurized school for the cream of the world's young musicians, and it was a theme park for classical music. It was Ozawa Hall and the Shed.

IF OZAWA is an enigma, he is at least an enigma with a friendly face. In his annual talk to students at the Music Center's opening exercises, he invariably becomes entangled in the English language, which, after nearly four decades in the West, he has yet to conquer. Students laugh not at him but with him. What he meant, he explains amid the hilarity, was—well, people know what he meant. Somehow, with students and others, his intention comes across without the finer points. There is something about his lithe, athletic body (he loves skiing and tennis), his mobile features (now showing their sixty years), his white Hanae Mori tunics, and even his fractured English that communicates in person as on the podium. Even his detractors—and there are a fair number of them in the BSO—will grant that he is a

Itzhak Perlman, Seiji Ozawa, and Yo-Yo Ma take a bow after the performance of Brahms's Double Concerto at the 1995 "Three Birthdays" concert. (Walter H. Scott)

"nice guy." Yet behind the mask lies an iron authoritarian streak, as some players and staff members have discovered to their sorrow. That trait, too, is perhaps Japanese.

Born in Manchuria to a Japanese dentist attached to the imperial army, Seiji Ozawa first came to Tanglewood and the United States in 1960 as a conducting student without money or acquaintances. After the solitary bus trip from the Boston airport through strange country to the Berkshires, he became a protégé of Charles Munch. The then-director of the BSO had encountered him the previous summer while attending the international conducting competition at Besançon, France, which Ozawa, an unknown Japanese tooling around Europe on a motor scooter, won.

One of the memories Ozawa likes to recount at the Music Center exercises is the impression made on him not only by music at Tanglewood—other students knew far more than he did, he says—but by the glories of the Berkshire countryside. Other glories lay ahead. He won the Koussevitzky Prize, the Music Center's top honor, and went on to serve apprenticeships with Leonard Bernstein at the New York Philharmonic and Herbert von Karajan at the Berlin Philharmonic. The two conductors became his mentors along with Munch; he spoke of all three as his "fathers" along with his real father and was devastated when each died. A man of loyalties to places as well as people, Ozawa retained his love of Tanglewood as his "first beginning" in the United States while ascending rapidly to the directorships of the Toronto and then San Francisco symphonies. In 1970, during the reign of William Steinberg, who was ailing and took little interest in Tanglewood, Ozawa became the festival's artistic director in a triumvirate that ran the summer programs. His partners—both of them his seniors in terms of recognition and experience—were Gunther Schuller and Leonard Bernstein. Schuller was in charge of the Music Center, while Bernstein held the title of adviser, serving as a kind of minister without portfolio. In 1972, upon Steinberg's retirement, Ozawa became the BSO's music adviser, or interim director. A year later he was crowned with the directorship.

Ozawa is the BSO's thirteenth music director and the fifth to preside over Tanglewood. Closing in on Koussevitzky's twenty-five-year record with the BSO, by 1995 he had already run Tanglewood longer than any of his predecessors, including Koussevitzky, who was its guiding spirit for the first thirteen years. By then Ozawa also held the longest record of service among current directors of major American orchestras.

Ozawa's BSO career can be marked off in stages. First came the brilliant, exotic young Japanese full of promise and wearing beads and long hair as trademarks. Then, perhaps inevitably, disenchantment set in and he was widely accused of superficiality in performances. ("Bland in Boston" was the memorable headline over one critical bombardment.) In the 1980s a new maturity and greater emotional range occurred, especially in the core Beethoven-to-Mahler repertory; he said that with the deaths of his "fathers," he learned to assume something of a father's responsibility for his players. Part of the liberating force came from the 1984 departure of concertmaster Joseph Silverstein, an unspoken rival for power, to pursue his own conducting career as director of the Utah Symphony. Bernstein's death, in 1990, may also have contributed to the growth, freeing Ozawa from the constraints of an authority figure who cast a longer shadow both at Tanglewood and in the outside world. But as Ozawa's career burgeoned in the 1990s, some backsliding, or sideslipping, seemed to take place in his work with the BSO. Especially at Tanglewood, where rehearsal time is shorter than in Symphony Hall and pressures are correspondingly greater, his conducting often seemed driven, as if he could bend the music to his will instead of finding its inner pulse. Now, with silver streaking his long black hair, he wore reading glasses instead of beads around his neck.

Nothing about Ozawa, however, is simple, especially to a Western mind. Even in the late 1970s and early 1980s, when the cries of superficiality were loudest in the land, he exercised a field marshal's command in large-scale symphonic and choral works—not only of their logistics but often of their content as well. Amid the pressurization in the 1990s he continued to demonstrate greater emotional depth in some performances, such as his Mahler *Resurrection*. And always he showed a particular identification with opera and choral works on devotional themes. His Boston performances of Berg's angst-ridden *Wozzeck* and Richard Strauss's gloriously decadent *Elektra*—he brought the latter to Tanglewood—were of a scorching intensity; yet he also found deep wells of meaning in Britten's *War Requiem*, perhaps the most profoundly antiwar music ever created. He began conducting regularly at the Vienna Opera and La Scala of Milan and finally made his Metropolitan Opera debut in 1992 (in Tchaikovsky's *Eugene Onegin*). His mastery of large-scale, complex works extended to contemporary music, which he conducted sparingly, like other foreign-born directors of major American orchestras, but with skill and comprehension. Under him the BSO commissioned works—more in anniversary seasons than in others—from both American and foreign composers. None were quickly recognized as masterworks, as were Stravinsky's *Symphony of Psalms* and Bartók's *Concerto for Orchestra*, both commissions under Koussevitzky. But neither were the newer commissions repeated year after year, as new music was under Koussevitzky, making understanding and appreciation easier.

Brought up by a Buddhist father and Christian mother, Ozawa seemed more attuned to the metaphysical struggles of the *Resurrection* Symphony than the niceties of Mozart or the introspection of, say, the later Mahler symphonies. It was as if something in him vibrated to the sublime and the elemental—the theatrical and the grand—more readily than the infinite gradations of emotion between. Without an extensive background in Western literature, art, and culture, he was never a well-read or intellectual conductor like the Europeans who had preceded him in Boston (and who continued to rule most of the country's other leading orchestras). Rather, instinct guided him. In that, he was in tune with the times and a festival that cultivated a popular audience without the need for musical literacy or depth.

By the time Ozawa arrived at Tanglewood as music director, the format of the summer BSO season had been established. From their beginnings in a tent in 1937, the concerts had increased from two to eight weekends of three programs each. Evolutionary change continued under Ozawa with the 1978 reestablishment of a weeknight chamber and recital series and inauguration of the Boston Symphony Chamber Players' pre-BSO weekend of chamber music.

In 1979, while the BSO embarked on its first European festival tour, the

New York Philharmonic, under Zubin Mehta (Tanglewood '58), played the final weekend's concerts. It became the first visiting orchestra to perform in the Shed. Among the ensembles that followed in subsequent years were the Cleveland, Minneapolis, Pittsburgh, and Montreal orchestras, the Israel Philharmonic, the Kirov Orchestra and Chorus from Saint Petersburg, the Academy of Saint Martin-in-the-Fields from London, and the Mostly Mozart Orchestra and the Orchestra of Saint Luke's, both from New York. Each, along with occasional celebrity recitalists, helped to spell the BSO for two or three of the twenty-four weekend dates. Shed recitalists included Itzhak Perlman, James Galway, Leontyne Price, and Yo-Yo Ma with Emanuel Ax. At the same time the BSO divided itself in half for four or five chamber orchestra programs scattered through the season. The changes were made partly to give BSO players more time off and relieve rehearsal pressures, but the influx of celebrity artists and visiting orchestras also heightened Tanglewood's profile and made it increasingly a mecca for audiences from the United States and abroad. Ozawa spoke of making Tanglewood an international festival along the lines of Salzburg.

In 1980 Ozawa made his boldest move: a revival of opera. But unlike the student program run largely under Boris Goldovsky from 1940 until 1961, and unlike Salzburg's fully staged productions in a theater, this was opera partially staged by the BSO in the Shed, performed with big-name soloists, and conducted by Ozawa himself. Critics scoffed, largely at the staging compromises that had to be made in a concert space that was designed for symphonic use, not opera. But on their limited terms the productions were musically successful more often than not (see chapter 6). Until financial and logistical pressures forced suspension of the series in 1992, *Tosca*, *Fidelio*, *Pique Dame*, *Orfeo ed Euridice*, *Elektra*, and even Bach's *Saint Matthew Passion* were among the annual productions. Mirella Freni, Frederica von Stade, Marilyn Horne, Philip Langridge, Sergei Leiferkus, and Sherrill Milnes figured prominently in the international casts.

Opera was a goal Ozawa had set for Tanglewood almost from the day he established himself in the Shed's green room. Although it took pressure by the faculty and staff to reestablish student opera, he said opera was necessary to make the festival all-inclusive and round out a program of student activity that extended to the art song but lacked a Goldovsky-like component. Opera also happened to be a personal goal. Ozawa felt he would never be a complete conductor until he knew the operatic as well as symphonic repertory—and in fact, the experiments with semistaged opera at Tanglewood, and later in Symphony Hall, probably contributed to his 1980s maturing as a conductor. (They also aided his growing operatic career in Europe.) But even as a variety of nonartistic problems put a stop to BSO opera both at Tanglewood and in Boston, in the early 1990s faculty-staff planning began for a new student opera program, possibly on the Goldovsky model. It would have to await restoration of the Theater-Concert Hall, which in turn awaited completion of Seiji Ozawa Hall. But by 1996 Tanglewood and Ozawa had taken a first giant step. In a partially restored Theater-Concert Hall he conducted a student production of Britten's *Peter Grimes*, commemorating the fiftieth anniversary of the opera's American premiere, which took place on that same stage with Leonard Bernstein conducting. As frequently happens, Tanglewood looked forward by looking back to past programs and glories.

Ozawa was the first jet-age conductor to head the BSO. All his predecessors were European-born and European-trained in an age when music directors stayed home and tended their flocks. Among his contemporaries, he was not alone in pursuing an itinerary that enabled him to conduct in the United States one night and begin rehearsal for another concert in Europe or Japan twenty-four hours later. His twenty weeks a year with the BSO—six of them at Tanglewood—was more than his counterparts spent with the country's other major orchestras, which lacked a comparable summer season. Otherwise the schedule was typical of the new breed of winged music director.

The schedule, however, produced strains for members of the clan and their orchestras. For Ozawa these difficulties were heightened when, in the 1980s, he decided to establish his family's principal residence in Japan so that his son and daughter could get a Japanese education. Not only did he seem torn, harried, or afflicted by health problems, especially respiratory ailments, but there were periodic tensions with the players over his absences. He would promise to spend more time on BSO affairs, only to continue on his globe-trotting ways. Sometimes he simply seemed overbooked. His loyalty to the BSO was not in doubt, but in his scurrying here and there he could seem like a puppet of Ronald Wilford, his manager and summer neighbor in the Berkshires. As president of Columbia Artists Management, Inc., which also controls many of the country's other conductors, Wilford bestrides the music-management scene in the United States and can make or break a conductor's career.[2] If the Berlin or Vienna Philharmonic wants Ozawa as a guest conductor, or if Wilford thinks it is in his or Ozawa's interest for them to have him as a guest conductor, Ozawa will probably go.

On the other hand, some of the tensions were of Ozawa's own making. In 1992 he founded his Saito Kinen Festival in Matsumoto, Japan, employing his Saito Kinen Orchestra. Reconstituted each year, the part-time orchestra is made up of fellow protégés of Ozawa's principal teacher in Japan, Hideo Saito. The ten-day festival had to be held in late August and early September, when most of these working musicians from the United States, Europe, and Japan were on vacation. To prepare for Matsumoto, Ozawa began taking his customary two weeks of vacation from Tanglewood at the end of the season instead of in the middle, when he would usually conduct at the Salzburg Festival. The calendar change meant he was no longer on hand to conduct Tanglewood's final concert—a minor but conspicuous sin in a music director. More incongruously, he would conduct the traditional farewell ceremony for retiring BSO members at his final Tanglewood appearance. Since the contract year ends on August 31, they would then go on to play their last two weeks of concerts under guest conductors before disappearing into the mists. Critics' and patrons' tongues clucked.

There is probably no orchestra in the world in which the players—notoriously an individualistic lot who think they can do the conductor's job better than he can—do not gripe about their music director. But in 1995 criticism of Ozawa welled up from an extraordinary source: concertmaster Malcolm Lowe, Ozawa's own choice for the position, and principal cellist Jules Eskin.

The year before, a group of dissident BSO players had started an in-house newsletter airing their criticisms of Ozawa and management. The third issue, published as Tanglewood was opening in 1995, featured a cover drawing of principal guest conductor Bernard Haitink and Boston Pops conductor Keith Lockhart—both newly appointed—aboard a BSO ship. The inscription read: "Welcome aboard, Maestro Haitink and Maestro Lockhart." Inside, a "letter to the editors" from Lowe and Eskin carried a distinctly different message for Ozawa, criticizing him (though not by name) as wasting time in rehearsals. The writers said he dealt with trivia instead of issues of balance, tempo, sound, style, "and a distinctly conveyed conception of the character wanted in each and every piece we play together."

Our music director is fond of saying that the relationship between a conductor and his/her orchestra is like a marriage, and that marriages end only in death. We all recognize that marriages do not all end in death; neither is it, nor should it be, the case with orchestras. We all do know, however, that some marriages linger on monotonously, with a lack of mutual regard, respect, and stimulation. Pablo Casals used to say repeatedly, "Monotony—enemy of music." For the health of the orchestra it is incumbent upon the musicians of the BSO not to let such a relationship linger on statically, but to address its problems.[3]

Though the letter went on to complain about a "demoralizing working environment caused by rehearsal mismanagement," it called for a "climate of greater openness and mutual responsiveness" rather than an outright divorce. Nevertheless, the controversy was sniffed out by the press and the damage compounded by publicity. Ozawa had nothing to say about the criticism publicly. But according to backstage reports, feelings on both sides were badly bruised and remained that way, with no resolution of the conflict. Meanwhile, other complaints festered, partly about such administrative matters as the scheduling of auditions and recording sessions but more seriously about the quality of performances. The Lowe-Eskin appeal for "a distinctly conveyed conception" of each piece was typical.

Amid the controversy Ozawa decided to lighten his Boston schedule the following year to give himself time for rest, reflection, and skiing at his mountain home in Japan. He told the press the sabbatical was a goal he had set for himself four years before, when he injured his arm and shoulder in a skiing accident and had to miss his first two weeks of Tanglewood concerts because of recurring physical problems. But characteristically he did not take a full sabbatical. Instead, he reduced his winter BSO schedule from nine weeks and eleven programs in 1995–96 to six weeks and nine programs in 1996–97. He also cut down his commitments with the New Japan Philharmonic, which he regularly guest-conducted in Tokyo, and turned over a BSO tour of the Canary Islands and Florida in early 1997 to André Previn. But after saying that he was refusing all other guest-conducting engagements for 1996–97, in the spring he led a series of European concerts with Mstislav Rostropovich for the cellist's seventieth birthday (they also gave a BSO program) and took the Saito Kinen Orchestra on a tour of Europe. He was not one to sit still.

Other troubles followed. At the end of the 1996 Tanglewood season, Ozawa took it upon himself to fire Richard Ortner, the Music Center's capable and widely respected administrative director for the last ten years (and second-in-command for twelve years before that).

Ortner was the almost indispensable staff person who, on a year-round basis, coordinated Music Center auditions, admissions, housing, performances, and related activities. Leon Fleisher, the school's artistic director, and Tanglewood manager Daniel Gustin, who had groomed Ortner, tried to argue Ozawa out of the dismissal. They said Ortner was faithfully carrying out policies set by the faculty. But Ozawa insisted that the administrator had been disloyal and self-aggrandizing, attempting to make the Music Center "his." Ozawa also declared that a "club" dictating the school's artistic policies out of personal interests had to be broken up. In the ensuing ruckus eighteen of the twenty-two full-time faculty members sent Ozawa a protest letter expressing "painful and powerful feelings in all of us and deep concern about the health and creative future of the Tanglewood Music Center." The letter was circulated by faculty chairman Gilbert Kalish.

The spark for the controversy was apparently Ortner's objections, along with opposition by Gustin, Fleisher, Kalish, and other Music Center leaders, to a 1994 television project that teamed Ozawa and the Music Center Orchestra with trumpeter Wynton Marsalis and his jazz band. Ozawa had pushed hard for the project, which was filmed by Sony Classical for PBS and commercial distribution. Where he saw educational merit in the two weeks of shooting, however, the Music Center leaders saw commercial and time-consuming interference with the school's time-honored mission. (For a fuller discussion of the four-part series that was ultimately filmed and of the problems it caused, see chapter 7.) Two years later, Ortner apparently antagonized Ozawa again by trying to alter some of the arrangements for the staging of *Peter Grimes*, another Ozawa project.

Beyond those specific points of friction, Ozawa was unhappy with the traditionalist stance of the Music Center, which since its beginning under Koussevitzky had been dedicated to ensemble performance and the art of music rather than solo careers and glorification of the performer. Wanting to open the festival and school to such outside influences as jazz, Ozawa felt blocked by the "club," by which he apparently meant the leadership under Fleisher, Kalish, and Ortner. Since it would have been difficult to get rid of men like Fleisher and Kalish, who are nationally known pianists and teachers, Ortner evidently became the sacrificial victim. An unspoken concern behind the faculty letter was: in Ozawa's quest for change, would there be more Marsalis-type projects, and did the ax also await those who opposed such initiatives?

Again, Ozawa made no public comment on the challenge to his leadership. Nor—apart from some organizational changes in the student conducting program, on grounds that it was no longer turning out star-quality graduates like Michael Tilson Thomas—did he offer ideas for strengthening the school. Indeed, through a questionnaire he solicited BSO and faculty members' ideas on how they thought the program could be improved. The immediate tensions were relieved when Ozawa called in leaders of the protest for one-on-one meetings, at which he gave a respectful hearing to their views. Then in the spring Ellen Highstein, executive director of the Concert Artists Guild, a New York organization that assists promising young musicians in building careers, was appointed Ortner's interim successor. Kalish took part in the selection process along with Ozawa and others from the BSO and faculty, and the 1997 summer proceeded more or less as usual. Dissatisfaction still simmered beneath the surface. It broke out in public

Seiji Ozawa addresses students at the Tanglewood Music Center's opening exercises. (Walter H. Scott)

at the Music Center's 1997 opening exercises when Fleisher, delivering the main address, went out of his way to lament the loss of Ortner and praise Kalish. In Ozawa's presence, he said Ortner's "dedication to this place that is Tanglewood is encrypted in every brick and on every blade of grass that is here," and Kalish's "stability, reliability, compassion, and allegiance to Tanglewood is a beacon for us all." Fleisher, however, sought to put the controversy behind him and get on with the summer's tasks. The changes, he said, "mean an opportunity for growth, an opportunity for development and progress." Taking the rostrum after Fleisher, Ozawa ignored the implicit challenge, speaking instead about music as "spiritual food."

Fleisher's summer of growth was not to be. During a series of apparently strained meetings with Ozawa, the faculty tried to get at specific sources of his discontent and find ways of satisfying them. At BSO players' request he did obtain a larger role for them in the coaching of student ensembles. He also asked to be kept informed about proposed policy and personnel changes at the school. (There was an implicit threat of a veto.) The faculty agreed to these requests, hoping for an improved relationship among music director, BSO, and school. The summer ended in a standoff, however, leaving unresolved several key issues, including auditions for the following summer's students and appointment of a 1998 composer in residence.

In late October the frustrations boiled over with the resignation of Kalish as faculty chairman and, a few days later, Ozawa's appointment of Ellen Highstein to the newly created position of Music Center director. More than a replacement for Ortner, she was given unprecedented control over artistic and faculty affairs—formerly the provinces of Fleisher and Kalish—as well as administration. Not only had Fleisher, Kalish, and Gustin been stripped of responsibilities; they were not consulted about the appointment of a newcomer to supplant them. In an angry letter of resignation addressed to Ozawa and the BSO trustees, the usually mild-mannered Kalish wrote that Ozawa's "arbitrary actions have transformed a loving family into a coldly heartless corporation with no communication, no collaboration, and no loyalty."

Fleisher and Kalish had distinguished careers as pianists and teachers to fall back on; Kalish, in fact, was the regular pianist of the Boston Symphony Chamber Players, a position left unresolved by the Tanglewood resignation. Gustin, however, was a BSO career man, much of whose thirty years of service had been devoted to the Music Center.

Ozawa was conducting the Berlin Philharmonic when the crisis broke. From Germany he sent back a statement saying he was "very excited" about the Highstein appointment and "sorry and mystified at the vehemence" of Kalish's letter.

"If we are to keep the Tanglewood Music Center in its place as the top training ground for young classical musicians," Ozawa said in a formal statement naming Highstein to the new position, "we must continue to respect our tradition, but also embrace innovation in order to keep the school vital and alive." He did not specify what kind of innovation he had in mind. Ozawa had, in fact, never stated a vision for either the individual teaching programs or the school as a whole. His only change was to bring about the resignation of the respected Gustav Meier as head of conducting activities, scale back the program of seminars and hands-on experience in 1997, and plan to resume an interim program in 1998 and start over in 1999 with the respected but younger Robert Spano in charge. As for other reforms, Kalish wrote that during the summer the faculty had tried to understand and respond to Ozawa's dissatisfaction through "endless meetings, discussions, memos, surveys, and mission statements," but Ozawa followed "a seemingly predetermined agenda that made a mockery of all of our efforts." Indeed, he insulated himself behind a "wall of absolute silence," Kalish said. Nowhere in his response did Ozawa address the charges, the accuracy of which other faculty members confirmed.

A month later Fleisher quit, accusing both Ozawa and Highstein of "unprofessional, unprincipled, duplicitous, and totally self-serving" behavior in carrying on pointless discussions with the faculty while preparing for the restructuring under Highstein. In a letter alternating between anger and avuncular advice, Fleisher warned Ozawa that he had set out on "the dangerous slope" of commercialism through pursuit of "the criteria of the marketplace," an apparent allusion to both the Marsalis project and gala events with the BSO. True innovation—the "Tabasco sauce" that Ozawa said was needed—would come only through greater commitment to Music Center activities by Ozawa himself, Fleisher wrote. "It's not going to come from more and more distinguished guests and blockbuster events; they are one-shot deals. The lineage that started with Koussevitzky and continued down through Leonard Bernstein now rests on your shoulders."

Ozawa, who was conducting in Boston, offered no public response. But in a letter to Fleisher, BSO president Nicholas T. Zervas and managing director Mark Volpe replied that it was Koussevitzky's vision "to innovate, to embrace the future, to take risks." They said Ozawa had offered, "out of deep loyalty" to Fleisher, to keep him on as a chamber music coach and senior faculty figure. The reconfigured position, they wrote, "would capitalize on your strengths while reducing your involvement in areas where you were less effective."

Commenting on the offer in his own letter, Fleisher sardonically told Ozawa: "A rather curious position for me to be in, wouldn't you say? Somewhat akin to having my legs chopped off at the knees, you then gently taking me by the arm and inviting me for a stroll."

In December, a week after Fleisher's widely publicized resignation, Ozawa announced his program for the school. Devised in large part by Highstein, it consisted of an elaborate—and probably expensive—mix of new or enlarged activities along with an expanded faculty role for BSO members. The initiatives included an interdisciplinary "Lives in Music" project, focusing in the first year on composing for film, and residencies by the Juilliard and Guarneri String Quartets. Tanglewood, meanwhile, would assume students' room and board costs in addition to tuition, which had been free since the 1960s. BSO players were to take charge of coaching their student counterparts in most phases of performance and conduct most of the annual auditions for applicants. More than the initiatives themselves, many of which were refinements or repackagings of existing programs, the scheduling of the eight-week season spelled a break with the past. Instead of more or less continuous studies in composition or performance, there would be clusters of activities—chamber music one week, orchestra the next, perhaps contemporary music after that—throughout the summer.

Ozawa said the cluster approach would provide "more focus" and "maximum concentration" in each area. The heightened involvement of BSO players, he said, would restore the BSO-school relationship that had prevailed under Koussevitzky.

Many details of the program remained to be worked out, not least of which was choosing qualified BSO players to audition and teach and arranging time off from rehearsal and performance for their added duties. Looking further ahead, Ozawa listed as "dreams" for the future a student dormitory on the grounds, summer performances by the Music Center Orchestra in Boston and New York, and a series of international exchanges, including a visit by the Mahler Youth Orchestra of Europe under its conductor, Claudio Abbado. The goal, Ozawa and Highstein said, was to help Tanglewood compete for the best students against such other festivals as Aspen, in Colorado, and Marlboro, in Vermont; active recruitment in the conservatories would be part of the strategy. It was also necessary, Highstein said, to prepare musicians for a job marketplace in which they would be called on to do many things instead of simply being orchestral or chamber players. Highstein described Tanglewood as "a victim of its own success," coasting on its reputation. "It takes a certain amount of courage and a certain amount of grit to be able to re-examine yourself when you're on top," she said.

Nowhere was Tanglewood's clash between tradition and change more sharply defined than on this battlefront, which the music world followed with avid attention in the press and on the Internet. On one side were arrayed Kalish and Fleisher, both in their sixties, who saw themselves as upholding what Fleisher described as "the purity and idealism of Koussevitzky's dream": a place where young and experienced musicians, working together, could dedicate themselves to the highest ideals of their art without the financial and commercial pressures that awaited outside the gates. On the other side were Highstein and Ozawa (also in his sixties), who maintained, as he put it in a press release, that Koussevitzky "saw the school as a 'laboratory,' a place for creativity, experimentation, and risk-taking." In the middle were the BSO's trustees, who, with a $130 million capital fund drive under way and Ozawa's twenty-fifth anniversary season on the horizon, had little choice but to cast their lot with the music director. To do otherwise was to risk scandal at a time when they could little afford it.

Both views—Ozawa's and Fleisher's—of the Koussevitzky vision were correct. The Music Center had innovated many times before, once when Erich Leinsdorf introduced tuition-free study, most recently with Ozawa's 1996 reintroduction of student opera. But the past changes, under Koussevitzky and others, had been driven primarily by artistic concerns such as new developments in composition. Ozawa's innovations also reflected the market-driven strategies that symphony orchestras and arts organizations in general were pursuing as they sought to draw audiences in the late twentieth century—the target audience in this case being students. Certainly there was merit in teaching film music, along with music for dance, opera, and visual arts, future areas envisioned for the "Lives in Music" project. Undoubtedly, too, BSO players, like other faculty members, could become mentors to young musicians who might wind up in orchestral careers. But like the Marsalis project, the new activities risked diluting a program that had drawn fifty-seven years of students, including Bernstein and Ozawa, not for timely ideas or a smorgasbord curriculum, but for the enduring values that the Music Center embodied.

The full-time summer faculty includes such well-known musicians as soprano Phyllis Curtin, pianist–vocal coach Margo Garrett (who resigned in 1997), conductor Reinbert de Leeuw, and composer Yehudi Wyner, all of whom signed Kalish's original protest letter, as well as pianist Peter Serkin, who did not sign. In addition, a varying number of BSO members and guest artists, such as Yo-Yo Ma, have regularly taught part-time. A smattering of sympathy resignations, including that of the noted double bassist Julius Levine, accompanied those of Kalish and Fleisher. Among those who remained on the full-time faculty, there was also a feeling that with Ozawa's widening activities in Europe and Japan he was losing touch with the institution that had given him his "first beginning." Whatever else his demand for change portended, it showed he was still in charge. It also showed there was no room for an old guard that had led the Music Center during two or more decades of dedicated service.

Indeed, as his international career expanded in the 1980s and 1990s, and especially with the founding of Saito Kinen, Ozawa had to scale back his commitments at the Music Center. Where once he had personally taken the first two weeks of the student conducting and orchestral program, he continued to prepare and lead the Music Center Orchestra's first concert but delegated the important classroom sessions to others. His absence was felt the more keenly because he was regarded as a good teacher of the basics of score and baton. Though he was less effective in teaching composers' styles, the nuts-and-bolts approach served as a corrective to the podium choreography that is often a primary concern of the novice trying to make a strong impression.

The reinstitution of student opera with the 1996 *Peter Grimes* brought Ozawa back into the heart of Music Center activity for three to four weeks of the season. His commitment to the project was unstinting. He prepared and conducted both sets of performances in the double-cast production—a contribution of time and energy beyond anything he had done at the Music Center before. But otherwise he remained at a distance from school activities. Though he continued to attend some of the Music Center Orchestra's other programs, he was rarely seen at the students' more numerous chamber and vocal concerts or at the Festival of Contemporary Music, in which students give most of the performances. His diverging allegiances showed in other ways as well. When a staff member suggested a weeklong festival of American music to inaugurate the hall that would bear his name, Ozawa chose the star-studded one-night gala instead. His rationale was that Tanglewood had to be an international festival.

The Ortner affair had a bizarre sequel. Ozawa is a sports lover and New England Patriots fan. His return from Japan for a set of BSO concerts in January 1997 coincided with the Super Bowl, in which the Patriots played (and lost to) the Green Bay Packers in New Orleans for the football championship. Ozawa obtained a ticket for the sold-out game from the Patriots' owner, Robert Kraft, and arranged for an airline flight down. He planned to fit in the Sunday evening spectacle between a Saturday night concert and a Monday afternoon rehearsal for a Monday night television taping.

Everything went according to plan until Monday morning, when he was to return on a private plane provided by a Boston banker and BSO overseer. Amid the post-game crush the plane couldn't get clearance to leave the New Orleans airport on time. Learning of the delay, Symphony Hall enlisted high-level assistance that led finally to Senator Edward Kennedy and the Federal Aviation Administration. Their intervention had the plane moved up in the runway queue. But it was too late. Ozawa missed the rehearsal, and when he did finally land at an airport in the Boston suburbs, a state police cruiser was waiting to rush him to Symphony Hall for the Monday evening taping.

There was no direct connection with the Ortner incident, but the caper took place a month after the faculty revolt had culminated in the protest letter, which aroused Ozawa to no such exertions. In both instances he appeared to put a personal agenda ahead of the institution he served. He clearly had no intention of hurting that institution. But, jetting from city to city and continent to continent, the once humble, media-shy young man from Japan now saw the world from the perspective of the international concert and celebrity circuit.

Meanwhile, word of the players' dissatisfaction spread through musical circles, always fertile ground for gossip. In the *New York Times*, senior critic

Bernard Holland revived an old rumor that Simon Rattle, then preparing to end a successful eighteen-year directorship of the City of Birmingham Symphony Orchestra in England, was impatiently waiting in the wings until the BSO management could dump Ozawa and name Rattle the successor.[4]

A good yarn, but not likely, at least on the BSO side. The BSO trustees and management were making big plans, including commissions to leading composers, for Ozawa's twenty-fifth anniversary with the orchestra, in 1998-99, and for his participation in the centennial of Symphony Hall the following year. Besides standing by their music director, the trustees received added value in his ability to attract millions of dollars to the BSO from such Japanese corporations as NEC and Lexus, as well as Norio Ohga's personal $2 million for Ozawa Hall.

Torn though he was among three continents, Ozawa had an open-ended contract that guaranteed his BSO incumbency as long as he wanted it, and he gave every sign of wanting it at least through those celebrations. From them he would emerge as the longest-tenured director in the orchestra's 120-year history—longer even than Koussevitzky, with his twenty-five-year reign.

*J*UST WHEN Ozawa's fortunes with his players hit these bumps in Boston, they broke through a wall in Japan. He returned in triumph to conduct the NHK (Nikon Hoso Kyokai, or Japanese Broadcasting Corporation) Symphony, Japan's finest. It had humiliated him thirty-two years before for the same reason that it lionized him now: he had made good in the West.

The trouble began in December 1962, when Ozawa, fresh from his early successes in the United States and Europe, returned to lead the NHK Symphony in a series of concerts. At first the players welcomed him as a disciple of Karajan, who was revered in Japan. But the twenty-seven-year-old with hippie airs soon made himself unpopular by exerting Karajan-like authority over players—many of them German-trained—who were his elders. His long hair and beads, his last-minute arrival at rehearsals, his Western ideas of technique and interpretation: all stamped him an upstart who had forgotten his origins. He was not *nakami doshi*—"one of us."

The orchestra delivered the ultimate snub: it canceled Ozawa's final concerts, notified ticketholders, but didn't notify him. One of the canceled programs was a New Year's Eve performance of Beethoven's Ninth Symphony, a year-end ritual in Japan. Alerted to the ruse when the press called for comment, Ozawa went to the hall at concert time with reporters and photographers in his train. He said he was honoring his contract. In the ensuing war of words, both sides claimed to be defending the honor of art. Ozawa swore he would never go back.

And he didn't return to the NHK. He did, however, obtain a base with the New Japan Philharmonic, which invited him to begin a series of guest-conducting engagements even before he went into his self-imposed exile. Then in 1978 he came back with his BSO as part of an Asian tour. Although he had led the New Japan Philharmonic and other touring Western orchestras in Japan in the interim, the Japanese knew the BSO only from one earlier tour under Munch. They were not prepared for the positive impact a seasoned Ozawa would make when conducting a first-class orchestra. In *Conductors: A New Generation* Philip Hart recounts:

When he went to Japan with the Boston Symphony, some questioned his holding so exalted a post as music director of the great Boston Symphony. Recalling what they regarded as the "golden age" of the orchestra under Charles Munch—Koussevitzky had never conducted in Japan—the Japanese could not conceive that they would hear it under Ozawa as anything but an orchestra that had seen better days.[5]

The concerts, however, were a triumph and vindication; even the most skeptical critics were swept away by Ozawa's Berlioz and Brahms. At the end of the farewell program, he received the customary floral tributes on-stage. With a keen sense of theater that has stayed with him, he performed a Japanese gesture that came from the heart yet also went to his countrymen's hearts: he walked down into the audience and placed a bouquet before a portrait of his teacher, Saito, that sat in an empty chair next to Saito's widow. His welcome thereafter in Japan was assured, and the next year he repeated the triumph with the BSO in China. This was the first visit to his birth country by an American performing-arts organization since the post-Mao resumption of relations with the United States.

But Ozawa and the NHK still were not talking. It was not until 1993 that Hideo Edo, the ninety-one-year-old father of Ozawa's first wife, and Mstislav Rostropovich, a colleague and friend, persuaded him to make peace. The 1995 concert became part of a larger mission of hope and reconciliation. Before facing the NHK, Ozawa led his Saito Kinen Orchestra in a New Year's Day teletcast promoting peace and the New Japan Philharmonic in a benefit for the victims of the 1994 Kobe earthquake. The NHK program featured Bartók's *Concerto for Orchestra* and Dvořák's *Cello Concerto*, with Rostropovich as the soloist. At $170 a ticket, with the proceeds dedicated to disabled musicians, it sold out in twenty-five minutes. Conductor and players saw to it that harmony prevailed: Ozawa was *nakami doshi* now as never before. In retrospect, he conceded that he had made mistakes of his own in 1962. He was not a "nice boy," he told the *Boston Globe*, and had not been ready for the burden thrust upon him. He even termed the 1962 fiasco a blessing in disguise. He said it made him pursue his career in the West, where the orchestras and traditions were stronger.

"I am very Japanese," he told the *Globe* in Tokyo. "My family is here, my friends. I love Japanese food. If I didn't have this accident, this problem, whatever you call it, maybe I would not have pushed to go out, maybe I would have stayed as a very busy conductor in this city."[6]

Ozawa *is* very Japanese, and there is no escaping what it means for his career. In Boston he is on friendly terms with many of his players, but between him and Americans there is a screen that only partly has to do with the make-do quality of his English. The authoritarianism—even temper—that evidently antagonized the NHK in 1962 still flares up from time to time, as in the Ortner incident and other dismissals of staff members. In a particularly bitter instance involving a player, Ozawa tried in the 1980s to summarily dismiss principal trumpeter Charles Schlueter, whom the BSO had lured away from the Minnesota Orchestra. Ozawa's grounds were that Schlueter's playing was not up to BSO standards. After a protracted struggle an arbitrator in 1985 ruled in Schlueter's favor, although not on artistic grounds. He found that Ozawa had violated the players' union contract by failing to follow the prescribed disciplinary procedures. The dispute was dropped. Schlueter remained.

Ozawa is a different person when he is among his Saito Kinen players. During a Saito Kinen rehearsal in Vienna for a European tour, he dropped to his knees to plead for more expression from the violas during the slow movement of Brahms's Fourth Symphony. It was a humbling gesture he would not have made with the BSO. With the Saito Kinen, too, the fun-loving Ozawa pops out more readily. Both orchestras' postconcert parties on tour have the same sometimes madcap air of comradeship and letting go from tensions. But among the Japanese Ozawa plunges into a communal hot tub with the men, sits cross-legged on cushions on the floor, drinks Japanese beer, clowns, leaps up to make impromptu speeches or shout wise-cracks across the room, and gets the giggles. Describing the college-reunion spirit and babble of Japanese, English, and German on these occasions, he said, "We are like children when we are together."

The Saito Kinen Festival takes place in an ultramodern 2,000-seat, $75 million concert hall in Matsumoto, a sleepy city of 200,000 in the foothills of the Japanese Alps about 110 miles west of Tokyo. The ten-day event is Ozawa's attempt to show Japanese audiences that Japanese musicians can present Western music, including opera, at standards as high as those in the West.

The inaugural concert in 1992 was honored by the presence of Emperor Akihito and Empress Michiko, who, under heavy security, made one of their rare trips out of Tokyo for a cultural event. (Requiring lodgings for themselves and their retinue, the royal couple bumped the one-hundred-member orchestra from the city's best hotel for two nights.) The central event was Stravinsky's *Oedipus Rex*, conducted by Ozawa and staged with an international cast: Ozawa's admission that Japan could not yet supply front-rank opera singers or directors. Philip Langridge of England was the Oedipus, Jessye Norman of the United States the Jocasta, and the Japanese actress Kayoko Shiraishi the narrator; the No dancer Min Tanaka appeared as a double for Oedipus, performing in mime. The elaborate staging by Julie Taymor, an American, incorporated elements of kabuki theater, bunraku puppetry, and other Asian traditions, transforming the Greek drama into a spectacle of ancient arts. Each year thereafter, an Ozawa-led opera anchored the festival's symphonic and chamber concerts.

Receptive to Western music since the Meiji Restoration of 1868—Norio Ohga was a late manifestation—Japan nevertheless remained musically insular during the early post–World War II years, when Ozawa was growing up. By the 1990s the country still had no orchestra comparable to the BSO, much less an opera company to rank with the Metropolitan. As he aged, Ozawa felt a growing obligation to strengthen Japanese musical life during his remaining years. He told the *Globe* that the Japanese music world was still twenty or thirty years behind the West: "Very sad. There are so many music schools in Japan. Every year thousands of students who are graduated come out in the world. Wonderful soloists, wonderful pianists, wonderful musicians. They go out and sometimes, usually, they don't come back."[7]

Saito Kinen—the orchestra and the festival—was Ozawa's main vehicle for change. Partly through his efforts, Japanese playing standards did indeed rise, and there was enough interest in Tokyo to support eight or nine professional orchestras, far more than in any American city. Not *nakami doshi* as a young man, Ozawa became a national hero and model for success, acclaimed not only by orchestras and audiences but by the emperor and empress, with whom he exchanged ceremonial visits at concerts and in their palace. He seemed more a hero in Japan, in fact, than he did in Boston, where BSO recording activity was drying up—a fact duly noted in the players' newsletter—and some players admired him but many thought he was overextended and had overstayed his time.

Ozawa was clearly overextended when he joined the BSO in London in

December 1993 for a seven-city European tour. The month before, he had led the Vienna Philharmonic on a European tour taking in three of the same cities, London, Paris, and Munich. He returned to Tokyo from that journey suffering from a heavy flu, one of a series of respiratory ailments that had plagued him in recent years and resulted in concert cancelations. He was still under the weather when he arrived in London, and the early BSO programs, in London and Paris, did not show the orchestra at its best. Although audiences and critics cheered, there was grumbling within the musicians' ranks. The BSO, they said, had to take what was left of its music director after another orchestra had wrung him out.

Ozawa said he had not wanted to go on tour with the Viennese, but the Philharmonic was beginning a five-year touring cycle in Europe and Japan, each year with a different conductor, "and they picked me first. I couldn't say no. I think it's too bad I got sick, but my Boston Symphony played wonderfully."

The repertory for the BSO tour, all of it concert-tested in Boston, centered on Berlioz's *Symphonie fantastique* (an old Munch specialty) and Beethoven's and Mahler's Fourth Symphonies. In Paris Ozawa led Berlioz's *Requiem* in one of two all-Berlioz programs. The other paired the popular *Symphonie fantastique* with its sequel, *Lelio*, rarely performed even in Berlioz's France. Although bringing Berlioz from America to Paris was like serving the French a California wine, Jacques Doucelin, in *Le Figaro*, said that unlike the "admirable machines" of the Chicago, Philadelphia, and Cleveland orchestras, the BSO added emotion to the mix and went "beyond music."

The stops after Paris were Madrid, Vienna, Munich, and Milan, with the single Milanese concert given in La Scala opera house. Vienna, the home of Beethoven and Mahler, heard the Beethoven-Mahler program twice. The audiences were more enthusiastic than the critics. The final stop was Prague, where, in the BSO's first visit since 1956, the television cameras awaited. The occasion was an all-Dvořák program, to be performed in the faded art nouveau splendor of Smetana Hall. The date was December 16, 1993: the hundredth anniversary, to the day, of the first performance of Dvořák's *New World* Symphony, given in New York by the New York Philharmonic.

On this peg the BSO hung a made-for-television gala employing the services of three starry American soloists, Itzhak Perlman, Yo-Yo Ma, and soprano Frederica von Stade, and the Czech-American pianist Rudolf Firkušný. A black-tie audience paid $100 to $170 a ticket—steep by Czech standards—to hear an assemblage of Dvořák star turns and hits. The *New World* itself was represented by only one movement, the familiar Largo. As if to justify the pops-style American approach to Czechoslovakia's greatest composer, the program notes suggested that the "blend of great art and entertainment" would (presumably via television) "provide a bridge to those citizens of our planet who will be hearing Dvořák's music for the very first time."

The evening's most dramatic moment came at the outset, when a fanfare by Smetana ushered in Czech president Václav Havel and his wife, Olga Havlova. As the audience stood in respect, the couple made their way into the presidential box overlooking the stage, where they heard the entire concert. For the final ovations the Havels joined Ozawa and the soloists on the flower-decked stage. A particularly emotional moment occurred when Havel, the architect of post-Communist Czech democracy, embraced Firkušný, who had refused to play in Czechoslovakia while it was controlled by the Communists.

Ozawa, fully recovered, was in fine form. The audience responded with generous ovations, and the BSO's playing was remarkably good for an orchestra that had whipped the nonstandard program into shape in two rehearsals at the end of a grueling two-week trip. Yet the evening was a hodgepodge, roundly attacked as such by the Czech critics. The musical nuggets ranged from the famous *Humoresque*, in an arrangement for violin, cello, and orchestra, to two *Gypsy Melodies*, sung by von Stade, and a movement from the *Dumky* Trio, played in unmatched styles by Perlman, Ma, and Firkušný. The evening's most conspicuous presence, overshadowing even Havel, was the busy bank of television cameras. Most conspicuously of all, one dangled like a snout from a huge boom that periodically rolled up and down the center aisle, hungering for closeups and fadeouts. Even so, several performances were not satisfactory for commercial distribution and had to be reshot in the empty hall after the concert, further prolonging the exhausted musicians' travails.

The program was produced by Peter Gelb, who was also the producer for the Marsalis project at Tanglewood. A former BSO assistant manager, Gelb went on to Columbia Artists and, later, Sony Classical, at both of which he oversaw the BSO's television fortunes and channeled artists into Boston.[8] Designed to television's specifications, the Prague gala was shown live in Europe and taped for later broadcast in the United States. Video cassette and compact-disc versions were also released by Sony. Both—surprisingly for the video—omitted the drama of Havel's entry, Kenneth Haas, then the BSO's managing director, said the orchestra tried to include a television gala on each of its foreign tours. The format of excerpts and stars, he said, is "the way classical music goes on television these days," and the collaboration with Europe's national TV networks made the show less expensive for all.

Except for the occasional shot of the ornate hall, the program could have been any orchestra playing Dvořák excerpts for a black-tie audience anywhere. Television's needs, complete with superstar soloists, snaking cameras, and blinding lights, had become the tail that wagged the dog. And whether in Prague or at Tanglewood, Ozawa stood ready to accommodate the cameras. There was nothing particularly venal or out of the ordinary about it. As Haas said, it was the way classical music was going.

AT TANGLEWOOD music was also going the celebrity route with stars like Perlman and Ma, who provided surefire box office to offset the occasional gamble on new faces and new works. The twin idols were on the BSO schedule every summer, but the "Three Birthdays" program in 1995 reunited them and Ozawa as a team for the first time since Prague.

The gala grew out of discussions of how to celebrate Ozawa's sixtieth, which fell on September 1. The date lies between the BSO's Tanglewood and Boston seasons, and Ozawa had already decided to spend his birthday in Tokyo, where he would conduct another benefit for victims of the Kobe earthquake. As BSO program planners discussed other options open to them, it dawned on them that Perlman's fiftieth fell on August 31 and Ma's fortieth on October 7. At that point, Tanglewood manager Daniel Gustin said, the three-birthdays idea "just steamrollered along. It was just irresistible." It was so irresistible that the BSO invited President and Mrs. Clinton to attend. The First Couple politely declined.

The birthday party was a gala to outdo all Tanglewood galas except the four-hour seventieth-birthday salute to Leonard Bernstein in 1988. It opened with Brahms's *Academic Festival* Overture and Double Concerto in slapped-together performances like some in Prague. But monumental Brahms was not the point. After intermission the three guests of honor took seats in chairs drawn up in front of the podium, and conductor-composer André Previn sauntered onstage in a spiffy jacket and bow tie as master of ceremonies. Reading from a script, he described Ozawa, Perlman, and Ma as "three musical giants." In his praises of Ozawa, however, he observed that in Japan, at sixty "everything's complete."

Ozawa, who can mug with a comedian's perfect sense of timing, jumped out of his chair and began shaking a fist. As laughter spread through the throng, Previn calmly read on, "At sixty Seiji now represents the master musician. Nothing's missing, everything's complete." That set the tone, amused and affectionate, for the variety show that followed.

There were birthday presents, proffered by a conductorless BSO: for Ma, Rachmaninoff's Vocalise, played by six Music Center cellists as soloists; for Perlman, "At the Fireplace," a Yiddish folk song; for Ozawa, Berlioz's "Dance of the Sylphs," recalling his French tutelage under Munch. The gifts set off a round of surprises and other party acts. In one, Leon Fleisher made a comeback as a two-handed pianist, performing a movement from Brahms's Trio, op. 8, with Perlman and Ma. Taking the microphone, Ma told the crowd, "This is the fulfillment of a childhood dream: to be able to one day play something with Leon." The date, July 23, actually was Fleisher's birthday—his sixty-seventh. He joined the three other celebrants in a guest of honor's chair.

Ma and Doriot Anthony Dwyer, the BSO's former principal flutist, played the posthumous world premiere of Bernstein's Variations on an Octatonic Scale, apparently his last remaining unperformed work. Pop stars Bernadette Peters and James Taylor joined Senator Edward Kennedy in singing a birthday version of Cole Porter's "You're the Top." The new lyrics, penned for the occasion by the Boston Pops's laureate conductor, John Williams, included this politically dubious tribute to Ozawa, croaked out by Kennedy: "You're standing tall, you've done it all—*without Bob Dole!*" When the last laugh faded and the last tear was shed, the four thousand colored balloons fell and enthusiasts in the audience ran through the aisles, grabbing at and popping them.

Like a photographic positive and negative, the war memorial concerts two weeks later showed the two sides of Ozawa—master of control, spiritual pilgrim—in direct contrast. His Berlioz *Requiem*, with Vinson Cole as the tenor soloist, was rigidly controlled and sputtered into life only in the singing of the chorus. He, the BSO, and Cole had performed the work repeatedly in the previous two seasons, most recently on tour in Asia, and the performance seemed to have gone stale. The next afternoon his Mahler Second, which had Barbara Bonney and Florence Quivar as the vocal soloists, enjoyed the freedom that the Berlioz had lacked. Tempos and dynamics tended toward extremes, and the veering from one to the next could be dizzying. But these effects—this willingness to take chances—grew out of a passionate response that bound the intimate details and the resurrection finale together in a musical and emotional vision.

The Berlioz and Mahler works do not make a natural pair. The former was completed by a Catholic and Frenchman in 1837, the latter by a Jew and adoptive Austrian in 1894. A world of differences, both stylistic and philosophical, separates them. Religious ritual in Berlioz yields in Mahler to a faith that rushes outdoors to embrace the entire universe. Yet there are links, too, especially appropriate to one of history's most momentous dates. The Berlioz was actually composed as a memorial to victims of war and ends with a rumble of funeral drums. The Mahler, seeming to pick up where the Berlioz leaves off, begins with an enormous set of funeral marches and ends in an affirmation that the dead will live again.

As Ozawa realized, the two works fit together as a monumental statement. Dedicate the performances to the memory of all war dead, ally and enemy alike, and you have a giant gesture of reconciliation, made by a Japanese conductor in the former enemy nation where he has made his name.

Then ten years of age, Ozawa was living in Tachikawa, a suburb of Tokyo, when the Hiroshima and Nagasaki bombs fell and Japan surrendered. Three of his classmates died in American air raids, and his two teenage brothers were conscripted as military laborers. He himself once thought an American fighter-bomber was attacking him outside his house. (It was actually swooping in to bomb and machine-gun a nearby military base, but it was so close that Ozawa can recall seeing the pilot's eyes.) Yet he remembers the war's end as a happy time. After the hate propaganda about Americans, he said, Japanese children were happily surprised to find themselves treated well by an enemy made up of easygoing men who chewed gum and smoked Lucky Strikes.

But "the big thing," he admitted, was that his father said they could play baseball and his mother made him a mitt. Baseball had been forbidden because it was an American sport.

The public likes to see its leaders and heroes come down from their pedestals. Ozawa, a fan of Boston's Red Sox, Patriots, Celtics, and Bruins, occasionally obliges by leading bands at Red Sox and Patriots games. But his pacifist convictions take him on an itinerary far from the patriotic truths that Fenway Park's sometimes rowdy fans hold dear. Before coming to Tanglewood in 1995, he conducted concerts in Vienna, Florence, Tokyo, and Nagasaki to commemorate the World War II anniversary. Each, like the Tanglewood observance, served as a plea for peace and reconciliation.

The New Year's Day telecast from Tokyo, with the Saito Kinen Orchestra, featured an international cast of performers and speakers that included Nobel peace laureate Nelson Mandela and Nobel literature laureate Kenzaburo Oe, former president Jimmy Carter, Yo-Yo Ma, filmmaker Steven Spielberg, and scat singer Bobby McFerrin. The Vienna concert, Mahler's *Resurrection* Symphony performed with the Vienna Philharmonic in the city's historic opera house, also marked the fortieth anniversary of Austria's post–World War II independence. The Nagasaki program was the *Resurrection* Symphony with the New Japan Philharmonic and singers from Tokyo. The "wonderful thing" about that performance, Ozawa explained, was that a local committee sponsored it as a nondenominational gesture for peace in a normally sectarian Roman Catholic church.

Ozawa said he avoided a Hiroshima concert on the anniversary of the bombing not only because of the political implications but because too many other organizations were planning observances in the city on that date. The Nagasaki group that invited him to conduct, he said, took the right way, steering clear of controversy and declaring, in effect: "We want peace. We want new life, against the atomic bomb." He said the attack on Pearl Harbor had been unfair, a mistake made worse by the failure of the Japanese ambassador in Washington to deliver a warning sent from Tokyo. So now the Japanese, having suffered the consequences of starting a war—not the United States for having dropped the Hiroshima and Nagasaki bombs—had an obligation to right a wrong: "The Japanese people should now speak out more strongly against atomic arms because we saw two atomic bombs. The Japanese government is not so strong about that. I think that's not right. Nagasaki and Hiroshima people feel more strongly."

The Tanglewood war memorial weekend climaxed a yearlong BSO retrospective of works—many by men banned, exiled, or murdered by the Nazis—composed in the shadow of World War II. The Boston centerpiece, conducted by Ozawa, was Britten's pacifist *War Requiem,* one of those devotional works that strike a deeply resonant chord within him. (The work received its American premiere at Tanglewood in 1963 under Erich Leinsdorf's direction; Ozawa conducted a profoundly moving 1986 performance at Tanglewood as part of a fortieth-anniversary Hiroshima commemoration in the United States, Japan, and Europe.) The Mahler part of the Tanglewood weekend opened with an unusual variation on the resurrection theme. For another fiftieth anniversary—that of his debut—Fleisher returned to the two-hand concerto repertory in Mozart's K. 414. The performance, a sequel to his Brahms with Perlman and Ma two weeks before, was the more moving for unshackling musical powers that had been largely silenced for three decades. Ozawa conducted, as he had many times before for Fleisher in the left-hand concerto repertory; two years later Ozawa's determination to remake the Music Center ruptured the partnership.

Some BSO players criticize Ozawa as seeking to advance his own career at the expense of the music and his orchestra. There is evidence for this in his absences from Boston and his occasionally careless, highhanded, or erratic behavior, the Music Center upheaval being a prime example. Yet there

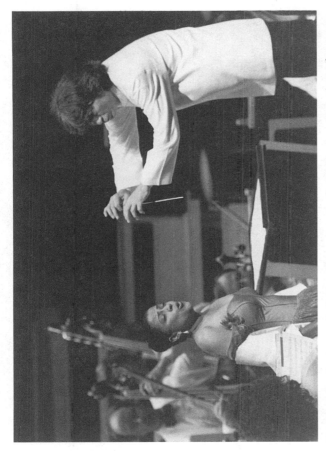

Kathleen Battle sings as Seiji Ozawa conducts in the BSO's 1995 opening-night concert. (Walter H. Scott)

could be no doubting his commitment to music and the cause of peace on that Sunday afternoon in August when resurrection resonated in the Berkshire air. As occasionally happens in the best music making, the personal and the transcendent merged to produce an entity larger than either.

THE BSO'S OPENING-NIGHT GALA that summer had been a more earthbound affair. It featured Kathleen Battle in a crowd-pleaser program that culminated in Orff's *Carmina burana*, an Ozawa parade piece. He stepped up the built-in voltage even higher by taking the *faux* medieval cantata, with its driving rhythms, ersatz primitivism, and choral celebrations of boozing and sex, at a supercharged pace.

Not for the first time, Tanglewood's love affair with stars kicked up a fuss. Battle, recently banished from the Metropolitan Opera for rehearsal behavior unbecoming even to a diva, acted up again in rehearsal with Ozawa. She ordered vocal students, who regularly sit in on BSO singers' rehearsals, out of the Shed and lectured Ozawa on the music. Then she sang indifferently in the concert. But Tanglewood can take its music seriously even when it puts on a show. Songs from the original *Carmina burana* manuscript were scheduled for the night before the Orff work. The medieval version was performed in Ozawa Hall by the Boston Camerata.

Other notable events in the season included Keith Lockhar's Tanglewood debut as conductor of the Boston Pops; a marathon of the six Bartók quartets, performed in a single evening by the Emerson String Quartet; a stimulating and diverse Festival of Contemporary Music, and BSO conducting appearances by John Nelson, Marek Janowski, Jeffrey Tate, and Christoph Eschenbach. One of the players' favorite guest conductors, along with Bernard Haitink, Eschenbach ended the season with a moving Verdi *Requiem.* Ozawa was already in Japan. The Hiroshima day concert had been his last of the season.

For the earthquake benefit given in Tokyo on his birthday, Ozawa conducted members of American and European orchestras he regularly worked with, including the BSO, and again had Rostropovich as a soloist. By coincidence September 1 was also a national day of disaster preparedness. "Everybody understood that this is going to be not just 'happy, happy birthday,' but life and death, death and life," Ozawa said of his concert. He went on from Tokyo to the Saito Kinen Festival, where he conducted winter in a rebirth of semistaged BSO opera. Two weeks after Saito Kinen he was back in Boston to begin rehearsals for the opening of the winter BSO season.

Technically the BSO was playing at a high level, though the principal flutist's position had remained unfilled from Dwyer's retirement in 1990 until Jacques Zoon of the Netherlands took up the position (having earlier refused it) in September 1997. Technically, too, Ozawa's baton work was clear and graphic, like a beacon to guide players in even the heaviest orchestral seas. He was a skillful accompanist—he had steered the orchestra past many a perilous shoal with soloists like Jessye Norman and Battle—and he claimed to have instilled a deeper, more Germanic sound in an orchestra traditionally thought of as having inherited a more transparent French quality from its years under Pierre Monteux, Koussevitzky, and Munch. The alteration (if alteration it was) seemed a part of the homogenization taking place as national and local characteristics disappeared from orchestras across the world. But at its best the BSO was as good as any in the world. In repertory and soloists it tended to travel the safe side of the street with audience-pleasing choices—but so did most other American orchestras. Then in 1994 Ozawa brought in Anthony Fogg, an Australian, as his artistic administrator, or assistant for artists and repertory. At Tanglewood Fogg began gradually weighting the programming toward a less-familiar repertory, including more American works, and programs with thematic connections.

Tanglewood programming would always be constrained by a BSO rehearsal schedule that required preparation of three different programs in most weeks. (In Symphony Hall, by contrast, a single program each week receives as many as six rehearsals and three or four performances.) That meant a continuing reliance on standard repertory, which the orchestra could brush up quickly, and a limit on the number of out-of-the-way or contemporary works. Nor would the Shed audience have wanted it any other way. Nor did that audience share critics' remaining qualms about Ozawa, in whom the doubters still found a certain slickness. In his ovations at concerts as in his reception at fund-raising events and other BSO functions, he was as much a hero as he was in Japan.

As with his Berkshire home, which clings to a hillside with panoramic views of the rolling hills to the south and west, Ozawa has carved out a Japanese space within an American environment. White and New England-plain on the outside, the two-story house has only a tennis court to distinguish it from its neighbors. Inside, much of the furniture is American but the ambiance is Japanese. When Ozawa's Russian-born wife, Vera, their two children, and his mother come from Japan to be with him during the last two weeks of his Tanglewood stay, chatter in Japanese fills the rooms. BSO functionaries, soloists, and other visitors shuttle in and out on what begins as a rigid schedule but soon breaks down as Ozawa keeps each to chat. If the conversation becomes social, gin is likely to appear. Yet while on a first-name basis with nearly everyone, Ozawa is not *nakami doshi*—"one of us"—in America. The music and talk about music may be Western, but in gesture, speech, and thought he remains rooted to another culture.

In one sense Ozawa is a mirror of the late-twentieth-century music director, torn between the tugs of his own orchestra and other podiums around the world, seduced by fees that in his case total $1 million or more a year, and faced with the necessity to haul a nineteenth-century institution into the twenty-first century. In another sense he is a special case, formed by and pulled back to a country that came late to Western music and culture.

Yet everything was not "complete" (in André Previn's term) for him, in either Japan or the United States. In both standard and contemporary works, he put a high charge of electricity or tension on the music's surface—a sure way to win over an audience—yet frequently left finer points untouched beneath. He attracted audiences and money to the BSO, and the guest conductors who deputized for him included some, like Haitink, who brought distinction as well as variety to the podium. But he is not another Koussevitzky, living with his orchestra day in and day out through the year and raising it and himself to greatness together. Nor is he another Bernstein who touches each orchestra he conducts with greatness, however transitory. In the era of the jet, the television camera, the million-dollar pay scale, and the idolatrous crowd, perhaps it is too late for other Koussevitzkys and Bernsteins to arise. Perhaps excellence is all that can be expected in a conductor.

And in some ways Ozawa is excellent. If he has blind spots in his repertory, so does every other conductor. (Mozart's music was one of Koussevitzky's weaker points, as it is for Ozawa.) Yet something in Ozawa falls short of the promise that Munch and others saw in 1960 when he arrived, nearly penniless, from Japan. Everything might be complete at sixty in Japan, but the greatest conductors continue to grow until, paradoxically, they are at the height of their powers just when death or debility steals the baton from their hands. On the verge of becoming the BSO's longest-tenured director, Ozawa seems to have overstayed his time: neither he nor the orchestra is growing. Perhaps at sixty, with a hall named in his honor, he has been seduced by the tinsel of power and celebrity. Perhaps the Japanese in him misunderstands the finer nuances of Western thought and life. Perhaps he belongs in opera, perhaps with another orchestra; perhaps he enjoys his greatest success on the road as a guest conductor, with no further responsibilities to an orchestra. Or perhaps he simply falls between two worlds: the worlds of spirit and commerce, of freedom and control, of culture and celebrity, of East and West. Perhaps the day is coming when he will retire from the BSO in glory with laureate status and give himself fully to the bettering of music in Japan. There he might find the completion that has eluded him in America.

3

The
Riderless
Horse

"In my end is my beginning," Leonard Bernstein said, quoting T. S. Eliot's *Four Quartets* (which was quoting Guillaume de Machaut), when Tanglewood staged a four-day party for his seventieth birthday in 1988. He was a better prophet than he could have known. Just as he had begun his conducting career at Tanglewood in 1940 under Koussevitzky, he ended it there with his Boston Symphony Orchestra concert of August 19, 1990. On October 14 he was dead.

The concert took place on a cold, cloudy Sunday afternoon six days before Bernstein's seventy-second birthday. In his summer tux—white jacket, black trousers—he made his way painfully to the podium, seeming to drag a terrible weight behind him. The fire was gone from his sunken eyes; his face and body were at once bloated and gaunt, like a gnome's. The Shed audience, huddling under raincoats and sweaters, rose and applauded in tribute to the man and his gallantry in the face of disease. He was even sicker than the audience knew, despite his much-publicized travails. In rehearsal a few days before with the Tanglewood Music Center Orchestra, he had spoken of his death and likened his trials to Job's.

A chain-smoker, Bernstein had suffered for years from emphysema and related troubles, including the side effects of his dependence on painkillers. But always something—friends, music, work with the young, Scotch, the cigarettes that had brought on his afflictions—had kept him going. A month before Tanglewood he had given up the Pacific Music Festival, a summer concert series and academy he had helped to found on the Tanglewood model in Sapporo, Japan. In Tokyo for the festival, he collapsed in his hotel suite. He canceled his six remaining Japanese concerts and was flown back to New York to see his doctor.

A month's rest at his Connecticut estate refreshed him but produced no miracles. Nevertheless, Bernstein wanted to go on with his annual teaching and conducting sojourn at Tanglewood, and his physician, Dr. Kevin Cahill, agreed that work might be the best medicine. The visit was to be more onerous than usual. On the day after the climactic BSO concert, Bernstein planned to embark on a twelve-day tour of Europe with the Music Center Orchestra, repeating the program they would give at Tanglewood. He had proposed the trip. It was to be his salute to the Music Center on its fiftieth anniversary and the crowning event in a summer-long jubilee.

The BSO program consisted of the Four Sea Interludes from Benjamin Britten's *Peter Grimes*; Bernstein's first performance of his own *Arias and Barcarolles* in an orchestration by the young Chinese-American composer Bright Sheng, one of Bernstein's many Tanglewood protégés; and Beethoven's Seventh Symphony. It was no coincidence that Britten's music was receiving its first Tanglewood performance since Bernstein conducted the opera's American premiere in the Theater-Concert Hall in 1946. With the BSO at Tanglewood, he always programmed a work associated with Serge Koussevitzky and the festival's beginnings.

Like Bernstein himself the Sea Interludes performance was slow and full of pain: almost an icy premonition of death. The orchestral version of his own song cycle, which originally had a two-piano accompaniment, took even more out of him. Too weakened to learn and rehearse it, he turned over the baton to another in the long line of Tanglewood protégés, BSO assistant conductor Carl St. Clair. Two other favorites, Judy Kaye and Kurt Ollmann, were the vocalists. Bernstein listened to the performance in the radio control booth. Waiting backstage when St. Clair finished, Bernstein embraced this Texas boy who had been inspired to take up conducting by watching him in a delayed telecast from Tanglewood. Then he retired to his dressing room for a massage. When the audience had reassembled in the afternoon chill, he repeated his laborious trek to the podium to conduct the Beethoven symphony.

The performance was slow—at times, almost to the point of stopping. That was no surprise: most of Bernstein's performances in recent years had been slow. But where other performances had used the time to explore the music's innermost workings and meanings, this one lost momentum and turned ragged. During the third movement an almost audible gasp ran through the audience: Bernstein was seized by a coughing fit. Leaning back on the podium rail for support, coughing uncontrollably into a red bandanna from his back pocket, he nodded to keep the orchestra going. It was a device he had used often in the past to propel a performance upward and outward beyond gravity. Now it was a desperate expedient. The audience,

Leonard Bernstein takes his last bow at the end of his 1990 BSO concert. (Walter H. Scott)

which included his mother, his three children, friends from New York, and about 225 Music Center alumni gathered for a fiftieth-anniversary reunion, looked on in horror. The thought in many minds was, *Would he be able to go on?*

The spell lasted only a minute or so but seemed an eternity. Slowly, painfully, while the orchestra took over for him, Bernstein got his coughing under control, stuffed the bandanna back into a pocket, and returned to his task. He threw himself into the finale with almost manic energy, as if to prove he was still had it in him. At the end a thunderous ovation followed him as he limped off the stage. In the wings a lighted cigarette awaited him; he also needed oxygen to revive him. They weren't enough. That night he canceled the Music Center Orchestra tour of Europe. It would have been the student ensemble's first appearance outside Tanglewood in the fifty years since he had stood before it as a Koussevitzky protégé in its maiden concert.

Bernstein's death severed Tanglewood's last direct link with the founder. After Koussevitzky's death in 1951, while Bernstein was busy elsewhere (everywhere, it sometimes seemed) as a composer and conductor, Koussevitzky's widow, Olga, had been the bearer of his memory at ceremonial occasions. When she died in 1978, the mantle fell not to Seiji Ozawa, who had been a protégé of Charles Munch, but to Bernstein. It was a responsibility Ozawa was willing to cede and Bernstein was ready to assume, both figuratively and literally. Already he wore the master's cape and cuff links to concerts and other public events, and he often slept in Koussevitzky's bedroom on visits to Tanglewood. In that role he was to speak for Koussevitzky. Henceforth he would speak for Tanglewood and the world outside the gates even as the rise of consumerism and pop culture threatened to make those ideals obsolete.

Unlike the ties with Koussevitzky and Tanglewood, the Bernstein-BSO relationship was not always a close or comfortable one.

Born in Lawrence, Massachusetts, to middle-class parents who had no ear for serious music, Bernstein went to Tanglewood in 1940 as a brash, piano-playing, jazz-loving Harvard graduate who for the last year had studied conducting with the crusty Fritz Reiner at the Curtis Institute of Music in Philadelphia. (Fellow students at Curtis, Bernstein recalled in his book *Findings*, regarded him "as a Harvard smart aleck, an intellectual big shot, a snob, and a show-off." By his own admission he probably was.)[1] He was one of five conducting fellows handpicked by Koussevitzky for the first Music Center class, along with Lukas Foss, Richard Bales, Thor Johnson, and Gaylord Browne. Bernstein and Foss, the only ones to go on to major careers, quickly became Koussevitzky's favorites, with Bernstein as the anointed one. He returned as a conducting fellow in 1941 and 1942. Then, after a hiatus caused by the war, he was back as Koussevitzky's assistant in 1946, conducting the *Peter Grimes* premiere recalled in the 1990 farewell.

Like many a musician and concertgoer after him, Bernstein fell under the spell of the place. In a letter home early in his first summer he wrote that "the inspiration of this Center is terrific enough to keep you going with no sleep at all."[2] Fellow students remembered him as a man consumed by his own talents and destiny even then. By 1988 he considered his destiny and Tanglewood's interlocked. Looking back at a press conference opening the seventieth-birthday fête, he said his Tanglewood roots were so strong that "I feel I built the bloody place." And Koussevitzky, he said, "was the light and soul of it," closely followed by Aaron Copland, the original faculty chairman, who in 1988 was ailing and unable to attend the seventieth-birthday bash.

In the main address opening the 1970 Music Center session, Bernstein recalled Koussevitzky in terms that could have described the heir himself. Koussevitzky, he said, was "a man possessed by music, by the ideas and ideals of music, and a man whose possessedness came at you like cosmic rays, whether from the podium or in a living room or in a theater like this." (Bernstein's own possessedness was such that, in his good looks and magnetic energy, he seemed lankier than he actually was.) Speaking in the Theater–Concert Hall, where Koussevitzky had first put him in front of an orchestra, Bernstein went on:

You see, in all the years I had lived and grown up in Boston, I had never met Koussevitzky; for me he was that distant, glamorous figure that I saw and heard from the dizzying height of the second balcony in Symphony Hall, and it was only after I had graduated from Harvard and had spent a long winter studying in Philadelphia that I read in the newspaper of the impending opening of this new Music Center at Tanglewood. I rushed up to Boston armed with letters of recommendation from anybody who would give me one, gained entry into the maestro's study, and—I must confess I was so awestruck I don't remember a moment of that interview, except his saying at the end of it, "Of course, my dear, I will except you in my class."[3]

Koussevitzky, whose Russian accent Bernstein mimicked fondly, called his protégé by the Russian diminutive "Lenyushka," became both a father and a friend to him, and groomed him to be his BSO successor. He was right in his appraisal of Bernstein's king-size talents but wrong in thinking the BSO was ready for an American conductor with one foot planted in Broadway. (He was also wrong in thinking that this composer-conductor wanted the BSO, Bernstein repeatedly insisted later in life. Sour grapes? Perhaps.) When Koussevitzky retired in 1949, the trustees turned instead to the fifty-eight-year-old Charles Munch.

Koussevitzky's death in 1951 further weakened the pull of Tanglewood. Later that year Bernstein married the Chilean-born actress Felicia Montealegre and began a high-profile celebrity life that reached a bizarre climax in the "radical chic" benefit party that the couple threw in 1970 for the revolutionary Black Panthers group. While Bernstein returned regularly to Tanglewood to conduct and to teach, his booming career and changing life drew him increasingly in other directions. The separation became a gap when he served as director of the New York Philharmonic from 1958 to 1969 and had even less time for his Berkshire alma mater. For the last six of those years, moreover, the BSO was directed by Erich Leinsdorf, Munch's successor. A hands-on Tanglewood leader, Leinsdorf had strong ideas of his own about the running of Koussevitzky's festival and would not have been receptive to a high-powered competitor.

It was the 1969 accession of William Steinberg, director of the Pittsburgh Symphony, as Leinsdorf's successor that drew Bernstein back into the fold. Seventy years old, infirm, and still conducting in Pittsburgh, Steinberg had neither time nor energy for Tanglewood. When the BSO named a triumvirate of Ozawa, Bernstein, and Gunther Schuller to direct the summer festival, beginning in 1970, Bernstein took a largely advisory, figurehead role. The appointment, however, began the series of annual residencies that lasted, with occasional interruptions, until his death. His visit quickly became one of each season's most eagerly awaited, provocative, and chaotic events. With an entourage of managers, assistants, press representatives, relatives, friends, a housekeeper, and beautiful young men, he descended on the place like a king with his court and stayed for ten days to two weeks, running everyone except himself into a frazzle with his open-ended rehearsals, supercharged performances, endless babble, indefatigable hugging and kissing, all-night parties, unquenchable appetite for Scotch and cigarettes, and all-round jiving. No one was better than he with the young, and no one fed more on their adulation. Shining light though he was in the season, management was always glad to see him depart.

No wonder there were absences and squabbles. Virtually alone among BSO conductors, Bernstein routinely demanded overtime at rehearsals—a costly matter for an orchestra—and could create an ugly scene if he did not get it. Not only did he feel as if he had built the bloody place; he sometimes acted that way, too. The low point came in 1981–82 with a year-long boycott of the BSO. Bernstein was angered by the orchestra's refusal to record Gershwin's *Rhapsody in Blue* with him as the conductor and pianist after a 1981 Tanglewood performance. Along with his 1982 Tanglewood date he canceled three winter appearances in the orchestra's 1981–82 centennial celebration. He spent the summer of 1982 as a codirector of the inaugural session of the Los Angeles Philharmonic Institute, another Tanglewood Music Center clone he had helped to found. His fellow director was Michael Tilson Thomas, another Tanglewood alumnus and Bernstein protégé. To seal the estrangement, he recorded Gershwin's *Rhapsody* with the Los Angeles Philharmonic.

Whatever Bernstein felt about the BSO, his loyalty to Tanglewood never faltered. In 1978, after his wife's death, he canceled his summer BSO engagement but went to Tanglewood anyway to work with students and conduct the Music Center Orchestra. He missed the summer of 1980 altogether

while on a sabbatical to devote himself to composing. After the 1982 contre-
temps he returned every year, drawing crowds of students, auditors, and
starry-eyed BSO followers to his rehearsals and conducting classes. Each
year there would be two concerts, one with the BSO and one with the student orchestra. Following the format established by Koussevitzky and
adopted by professional conductors ever since, he would prepare two or
three student conductors in shorter works to open the Music Center Orchestra program and then lead the symphony or other major work himself.
He and the BSO put their differences behind them. In fact, he now conducted the BSO only at Tanglewood. To the end he accepted no fee for his
Tanglewood engagements, but rebated the money—probably in the vicinity
of $50,000—to the Music Center, creating an endowment to support future
generations of students.

The love fest culminated in the seventieth-birthday party in 1988. The
four-day round of concerts and related events attracted pop and classical
celebrities from the United States and Europe, many of them for no more
than walk-on appearances in the four-hour gala on the actual birth date. In
tears at the end of a performance of his *Mass* two nights later by the Indiana
University Opera Theater, Bernstein made his way from his box seat to the
stage. After hugging and kissing cast members right and left, he turned to
the audience and a waiting microphone, and in an emotion-choked voice
declared the performance "a miracle—a miracle of youth, first of all; a miracle of faith, a ceaseless miracle of America, and I hope a ceaseless miracle
of Tanglewood."

Bernstein himself conducted the BSO in the climactic event, the Serge
and Olga Koussevitzky Memorial Concert, the next afternoon. On the program were two Koussevitzky specialties, Haydn's Symphony No. 88 and
Tchaikovsky's Fifth. In between Seiji Ozawa conducted a birthday garland
of eight variations on Bernstein's tune "New York, New York," each by
a different composer. The adulatory crowd of fourteen thousand included
governor and presidential candidate Michael S. Dukakis and Secretary of
State George P. Shultz.

The love fest belonged to the media, too. There was such a deluge of
reporters and cameras that it required reinforcement of the BSO's public
relations staff and put Tanglewood permanently on the television map, an
eminence that heightened its desirability on the tourist map. The coverage
included live concert broadcasts back to Europe by European television. In
an earlier time—when Bernstein was spreading the gospel of classical music
to a general audience via his televised "Omnibus" shows and "Young

People's Concerts," for example—such a thing might also have been possible in the United States. Now the homeland of Bernstein and Tanglewood saw only celebrity highlights on the networks. The concert programming did not arrive until several months later, and then in a taped, edited version of the European production shown on PBS.

Bernstein never had a permanent relationship with the BSO such as he had with the New York, Vienna, and Israel Philharmonics. But he never forgot old friends, and Tanglewood held a place in his life more personal in some ways than those exalted podiums elsewhere. His annual BSO assignment, fittingly, was the Koussevitzky Memorial Concert. Each year, reexamining a standard work or works usually associated in some way with Koussevitzky, he lit fires that glowed as brightly as anything on the musical horizon. Especially searing performances in this series included a Beethoven *Missa solemnis* (1971), a Mahler Ninth Symphony (1979; the only time the BSO ever performed this Bernstein specialty with him), and a Brahms First (1985). In 1989, Tanglewood's Copland year, he turned the program into a tribute to his shut-in friend and comrade in arms, leading his *Music for the Theatre* and *Dance Symphony* in the final day's concert, along with Shostakovich's Fifth Symphony.

Symphony musicians are notorious complainers, and in the BSO Bernstein generated generous garlands of gripes with his overtime rehearsals, hugging and kissing, and all-round grandstanding and showboating. Yet musicians, like athletes, want to deliver, and they recognize quality. The BSO consistently gave its best and its all for Bernstein, even when his partying had taken a toll, as it did on the night in 1987 when he showed up for a Sibelius Fifth considerably the worse for wear. As in the final concert, the BSO did both its work and his. The audience never knew.

Orchestra members felt the impact of his performances. Recalling the open rehearsal of the 1985 Brahms First, James Orleans, a BSO double bassist, wrote on the occasion of the 1988 birthday celebration:

From the opening C-minor chords of this symphony, I felt it was destined to be a momentous event. The involvement onstage was total. I felt the energy from every member of the orchestra. I remember distinctly the B-major chord of the first movement's second ending appearing to me for the first time as emanating from a great pipe organ, the sonority of the orchestra was so astonishingly rich. The finale was even more remarkable. . . .

Not a soul in the orchestra was left untouched by the experience. They had all been moved to involve themselves completely, to spend themselves fully in service to the music and Bernstein's vision of it. I noticed much head-shaking amongst

the players backstage in utter amazement at the miracle that had just happened.
How we were going to do it again in the evening was an unspoken question.[4]

If beads became a symbol of hipness in the 1960s and 1970s, the Music Center was as close to the eternally hip Bernstein's heart as the beads he affected during that era. The Music Center was where his beginnings lay, and it was where he fired the imaginations of the young and they repaid him with worship and adulation. As a teacher and conductor Bernstein could be both maddening and revelatory. In his classes he would stop for political, philosophical, or personal monologues, in which, politically, he simply repeated the left-liberal commonplaces of the day. He also had a rabbinical streak, preaching as well as teaching. But when he got down to the business of music—how to beat a measure, get players to do what you wanted them to do, find the meat of a composer's intent—he had no equal.

Marin Alsop, one of the tribe of protégés, once recalled how Bernstein had put her through her paces in preparing Roy Harris's Third Symphony for a Music Center Orchestra concert. It was a work Alsop had never before heard, much less conducted. After two rehearsals in which "he knew, and I sensed, that something was missing," he put his arm around her at the next rehearsal and said, "You must forget about conducting now. . . . The inner music will lead you." Alsop recalled: "It wasn't so much what he said but the depth of caring in his expression. He knew that I had more to give, and his sole desire was to free me." When she returned to the podium, "all had changed—it was all new." As the concert was about to begin, Bernstein stood with her in the wings, wearing his Koussevitzky cape, and took her arm. "Very quietly he began concentrating and humming the opening of the Harris symphony—willing his love for the piece into me. And then the door opened and he playfully pushed me onstage. 'It's all yours, baby.'"[5]

His generosity with students was matched by a generosity with friends. Many musicians were the beneficiaries of his financial or moral support. Other friends would receive phone calls—sometimes from far points of the planet—or visits during times of sickness or other troubles.

Bernstein had a darker angel, too, and it was a side of him that the dazzled young didn't readily see. All-consuming as his performances could be, they depended on more than the usual amount of conductor's license. Indeed, he frequently said that when conducting, he *became* the composer.[6] He could take liberties, in other words, because he was a composer himself and could penetrate a fellow composer's mind and soul.

That sense of an all-seeing, all-knowing self could also manifest itself in the classroom. It happened, for instance, in a 1987 conducting seminar when a young man from Scandinavia volunteered to lead the first movement of Mozart's G Minor Symphony, No. 40, to get the benefit of the master's advice.

The seminar took place, as usual, in the living room of Seranak, Koussevitzky's former mansion. Amid the overstuffed sofas and chairs under a benign portrait of Koussevitzky clutching his double bass, folding chairs had been set up to accommodate the twenty or so conducting students and auditors and fifty or so Bernstein admirers who invariably turned up at his supposedly closed classes. As a pair of pianists stood by to play the orchestral part, the student took his place at a music stand between them, Bernstein, chain-smoking and in dark glasses, white pants, a green pullover, and a seersucker jacket, presided in an armchair at the side of the room.

The student begins, giving the opening upbeat hesitantly. Bernstein stops everything right there. He seizes upon the uncertainty to begin a Socratic dialogue with the class on what Mozart intended with his upbeat and how the conductor should treat it. The upshot: the introductory accompaniment is more important than the melody. Soon Bernstein is off on a discourse about vamps, the sometimes improvisatory introductions to popular tunes, and the lonely figure at the music stand, the pianists, and the rest of the class have become an audience at a performance. Stepping to a piano, Bernstein plays vamps from Schubert and "The Peanut Vendor," an old pop tune. "It pertains just as much to Mozart and Schubert as to pop music," he says. The crowd hangs on every word.

More discussion of the peculiarities of Mozart's opening. In the midst of the arcana and esoterica: "Jeffrey! I haven't seen you since Schleswig-Holstein [the Tanglewood-inspired music festival and school in northern Germany]! How are you?" The Bernstein mitt reaches across two rows of chairs to shake Jeffrey's flattered hand.

Back to the opening upbeat. Why is the irregular meter in Mozart's bass line "so poetic instead of just prose carrying information?" Bernstein asks. "Because," he answers himself, "we live in a world of asymmetries. We have two arms, two legs; some of us have two testicles and two breasts." Then again, that's not asymmetrical, even if it works in a sly sexual reference. "This breaks a rule, doesn't it? It breaks the duality principle." To the piano again to play the passage from Mozart with a wrong emphasis, turning it into bad jazz. "This is the way Schmoo-face Horowitz would have written it if he were living in the day of Mozart." The implication: you're a Schmoo-face if that's the way you conduct it.

By now Bernstein, pacing the floor, cigarette in hand, is delivering a monologue on Noam Chomsky's theories of linguistics, and the student who started it all is a forgotten man. Deletion is "one of the great Chomsky phenomena," Bernstein declares. Deletion in language means elimination of unnecessary words—"Seiji has to go home to do Seiji's homework" becomes Seiji doing "his homework"—and in music it means elimination of unnecessary emphases. A pun: "Any conductor who doesn't conduct in bars is going to conduct in bar phrases, and he should be disbarred."

And so on through sallies into Gilbert and Sullivan ("the greatest team before Rodgers and Hammerstein"), Stephen Sondheim's *Sweeney Todd,* festivals and schools he has visited, and more Chomsky rules, some of this in German, some in French. After half an hour the student gets a chance to start the symphony again. The lesson has taken hold; from this day forward he will be able to start Mozart's G Minor Symphony. "Atta baby!" Bernstein enthuses. "You've got it. You've got the lesson." Then an announcement: "My doctor told me I should not speak for the next two days because I have this laryngitis infection. But this is more important." It's time for the next student's burnt offering to the master.

Polymath or show-off? Wisdom or intellectual rubbish? Both in the same package, probably. Other conductor-teachers—Ozawa, for example—stick to the basics of what's in the score and how to help the players deliver it. Bernstein needed the adulation of the young the way he needed his whiskey and cigarettes. *Love me!* his words and actions shouted, even as they inspired. But for a musician love is something to be given, not received; self is a filter through which the music flows. To be a Bernstein with an outsized talent and omnivorous mind is one thing. To be an aspiring musician learning to separate music from ego is another.

*B*ERNSTEIN'S 1990 VISIT was timed to climax the Music Center's fiftieth-anniversary festivities. That summer-long series of events in turn culminated a four-year celebration, which included the Bernstein year in 1988 and the Copland year in 1989, of Tanglewood at the fifty-year mark. The jubilee tour, taking Bernstein, the student orchestra, two student conductors, two student chamber ensembles, and pianist Leon Fleisher to Kiel, Düsseldorf, East and West Berlin, Vienna, and Santander, Spain, was to be the triumphant finale to the summer's celebration. But in the months before, Bernstein's troubles had, as he said, multiplied like Job's.

In London in December 1989 he had recorded what he decided was to be the definitive version of his *Candide.* Despite a heavy flu he continued on to Berlin for a pair of "Freedom Concert" Beethoven Ninths—one each in the West and East—celebrating the fall of the Berlin Wall. (It was in these concerts that he hit upon the idea of substituting the German *Freibeit*, or freedom, for the *Freude*, or joy, of Schiller's ode. There was nothing like underlining the obvious.) Amid a series of ensuing concerts, including three with the Vienna Philharmonic in Carnegie Hall, his strength steadily ebbed and he began a series of treatments for what turned out to be cancer of the lining of the lung. In the spring he canceled an appearance at the Spoleto Festival in Charleston, South Carolina, but kept a date to lead a Beethoven Ninth at the Prague Festival. On his return from Czechoslovakia in June, he continued to weaken but decided to go to Japan anyway for the Pacific Music Festival, where Michael Tilson Thomas, again, was a founding codirector.

For Bernstein the new festival was a Japanese extension of Tanglewood. "There were," Humphrey Burton writes in his Bernstein biography, "young conductors to be coached and speeches to be made; he was to be the guiding spirit, the Koussevitzky figure, of the entire festival. . . . He loved conducting, he loved teaching, he loved the idea of sowing Tanglewood seeds in Japanese soil."[7] Besides, the emperor and empress were to attend his first concert in Tokyo, and Tilson Thomas and other young conductors, including Marin Alsop, would be available to help. "As always," Burton writes, "he was ready to gamble, not with his artistic reputation this time, but with his very life."

In Sapporo Bernstein conducted one concert each with the student orchestra and the London Symphony Orchestra, which, on a visiting basis, filled the role that the BSO does at Tanglewood. Then he and the London Symphony took their program to Tokyo for the concert before the emperor and empress.[8] Like the final Tanglewood concert, it consisted of Britten's Sea Interludes and the Beethoven Seventh, but with Bernstein's Serenade (Midori was the violin soloist) in place of *Arias and Barcarolles*. The Tokyo stay, which was to be followed by five more concerts in other cities, was marked by a series of increasingly desperate medical episodes and treatments. Finally, with Bernstein preparing for a second London Symphony concert in Tokyo, his longtime assistant Craig Urquhart found him on the floor of his hotel suite, where he had collapsed and was unable to move. There was nothing to do but put him on a plane and send him home. A hastily prepared press release identified his ailments as severe influenza, pleurisy, and pneumonia. Urquhart, according to Burton, confided despondently to his diary: "The real question is why he bothers at all. Here is a very sick man who knows he is doing his *danse macabre*."[9]

Bernstein and Dr. Cahill believed that, together with the month's rest before Tanglewood, the energy he drew from music and the young would get him through the visit and tour. Still, Bernstein was a weakened man, breathing with difficulty and dependent on painkilling drugs (and still smoking heavily), when he arrived at Tanglewood on Friday, August 10, for a ten-day stay. It didn't help his mood that his usual borrowed house in Great Barrington was unavailable and the BSO had found a damp, smelly replacement in Lenox. Bernstein promptly christened it the Mildew Palace.

Musically, too, the visit started badly. Bernstein began rehearsals with the Music Center Orchestra for Copland's Third Symphony, the work he would conduct in their concert. (He had also led it with the 1985 student orchestra for Copland's eighty-fifth birthday, the occasion for Copland's last Tanglewood visit.) The students were tired from having performed the final concert in the weeklong Festival of Contemporary Music the night before and then partied well into the morning hours, and their playing was rough. Bernstein got out of sorts, took an intermission, and didn't come back. Mark Stringer, a protégé who happened to be in that summer's conducting seminar, took over for him.

Bernstein also missed the next two days' rehearsals, leaving preparation of the Copland symphony to Stringer, who had not conducted it before but had studied it with Bernstein. On Monday, however, he returned and put in five hours with the orchestra, plus additional time with one of the conducting fellows who was to share the podium with him.

Like the Bernstein of yore, he came dressed in silver-tipped cowboy boots, a turtleneck, and jeans with an "LB" monogram emblazoned on the back pocket. He also sounded like the Lenny of old in the line of patter that Richard Dyer of the *Boston Globe* caught him using to coax and cajole his players: "Atta baby!" he would exclaim when something pleased him. "What more could an old guy ask for?" At another point, having mistaken a metronome mark for a rehearsal number, he told himself, "Stupido maestro!" He praised the piccolo player for having a beautiful sound—"which is not so easy to come by when you're playing a little, schlocky instrument like that." He asked for five different textures in a passage, then corrected himself: "Who am I to say that *I* want it? *Aaron* wants it." Satisfied with another passage, he declared, "Well, that's as good as I ever heard it."

Lukas Foss, back for the summer as composer in residence, caught the mood of the day when he went up to Bernstein during a rehearsal break and asked how he was feeling.

"I'm still upright," Bernstein replied wryly.

"You're better than a piano," the puckish Foss said. "You're both upright and grand."[10]

There was another rehearsal on Tuesday morning. On Tuesday night, amid lovely summer weather and continuing doubts whether the European tour could go on, the Shed began filling for the concert. (Because of the crowds he attracted, Bernstein was the only conductor since the festival's early years who enjoyed the privilege of leading student orchestra programs in the Shed rather than the Theater–Concert Hall.) The program was the one the orchestra would take on tour: Beethoven's *Leonore* Overture No. 3, Ravel's Concerto for Piano Left Hand, and Berlioz's *Roman Carnival* Overture before intermission, the Copland Third after. Stefan Anton Reck of Germany was the student conductor for the Beethoven, Stefan Asbury of England for the Ravel and Berlioz. Fleisher, who on the tour would represent Tanglewood in his capacity as artistic director of the Music Center, was the soloist in the Ravel. It was a work he had played countless times with countless orchestras in the quarter-century since losing the use of his right hand at the keyboard through injury.

For Bernstein the Copland Third was a memento of his Koussevitzky and Copland roots. It was also an example of the "noble" music that he found dying in America amid a Babel of new movements and styles ranging from the severe intellectualism of Elliott Carter to the pop-driven postmodernism of younger composers. When he walked out in his summer tux after the intermission, flicking his baton in an old gesture of recognition to his players, he looked old and tired—shockingly so to anyone who had not seen him since the previous summer. But after he had taken his bows and turned to his work, it was clear that the old fires still burned.

Ten minutes into the performance, according to Burton's biography, Bernstein began to feel the effects of oxygen deprivation. Stringer told Burton: "You would see his brain go click. It was sad, because it made the Copland extremely dogged."[11] That was not the impression from the audience. If there was less energy in his gestures, it concentrated the playing more brilliantly. Blended, bronzed, and burnished, the music resonated like a great organ. Now pushing ahead, now pulling back, probing for the "inner music" (as he had described it to Marin Alsop) Bernstein found ever-deeper levels of richness in the familiar sounds.

The Copland Third is usually considered an affirmation of American openness and optimism. This time the effect was different. The tender third movement was almost a hush. It was also very lonely. The fanfare that opens the big-as-all-outdoors finale, where Copland quotes his own *Fanfare for the Common Man*, spoke almost as much of resignation as affirmation. It was as if Mahler's world-weary Vienna had somehow found its way into Copland's hope-filled prairies and Brooklyn. Facing death, Bernstein made the music speak as much of his own condition as Copland's. Hadn't he said that when he conducted, he became the composer?

With that performance Bernstein seemed indomitable, the tour assured. But the concert took too much out of him. During rehearsals with the BSO over the next four days, he realized half an hour into *Arias and Barcarolles* that he couldn't do it, and Carl St. Clair, who was on standby as conductor, would have to do it for him. At the Sunday concert he showed flashes of the old magic, even managing a few leaps and dance steps on the podium. But his gestures were fewer than in the past, and those that he did use often lacked vigor or clarity.

The program, performed before a gray-day audience of seven thousand instead of the usual twelve thousand to fifteen thousand that thronged a Bernstein-BSO concert, was memorable not as a musical experience but a heroic drama. Like a line of great conductors before him, Bernstein refused to give in to infirmity. In recent years there had been the example of Herbert von Karajan, crippled by a back ailment and limping painfully to the podium. Earlier there had been Arturo Toscanini, pushing on despite failing eyes and failing legs until at last memory failed, and Wilhelm Furtwängler, who collapsed during a concert as his health gave out. Now Bernstein joined in that cortege. As the program progressed, many in the audience realized that he would never be seen on a podium again. When, enfeebled and exhausted, he walked halfway out to the podium at the end to acknowledge the cheers of the crowd, it was his farewell to the life and place he loved.

The usual postconcert reception was cranking up at Seranak, Koussevitzky's hillside retreat, where Bernstein had often wined, dined, and slept. He was driven there but was in no condition to party. Still, the tour was to begin the next day, and a decision had to be made whether it was on or off. Some members of his entourage wanted him to press on. But his children, Alexander, Nina, and Jamie Bernstein Thomas, who were among the guests—his eighty-nine-year-old mother, Jennie, was also there—insisted: Daddy was too sick. Daddy knew it. He left the party early and was driven in a limousine back to his New York apartment, where he would see his doctors in the morning.

Without Bernstein there was no tour. It had been conceived by him and planned around him. The itinerary had even been lightened for him when it was evident that his strength was fading. On Sunday night the musicians were convened at Miss Hall's School in Pittsfield, the girls' prep school where Tanglewood boards its students. Music Center administrator Richard Ortner made the announcement. Some students were in tears. All were devastated. They had auditioned for Tanglewood on the understanding that they would join Bernstein on the tour, and they had been picked to give him a showcase orchestra for Europe.

As a consolation the group was invited to stay on and take part in the BSO's performance of the Berlioz *Requiem* in the season's finale the next Sunday under Ozawa. Those who accepted replaced freelancers who normally provide the reinforcements required for Berlioz's monster orchestra.

In New York Bernstein underwent ever more stringent medical tests and treatments. The public was told he needed only rest and quiet to pull through. Then on October 9 his office announced by press release that he was retiring from the podium, had canceled all outstanding engagements, and would henceforth devote himself to composing, writing, and other projects. Although the release spoke of an eventual return to conducting, everybody who knew Bernstein knew that he would lay down his baton only when he could never lift it again. The end came five days later. In his New York apartment he died of a heart attack shortly after a visit from Bright Sheng, who was revising his orchestration of *Arias and Barcarolles*. The world's grief was encapsulated in a *Los Angeles Times* cartoon that showed the earth flying an eighth note's tail in a dark, starry sky. The caption read: "Leonard Bernstein lived here."

On December 2 Copland died after a long siege with Alzheimer's disease. The Koussevitzky lineage was at an end.

13 BERNSTEIN LIKED to recall that Koussevitzky had spoken of "the central line"—what Bernstein defined as "the line to be followed by the artist at any cost, the line leading to perpetual discovery, a mystical line to truth as it is revealed in the musical art."12 Tanglewood, he said, embodied this goal.

In 1970, on the Music Center's thirtieth anniversary, Bernstein pursued this idea in the opening address to the students. He entitled his talk "The Principle of Hope," after a book of that name by the German philosopher Ernst Bloch. It was the Vietnam era, and the youth of America was rebellious—"impatient," in Bernstein's word. "Does one dare, in 1970," he asked, "to speak of 'values' or of 'virtues' such as hard work, faith, mutual understanding, *patience?*"

"Well," he answered himself, "the answer is *yes*. One does dare."

Recalling the "heroic music" of his youth—affirmative, humane symphonies by such composers as Copland, Stravinsky, and William Schuman, with Koussevitzky "ready and eager to play them all"—Bernstein said that that musical era was past. Symphonic life still flourished, but it was "no longer fed by the noble symphony, nor is it fed by much of anything else, for that matter." Likewise politics and television and world affairs. Likewise new music: "Some of it is fascinating, some is titillating, some of it is touching and even beautiful, and some merely opportunistic—but one thing it almost never is is *noble*. And this negativism ranges right across the arts into almost all thinking disciplines, so that these university students I see and meet with hardly know where to turn." [13]

No wonder, he went on, students often told him "there's nothing to feel but irony and despair. So we drown ourselves in decibels of rock, we drop out with dope; we don't know what else to do." Then Bernstein delivered his charge to what he described as "the best generation in history." It is, he said, "the artists of the world, the feelers and the thinkers, who will ultimately save us; who can articulate, educate, defy, insist, sing and shout the big dreams." And it was the impatient young before him, who "with your new, atomic minds, your flaming, angry hope, and your secret weapon of art," would bring about the transformation.

On the Highwood lawn twenty years later, the day after the final Bernstein concert, 225 of those feelers and thinkers from fifty years of the Music Center gathered with families, friends, and many of 1990's students and teachers for a picnic supper. It was the final event in the reunion.

In some ways the gathering was like alumni reunions everywhere. Old friends and classmates, parted by the years, embraced and shared memories and histories. As in a singing of the alma mater, dewy-eyed old grads raised their glasses and voices in Randall Thompson's *Alleluia*, the work that students have sung every year to open their summer of studies. But the sky over Stockbridge Bowl was overcast, and so was the joy of renewal. Word had spread during the day: Lenny couldn't go. The tour was off. Students in the gathering were subdued, sometimes somber. Many of them should have been en route to Europe.

There were memorial concerts during the winter in New York, London, Tel Aviv, and other music capitals. Perhaps most memorably, there was a Carnegie Hall concert at which the orchestra, made up of members of the principal orchestras Bernstein had conducted over the years, played his *Candide* Overture without a conductor: the old idea of the riderless horse at the funeral, now carried over into music. The next summer Tanglewood opened its season with a Bernstein memorial weekend in which both the BSO and the Music Center Orchestra took part. Ozawa conducted Mahler's *Resurrection* Symphony, Bernstein's *Jeremiah* Symphony, and Brahms's *German Requiem*. Carl St. Clair was back on the Music Center Orchestra podium, and the weekend's starry array of soloists consisted of June Anderson, Hildegard Behrens, Jessye Norman, Thomas Hampson, and Itzhak Perlman.

From then on, a Bernstein Memorial Concert by the Music Center Orchestra in the Shed became, like the BSO's Koussevitzky Memorial Concert, an annual Tanglewood feature. It fell to Ozawa, as the BSO director, to conduct both programs. He was now the senior musician, the father figure, the link with tradition. But he was not a Bernstein—not an American-born conductor who, for the first and only time, became a world figure through the range of his musicianship and the sheer flamboyance of his personality. And after four years Ozawa, preoccupied with other affairs, including Tanglewood's revival of student opera, turned over the Bernstein memorial to another former BSO assistant conductor, the gifted Robert Spano. The memory of Koussevitzky was receding farther into the distance.

Asked at his 1988 press conference if there was anything he had left undone, Bernstein replied, "Oh, lord, yes, there's tons of music I haven't written yet. That's the main thing." It was a fair statement from a man who had achieved greatness as a conductor, shown how television could be used as a force for good in music, and inspired two generations of younger musicians, but had not—save for his Broadway shows—left an assuredly significant body of music.

Yet Bernstein lived to become a symbol of what was wrong with music in the late twentieth century as well as what was right with it. From a champion of American music, he turned, in his last decade, into a recycler of masterworks from the past. Britten, Shostakovich, and Copland—all from the century's middle years—were as far as he went. In his return to the Beethoven, Brahms, and Tchaikovsky symphonies associated with Koussevitzky, he delivered ever slower yet more penetrating performances. Those slower tempos made the fires burn more intensely, with the inner details aglow in vivid relief. Bernstein did not let celebrity turn him away from the music. But by endlessly repeating the old masterpieces, no matter how deeply considered the performances, he shifted the emphasis (as had Toscanini before him) from the music to the performer. By hobnobbing with presidents, royalty, and show-biz celebrities, and by frequently being pictured in the media with them, he further fed the public's mania for stars. The symphony orchestra, he often said, had become a "museum" preserving cultural artifacts of the past. With his huge gifts, appetites, and flaws, he helped to bring about the decline that he lamented in the institution that he loved. In his end was his beginning.

The gap he left in the BSO schedule was quickly filled with other conductors. The riderless horse stalked the Music Center. Outwardly, as on the old campus when Ozawa Hall opened, everything was the same. The student conducting program went on, with Gustav Meier as director, Ozawa and other BSO conductors coaching and leading concerts, and students from the Americas, Europe, and Asia beating on the door for admission. Other figures, especially Fleisher, invoked the ideals that Koussevitzky and Bernstein had invoked. Yet the Koussevitzky link, the larger-than-life force, was gone. No one could stand before students and make them sing and shout the big dreams as Bernstein had. Nor could anyone harangue them about Chomskian linguistics, install himself with a royal court, and insist on his right to overtime in rehearsals.

The transformation Bernstein had anticipated didn't happen. If anything, the forces turning great music into circuses, celebrity events, and background listening accelerated. In his "Young People's Concerts" and "Omnibus" shows of the 1950s, 1960s, and 1970s, Bernstein had been a master of television as a musical and educational forum. By the time of his seventieth-birthday party, he was just another celebrity, and Tanglewood just a picturesque backdrop, for a Hollywood-style gala on television. The Music Center remained an ideal world, largely untainted by commercial pressures, amid the real world of the BSO concerts in the Shed, where picnickers on the lawn sipped their wine. The "central line" was becoming ever harder to find amid the hoopla and hype of a media-saturated age. The loss—the eighth-note earth flying solitary in a darkened sky—was Bernstein's, Tanglewood's, and the world's.

4

Bearers

of

the

Torch

ONLY BERNSTEIN could wear Koussevitzky's cuff links and cape, but other important figures brought other fashions and influences to the festival after Bernstein's death. High among these musicians was Bernard Haitink, who not only favored conservative shirts and jackets but also lent a quieter distinction to the concerts.

The Dutch conductor's 1994 debut had been a long time in coming. Ever since 1985, when he began a round of annual guest-conducting stints in Boston, BSO management had been trying to tempt him to Tanglewood. One of the lures was repeats of his Boston programs, since he did not feel comfortable with Tanglewood's pressurized rehearsal schedule. But the reason he didn't come sooner, he said, was his commitments at the Glyndebourne and Salzburg festivals in Europe. He finally carved out time by scheduling his 1994 Salzburg concerts with the Vienna Philharmonic early in the season.

Haitink was sixty-five and the director of London's Royal Opera at Covent Garden when he arrived for two BSO programs and some readings (but no public concert) with the Music Center Orchestra. His 1985 Boston concerts had been such a success that 80 of the BSO's 105 members petitioned management to name him principal guest conductor, a position left unfilled when Colin Davis departed in 1984. Neither Haitink, who was busy in Europe, nor the BSO administration was yet ready to tie that knot. As his concerts sent players and critics into ever higher raptures, he consented, and the position was his in 1995. By coincidence Davis, an Englishman who had enjoyed similar BSO esteem in his day, was going to the New York Philharmonic at the same time in the same capacity.

At Tanglewood Haitink became, in his soft-spoken, professorial way, the new conductor with the most commanding voice in the post-Bernstein era. Unlike Roger Norrington, the English early-music specialist who had made his American symphonic debut at Tanglewood in 1988 and quickly risen to prominence with the BSO and other orchestras, Haitink was not a brand name in the United States. In fact, his occasional appearances with other American orchestras had met with generally tepid reviews. Norrington faded from the BSO scene after a few years. His over-the-limit tempos and sometimes outré dress on the podium—showing up for rehearsals in sandals and shorts, for example—began to pall on players. Haitink became a member of the family, a part of the establishment. His manners were relaxed, his tempos spacious; he drew from the BSO a warm, mellow sound more typically associated with European orchestras. "He lets us *play*," BSO members said.

Not only was he no Bernstein in manner and dress. He was no Ozawa, whose conducting was becoming more tightly controlled during the same period.

As he prepared to see the Tanglewood he had heard so much about, so favorably, in Europe, Haitink said in his Dutch-accented but comfortable English that the BSO was one of the two orchestras he felt closest to. The other was the Berlin Philharmonic, and he was somewhat less at ease with it because of what he described as its "Tiffany show-window" effect—its high-gloss sound and high-society character—dating from Herbert von Karajan's days. With the BSO, on the other hand, he felt "very much on the same wave length." The conductor-orchestra relationship would vary from city to city, but Boston, for him, was "very special. I don't have to use many words, which I never do and never can. I'm not very articulate. I think you have to do it [lead] with your hands. It's a very special relationship with the orchestra and the organization. They really take care of you. They're helpful and they make you feel at home."

Born in Amsterdam, Haitink became chief conductor of its Concertgebouw Orchestra in 1964. He remained there until his departure for Covent Garden in 1988, meanwhile serving as principal conductor of the London Philharmonic from 1967 to 1979. He added the directorship of the European Youth Orchestra to his portfolio in 1994. There was plenty to keep him busy in Europe, including large-scale recording projects such as *Ring* and Mahler cycles. But in 1989 he and the BSO began a series of recording projects with Ravel's complete *Daphnis et Chloé* in conjunction with their concerts. In the recording sessions they moved on to the four Brahms symphonies, which Ozawa was recording simultaneously—and for the same

Bernard Haitink rehearses the Tanglewood Music Center Orchestra for their 1994 concert. (Walter H. Scott)

label, Philips—with his Saito Kinen Orchestra in Japan. Brahms's two piano concertos, with Emanuel Ax as the soloist, and the rest of Ravel's orchestral music were to follow.

As management had promised, Haitink's Tanglewood debut programs were largely repeats from Boston in the spring. On a Friday night he led a concert version of the third act of Wagner's *Götterdämmerung,* with Jane Eaglen (also in her debut) as the Brünnhilde and Gary Lakes as the Siegfried. Schubert's "Unfinished" Symphony opened the program in an unusually quiet reading: a cooling breeze before the fires of Valhalla. The Sunday afternoon sequel, which took place amid a thunderstorm, featured Sibelius's Violin Concerto (Gidon Kremer made his debut as the soloist) and Brahms's First Symphony. The rain's drumming on the Shed roof and hissing in the trees actually seemed in sympathy with the naturalness of the music making.

Haitink was fully booked for 1994–95 and did not return to either Tanglewood or Symphony Hall. In 1995–96 he was back for both spring and fall programs in Boston and for a pair in Tanglewood's last two weeks. In Boston, with *Daphnis* already behind them, he and the BSO began a two-year Ravel cycle in concert and on disc. For a Beethoven weekend at Tanglewood, he led a program pairing the Violin Concerto and Fifth Symphony. Deputizing for Ozawa, who was in Japan, he concluded the season with Mozart's Piano Concerto, K. 271, and a repeat of *Daphnis.* Pamela Frank was his soloist in the Beethoven concerto and Emanuel Ax played the Mozart, but the two programs were notable most of all for Haitink's ability to elicit strongly characterized playing from the orchestra in music of contrasting styles.

During a two-week residency Haitink also worked with the student conductors and led the Music Center Orchestra in its season finale. Summing up his impressions from the return visit, he said he was "still very enchanted with the place," but "when you love something you also have a critical eye." His critical eye saw a danger that the student orchestra was overworked, particularly with contemporary music.

Haitink came to the students just after their immersion in the weeklong Festival of Contemporary Music. Although he was pleased with the quality of their playing in his program, he was critical of "very venerable people in the management"—his fellow Dutchman Reinbert de Leeuw, director of the contemporary festival, was a clear target—who "have only one mission in life." He had discussed the problem the day before with Ozawa, who called from Tokyo. Ozawa, Haitink said, "cares enormously." But they agreed: "You have to be careful that Tanglewood doesn't become an ego trip, that Tanglewood stays a place where young talents can flourish." When he suggested changes, BSO management would tell him, "Oh, Seiji has the final decision." That was not right. "To be in charge of the Boston Symphony is an enormous task. To be in charge of Tanglewood, to be responsible for Tanglewood in combination with the BSO, is inhuman. He needs people who think with him on the same lines and not for their own hobbies."

The criticism may have been directed at de Leeuw, but it also foretold the fate of Richard Ortner, whom Ozawa was removing as the Music Center administrator during the same period.

Though Haitink was, in one sense, as far as Tanglewood could get from the flamboyant Bernstein, both men came out of an older generation that tempered a belief in the new with a reverence for the masterworks of the past: "the bread and butter of every musician," Haitink called them. Both men also believed in the power of music to reach people without compromising it through popularization tactics such as those the American Symphony Orchestra League recommended in its 1993 study. Haitink told how, for a performance of *Carmen*, he had once given the tickets for his Covent Garden conductor's box to the domestics who worked in his London home. "They were over the moon!" he recalled. "It was such an outing for them to be in an opera house. They said, 'Fantastic! Fantastic! I want to go more!'" The moral:

I find it a sort of disguised discrimination to play special music for people who are not used to coming to concerts. I think music is there and we should try to get them in, and then they should listen to that music. I don't think there are recipes in music to attract certain audiences. I don't think that playing a Carmen fantasy will attract a new audience. I don't think that is the right way to do it. I think one should do what one does with conviction and try to get people to listen to it.

At the millennium's end, as pressures mounted to bring music down to the level of the crowd, the issue was becoming crucial not just for Tanglewood or Covent Garden. The art of music itself was embattled, as Bernstein had foreseen in his charge to "the best generation in history." Amid Tanglewood's eternal tug of war between art and the picnic hamper, Koussevitzky's "central line" found a new standard-bearer in the gentleman-conductor from Europe.

And yet Tanglewood would not be Tanglewood, nor the BSO the BSO, without the Pops to put a happy face on music. The Boston Pops plays only two concerts a year at Tanglewood, but its salad of light classics and dressed-up pop attracts a large, lucrative audience that bears little resemblance to the parent orchestra's clientele.

In 1995, after three years of suspense worthy of a Red Sox pennant race, the BSO named Keith Lockhart to succeed John Williams as leader of the Pops. Lockhart was thirty-five, Williams sixty-three. But the difference between them was more than age. Williams was the composer of more than seventy-five film scores, which had brought him five Oscars (most recently for *Schindler's List*) and sixteen Grammies. By comparison Lockhart, then the associate conductor of the Cincinnati Symphony and Pops, seemed a stranger from the sticks. When news of the appointment leaked out, he was in Vienna and his telephone went into meltdown as the paparazzi and musical press besieged him with calls. He claimed he hid under his hotel room bed to escape the summonses to celebrity.

Among symphonic orchestras the Boston Pops is the nation's pet—"America's special beloved," Williams calls it. Even in Boston, where it established itself in 1885, the Pops is everybody's band, compared to the brahmin BSO. If Lockhart was an unexpected choice for the job, he was not much more unexpected than Williams had been when the BSO plucked him out of the Hollywood studios to succeed Arthur Fiedler, the crusty "Mr. Pops" for forty-nine years until his death in 1979. To Pops fans, who can be as boisterous as Red Sox fans, both Williams and Lockhart were entertainers in the Fiedler tradition. (Lockhart, a divorcé when he landed in Boston, was also a Hollywood-style heartthrob who was said to look like actor Hugh Grant.) Entertainers both men were and are. But both are also serious musicians who, looking beyond show tunes and Pops clowning and pizzazz, dip into the standard symphonic repertory.

Williams arrived in Boston in 1980. In 1992, on crossing the great divide of sixty, he took stock. A guest conductor of the Los Angeles Philharmonic and other major orchestras in the past, he had already cut out his conducting except in Hollywood and Boston. Now, in the time he had left, he wanted more freedom to compose, especially for the concert hall. And he wanted to do more of that composing around Tanglewood. He gave notice that he would be leaving in December 1993.

As a going-away present the BSO put Williams on the Tanglewood podium in 1993 to conduct his first full-length concert with the BSO proper. The program was a portrait in miniature of the departing conductor. It mixed two Pops-style pieces, Michael Tippett's pomp-and-circumstance *Suite for the Birthday of Prince Charles* and the finger-snapping Symphonic Dances from Bernstein's *West Side Story*, with two elegiac works from the classical repertory. The latter were Elgar's Cello Concerto, with Yo-Yo Ma as the soloist, and Bernstein's *Halil*, with Leone Buyse, the Pops' principal flutist, in the solo role. Two nights later Williams was back in his accustomed role, conducting the Pops in a postseason program of movie music, including his own.

Newly crowned with the title of artist in residence, the conductor with the neatly trimmed brush of gray beard and the red flower in his lapel returned to Tanglewood in the following summers as a teacher. He also came "for my own invigoration and inspiration and learning." He was even looking for a year-round retreat in the Berkshires to get him out of the Hollywood hustle.

Purists hold a sniffish view of Tanglewood as a music factory and tourist trap. Fourteen years of sold-out Pops concerts, tours before adoring throngs in the United States and Japan, and top-of-the-charts records, plus the Hollywood experience, gave Williams a different perspective. Taking in the view of lake and hills from Seranak, the Koussevitzky mansion above Tanglewood, he reflected:

I love the place. I love, first of all, what one sees and experiences here. And I'm still infatuated with it in the spiritual sense. Perhaps that's naïve on my part, but I still can sense Koussevitzky in this place. Bernstein in this place. It's especially meaningful for me—because I come from the commercial, profit-oriented film industry and music business—to come to a place where the spiritual, devotional idea of making music is still, at least for me, intact. I say to colleagues all around the country that I think the high place in American musical life is Tanglewood. This is a sort of Vatican.

There had been a difficult period in the early years when, unaccustomed to the Pops tradition of pranks in rehearsals as well as performances, Williams had resigned in a huff over some Boston rehearsal shenanigans—paper airplanes, wisecracks, and the like. It quickly became clear on both sides that the Pops needed Williams and he needed the Pops. The players apologized and the conductor tore up his resignation. Not only did harmony reign thereafter, but the musicians came to respect Williams as both a man and a musician. "Mensch" was the word often used, when he wasn't listening, to describe him. Upon his retirement the BSO appointed him Pops laureate conductor and signed him to return to both Boston and Tanglewood to guest-conduct.

In fact, unable to come up with a successor right away, the BSO had to name Williams Pops artistic adviser and call on him to guide the orchestra until a Keith Lockhart appeared. He and the BSO celebrated the relationship by recording his *Schindler's List* music together; it was the first time the BSO turned studio orchestra for a full-length sound track. When the summer of 1994 dawned, Williams was back at Tanglewood, leading the BSO and Ma in the premiere of his Cello Concerto for the inauguration of Seiji Ozawa Hall. His friend Steven Spielberg, who had directed *Schindler's List* and many other Williams-scored films, sat in the audience with the conductor's photographer wife, Samantha.

Williams continued to conduct the BSO once a year, lead one of the two Pops concerts, take part in the "Tanglewood on Parade" gala, and give occasional "chat sessions" for composition students, discussing orchestration and synchronization of music with film. In a rented hideaway he worked on his scores. "All through the last thirty years I've done so much composing, but most of it's been to order—film music and background music of a kind of utilitarian nature," he said. Now he had "time and the opportunity for a little more thoughtful composition." His output included commissioned bassoon and trumpet concertos as well as music for films (*Jurassic Park* among them) and the theme music for the 1996 Summer Olympics. Repeated attempts to engage him for more teaching ran up against his composition schedule. If Tanglewood was a Vatican, he was a reclusive member of the College of Cardinals.

There are actually not one but two Boston Pops orchestras: the BSO Pops (the BSO minus its first-chair players) and the Boston Pops Esplanade Orchestra, a freelance band that takes over when the parent group is on vacation or at Tanglewood. The Esplanade band is a younger group, more attuned to the beat of America in the 1990s. BSO players might respect their Pops conductor and jealously guard the identity of their Pops against the Esplanade group's, but they cut their teeth on the classics and sometimes take leave without pay during Pops season to perform chamber music or simply get away from it all. Substitutes—often willing recruits from the Esplanade Orchestra—replenish the ranks.

Williams termed both groups national treasures. Reflecting on the reception either orchestra receives on the Pops' annual American tour, he said that "if Boston people could come on these tours with us once to see the affection with which this orchestra is held—both orchestras really; I don't think it's too corny to say it's America's special beloved. There are other pops orchestras in other cities, but none like this in the hearts of people."

This was the institution Lockhart inherited when he arrived in Boston in 1995. He came with two memories of Tanglewood. In one, as a high school student in the 1970s, he piled into a car with some friends in Poughkeepsie, New York, where he grew up, and drove up for a weekend concert. Mixing with the crowd and taking in the ambience, he discovered that there was a large audience for classical music and that the young as well as the old could enjoy it.

In the later recollection the Music Center, unimpressed by his credentials, turned him down in 1989 as a conducting fellow. Although it offered him entry into the lower-level conducting seminar, he enrolled instead in the Los Angeles Philharmonic Institute's Tanglewood-inspired conducting program. He drew the consolation that he had good company in his Tanglewood rejection: Simon Rattle met the same fate for the same reason, and Rattle, now Sir Simon in England, was on the world's most-wanted list as a conductor.

"Of all the different kinds of crystal-ball gazing in music," Lockhart mused as philosophically as he could in the midst of the hoopla attendant on his appointment, "I think looking at people's development curves as a conductor is one of the methods with the worst track record—worse than predicting the weather." Not all conductors, that is, are Bernsteins, ready to burst upon the world as full-blown talents. Neither are they Rattles or Lockharts, whose gifts reveal themselves more slowly or in unsuspected guises.

The world moved fast for Lockhart after his anointing in February 1995. In addition to the spring Pops season in Boston, he faced the Pops' man-moth July Fourth celebration on Boston's Esplanade, his Tanglewood debut, and a nine-city American tour with the Esplanade Orchestra. Meanwhile he was caught up in a whirlwind of meetings, planning, travel, Cincinnati rehearsals and concerts, and publicity. His face appeared so often on television and in the papers—he was gawked at so often in the streets and he signed so many autographs—that he came to think of himself, sarcastically, as "the poster-child conductor," with his picture plastered on the sides of buses.

Dealing with celebrity became the hardest part of his job. There was, for example, his opening-night Pops concert:

I won't say conducting is easy. But the conducting is what I love doing. People ask, "Gee, that opening thing—were you nervous?" It's a concert. I love doing concerts. If I didn't love doing concerts, I'd have made a pathetically wrong career choice. But it's the stuff around it that gets me on edge and that I find my stress level rising, dealing with. Always being on. And very little room, especially in my own conception, for a misstep.

Lockhart didn't apply to follow Williams. The job went looking for him. Brought to the BSO's attention by its librarian, Marshall Burlingame, who used to be with the Cincinnati Symphony, Lockhart was one of about twenty candidates whom the BSO invited to conduct the Pops in what was, in effect, a public audition process. After his debut in 1993 he was brought back for three more programs, all impressive. At that point in 1994 BSO managing director Kenneth Haas and Seiji Ozawa called him in for interviews. On May 10, 1995, he went before the Symphony Hall audience and television cameras for his first concert as the new Mr. Pops. Settling in for what appeared to be a long stay, he bought a condo in Boston and, in September 1995, sneaked off to his cabin in Maine to marry Lucia Lin, a BSO violinist. His days as one of the city's most eligible men were over.

Lockhart inherited a three-part concert format that had become as much a Boston institution as cod. A Pops program opens with light symphonic favorites, moves on after an intermission to a concerto or other music with a soloist (often a vocalist), and concludes, after another intermission, with jazz, show tunes, movie music, and other popular goodies. Lockhart made haste slowly in bringing change to the time-honored formula, but his opening program offered a taste of things to come: pop vocalist Mandy Patinkin sharing the bill with a selection from the BSO repertory, "Siegfried's Rhine Journey" from Wagner's *Götterdämmerung*. His Tanglewood debut two months later was an omelet made of Copland's *El Salón México*, Gershwin's *An American in Paris*, shorter selections by Bernstein and Williams, and an

Keith Lockhart addresses the audience during his Tanglewood debut with the Boston Pops. (Walter H. Scott)

assortment of jazz and swing classics. The "creative energy" that comes from that kind of mix attracts a broad spectrum of listeners and helps both kinds of music, he said. The usual complaint about Pops, he observed, is that it is neither classical nor cutting-edge pop—neither here nor there:

I would love to have the Pops be, instead of neither here nor there, both here and there. Pops is the only place where you have the freedom to put Elton John on the same program with Mahler. It's the only place where the boundaries don't exist to preclude you from doing that. And I think that's what's wonderful about it.

The honeymoon lasted about six months: average as conductors' honeymoons go. Then players began complaining, as players will. The criticism had less to do with repertory and ability than with the still somewhat tense, boyish Lockhart's not having Williams's musical and personal depth—not being a "mensch," in other words. Richard Dyer of the *Boston Globe*, an early Lockhart booster, chimed in. Reviewing the opening concert of the 1996 Christmas Pops season, he said that "the program did not show the Pops at its best, or represent what ought to be the unvarying standard of enterprises sponsored by the Boston Symphony Orchestra." He especially criticized the musical arrangements, one of which wedged "Jingle Bells" into a medley with "Silent Night" and "O Come, All Ye Faithful." [1]

"Christmas Pops," Dyer concluded, "is doing what it is supposed to; nearly two dozen performances are sold out. But selling out artistically is not part of its mission; Christmas Pops ought to represent something more than a cash cow lowing at the manger."

As Dyer indelicately suggested, on top of everything else Pops is a money-maker for the BSO. (It brought in $8.8 million, or 29 percent, of the BSO's $30.7 million in earned income during 1996.) In both Boston and Lock-hart's annual Tanglewood concert, having a poster-child conductor who could program Elton John and make television commentators gaga was clearly good business in addition to whatever it might have been as art. But like Williams, Lockhart refused to be pigeonholed as a Pops conductor. "What I like to think I do is conduct and bring lots of wonderful orchestral music to people," he said. "I don't think it's a handicap that I know a lot of Sondheim. I think it's an advantage that I know a lot of Sondheim, and I think it helps my Stravinsky and Mahler."

The big "if" was whether fans of Sondheim and Elton John would gradu-ate into the loftier pleasures of Stravinsky, Mahler, and the rest of the "classi-cal" fraternity. Without that, having Pops concerts fill stadiums with cheer-ing fans all across the country would do nothing to get orchestras out of their artistic predicament.

Ꮪ IMON RATTLE needed no Pops to make him a poster-boy conductor. His bushy hair graying, the former wunderkind from England had already clambered to the top of the heap when, at the age of thirty-eight, he rolled in to Tanglewood in 1993 on one of his periodic visits to conduct and teach. He was making the same pilgrimage made by Bernstein and other guest conductors right up through Haitink. He did not, however, fit into the 1990s globe-trotter pattern. Neither did his conducting. It was a kind of high-wire act that took music to dizzying places and somehow got musicians to risk their necks with him.

Perhaps it was that taste for adventure that made Rattle, like Lockhart, one of Tanglewood's rejects as a conducting student. In England in 1980, at the age of twenty-five, he took over the City of Birmingham Symphony Orchestra, then a provincial group. Through improved performance standards and innovative programming, it began to attract more music-world attention than the better-known orchestras in London. Soon Rattle was in demand everywhere as a guest conductor, and offers of music directorships followed—though not from Boston, to which rumor persistently linked him. Yet he refused more glamorous posts, accepting only occasional guest engagements, chiefly in Los Angeles but also, every few years, at Tanglewood and in Boston.

Like Koussevitzky and other conductors before the jet, Rattle pursued a full-time relationship with his own orchestra and enjoyed the freedom that the arrangement gave him to experiment with programming. Much of the repertory was contemporary. His current project in Birmingham was "Toward the Millennium," a decade-by-decade survey of music written in the twentieth century. Beginning with the 1900s in 1990, he would examine one decade per year—the 1910s in 1991, the 1920s in 1992, and so forth. When, in 1999, he got to music from the 1990s to usher in the new millennium, he would be playing works that had not been on paper when he started.

Perhaps only one or two American orchestras—neither of them in Boston—would or could touch such an idea. Among patrons and subscribers it would be poison at the box office and as fund-raising bait. More typically for an American orchestra, when the New York Philharmonic began "American Classics," a four-year survey of American music, in 1996, it looked backward to composers from the 1930s and 1940s such as Copland, William Schuman, and Samuel Barber. Their now easily digestible music, presented during the subscription season, was comfortably interspersed among pieces by the old European masters along with a representation of later twentieth-century works. Earlier in the same year the San Francisco Symphony presented a two-week "American Festival" devoted to music from colonial days to the present. Much of the repertory was ethnic or derived from pop, but the series, aimed at a younger audience, took place after the subscription season.

In person Rattle hardly fits an American's gouty image of a Knight Bachelor and Commander of the British Empire. He bounces around like a man on a spring, interrupts an interview to shout across the Tanglewood lawn to a friend, and looks in on a protégé from England, Daniel Harding, whom he has persuaded Tanglewood to accept as a conducting student at the tender age of seventeen. On the podium he is a dervish, swooping, crouching, blissfully cajoling. His Tanglewood programs during a two-week residency offered a kind of millennial experience of their own. With the BSO he conducted Haydn's *Creation* on a Sunday afternoon and a Mozart-Brahms-Elgar program the following Friday night. He also worked with the summer's six conducting students and shared a Music Center Orchestra program with two of them.

On paper the two BSO programs looked standard. But for *The Creation* Rattle replaced the standard German text with one in English and invested the playing with the snap characteristic of period-instrument orchestras. Drawing on recent scholarship, he also reinstituted much of the original ornamentation in the vocal solos. The often-performed work, with its untroubled praises of God, came across like a flight into unknown country. "That's part of the fun and spirit of the piece," Rattle said, "that one should not always know exactly what's going to happen."

The second program featured Elgar's *Enigma* Variations. Birmingham is Elgar country. Birminghamers are among the fourteen characters portrayed in the variations, and, Rattle pointed out with all due pride, Elgar conducted the Birmingham orchestra's inaugural concert and wrote many works, including his oratorio *The Dream of Gerontius*—perhaps his greatest achievement—for it. (The city was also Mendelssohn's second home, after Leipzig, and his *Elijah* had its premiere there, Rattle recalled.) "What is astonishing is that a piece like that [the *Enigma* Variations] should turn up after such an enormously fallow period in English music," Rattle said. He described it as "the first great masterpiece since Purcell," the seventeenth-century English composer. The performance certainly gave it the roundedness and depth of a masterwork.

Rattle's Music Center Orchestra program opened with student-led performances of Mozart's "Prague" Symphony and Alban Berg's Altenberg songs, the latter with Elise Ross, an American who was then Rattle's wife, as the soloist. Rattle assigned himself Bruckner's death-shadowed Ninth Symphony as the finale.

The choice of works was not haphazard. Finding the student orchestra "the really important part of the job here," Rattle set out to acquaint the players with styles outside the ordinary Beethoven-to-Bartók gamut for students. While it would have been fun to do Stravinsky's *Petrushka* or some Bartók with the group, he said, "in a way that's too easy. They need something which is further away from a young American's experience: the long-breathedness of Bruckner, for instance." The Mozart and Berg performances, coached by Rattle, also broke out of stylistic ruts. The "Prague" had the clarity and zip of his own *Creation* performance with the BSO; the Berg songs emerged with a voluptuousness that seemed born more of romanticism than atonality.

Rather than risk falling off the high wire, Rattle climbed off. In 1996 he resigned his Birmingham position, as of 1998. He would continue to conduct, record, and tour with the orchestra and finish the "Toward the Millennium" series, which he and the Birminghamers were playing in London and Vienna as well as at home. He would also continue to return to the BSO and Tanglewood. But, he said in his resignation announcement, "the position of music director requires 150 percent of anybody's energy and commitment, and there are only so many years that any one person can keep up the sheer intensity necessary." If Simon Rattle couldn't take the wear and tear, the conductor who remained wedded to one orchestra seemed indeed a thing of the past.

Rattle had eighteen years in Birmingham. When Lorin Maazel returned to Tanglewood in 1994, he was preparing to leave the Pittsburgh Symphony Orchestra after eight years. The pressures of office were not an issue. At the age of sixty-four he wanted to turn himself into a composer.

Among Tanglewood's prodigal sons, probably none was more prodigal than Lorin Maazel, class of 1951. His return in 1994 was his first since his student summer, and it was not to conduct the BSO. Instead he brought his own Pittsburghers. The one-time child prodigy, who created a sensation as a nine-year-old conductor at the 1939 New York World's Fair (and later paid in trauma for the premature exposure), had conducted the BSO exactly once, in 1961 in Boston. For years the BSO had tried to coax him back to Tanglewood. It had especially wanted him back for the 1990 Music Center jubilee, which presented many alumni in homecoming concerts. But Maazel was among the conspicuous absentees, along with Claudio Abbado, Zubin Mehta, and Michael Tilson Thomas. The word then was that he had set his fee too high, and that when the BSO offered to meet it if he would rebate all or part of the money to the Music Center as Bernstein regularly had, Maazel would not bargain. His fees were among music's highest, it was said.

Maazel, on the other hand, said there had been no time for Tanglewood because he usually spent his summers conducting at European festivals or vacationing. But when, during the summer of 1994, he would be taking the Pittsburgh on a European festival tour, Tanglewood was en route. A compromise was arranged. He would give two concerts with his orchestra while the BSO took the nights off.

All his life Maazel had kept a foot on each side of the Atlantic. Born in

Paris to American parents, he studied philosophy and literature—he speaks six languages—at the University of Pittsburgh and began his career as a Pittsburgh Symphony violinist. In due course he became director of the West Berlin Opera and Berlin Radio Symphony, successor to George Szell as director of the Cleveland Orchestra, principal guest conductor of the Philharmonia of London, manager and director of the Vienna State Opera for two politically tempestuous years, and director of the National Orchestra of France. He returned to Pittsburgh as music director in 1988.

Shortly before the Tanglewood trip, Maazel announced his intention to embark on a composer's career, beginning in 1996. He had not particularly thought of himself as a composer, he said, but he had "written quite a few little things just for fun." When he conducted flutist James Galway in one of those things, *Irish Vapours and Capers*, that spring with the Pittsburgh, the piece, "much to my surprise," proved a success. He realized that being a composer while heading the Pittsburgh Symphony and the Bavarian Radio Symphony, his German orchestra, was more than he could handle.

There is something about Tanglewood—the chance to show off in front of the competition perhaps—that makes visiting orchestras play their Sunday best. The Pittsburgh followed in that parade-ground tradition. The playing in the two programs (Rachmaninoff, Prokofiev, and Ravel on Friday night, Beethoven, Mahler, and Prokofiev in the Saturday sequel) was responsive and burnished. Maazel's ideas about the music could be wayward in their manipulation of tempo and rhythm, but at their best, as in Rachmaninoff's Third Symphony, the performances gave off an incandescent glow. During his two-day stay Maazel also worked with the conducting students and the Music Center Orchestra, going over the repertory he would conduct with the Pittsburgh but not leading a student concert. He said he liked to teach but could not spare the two weeks that conductors like Haitink and Rattle could for intensive coaching. The jet was waiting on the tarmac for the next concert.

As Maazel prepared to head off into his new calling, he left a legacy in Pittsburgh besides a virtuoso orchestra. Like the BSO the Pittsburgh had an extensive touring program and pops and youth series at home to reach new listeners, especially among the young. But unlike Rattle, and unlike Rattle with his visionary approach to the millennium, Maazel's orchestra had innovated with a "Breakthrough" series: three subscription programs each season that used video screens, staging, or other special effects to supply dramatic punch for listeners weaned on television. Despite periodic suggestions that Tanglewood install giant video screens on the lawn in rock-

Of all the stars in Tanglewood's post-Bernstein firmament, none shines more brightly than Itzhak Perlman. His annual visits incite crowds to frenzies of Perlmania. Defying weather, jacked-up ticket prices, traffic, and long lines at the food counters and toilets, fifteen thousand concergoers flood the gates for a single concert as much to see an idol as to hear him. The Tanglewood box office average is eight thousand to ten thousand.

Like Luciano Pavarotti's handkerchief, Perlman's entry onto the stage is his trademark. Crippled by polio at four, he walks in gamely, even proudly, on crutches while the conductor trails behind. He smiles to orchestra and audience, eases himself into a waiting chair beside the podium, and lays his crutches on the floor. Only then does he take up his Stradivarius or Guarneri, which the conductor (usually Seiji Ozawa at Tanglewood) or the concertmaster will have carried onstage. Then, to the audience's delight, he goes into a show of inspecting the instrument as if it might have received rough handling from his helper. The soloist rather than the music has already become the center of attention; even the conductor has been cast in the shadows. How can an audience resist?

Triumph over adversity is only part of the story. Since his 1958 appearance as a thirteen-year-old wunderkind on the "Ed Sullivan Show" and his subsequent discovery by violinist Isaac Stern, the Israeli-born Perlman has yoked a sunny personality, media savvy, and advocacy of popular causes—especially the handicapped and Israel—to an innate musicality. Not only has he appeared on countless concert telecasts, but his credits extend to the "David Letterman" and "Tonight" shows, "Sesame Street," "The Frugal Gourmet," the Grammy Awards, the "Three Tenors, Encore!" telecast (which he hosted), other public television specials (also sometimes as host), and American Express credit card commercials. His huge discography includes, in addition to concertos and sonatas, Bach arias with soprano Kathleen Battle, jazz with pianist Oscar Peterson, and klezmer music. His records have won fourteen Grammys; he plays the violin solos in John Williams's Oscar-winning sound track, recorded with the BSO, for *Schindler's List*. President Reagan awarded him the Medal of Liberty, London honored him with a "Definitive Perlman Experience" festival, and universities ranging from Harvard and Yale to Yeshiva and Jerusalem have conferred honorary degrees.

Then, when he begins to play, there is the tone: plush, gleaming, culti-

concert fashion, the festival's chief boon so far to the video age was galas and telecasts. It also had a not-so-secret weapon named Itzhak Perlman.

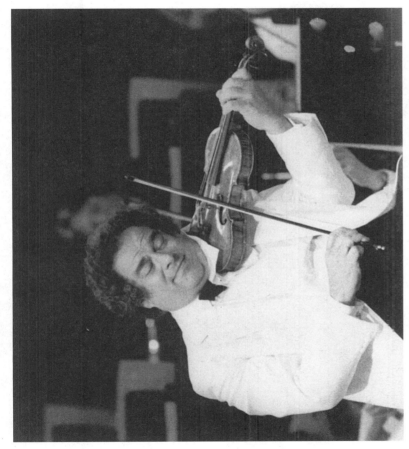

Itzhak Perlman radiates joy as he performs with the BSO. (Walter H. Scott)

vated. And the playing itself: suave and luxurious, like fine silk or leather. And the repertory: nearly always something familiar and beloved. Audiences have come to expect it of him, and he has come to deliver it.

At Tanglewood there is another attraction. Surveys have found that about half the audience comes from the heavily Jewish New York metropolitan area, including Connecticut, Long Island, and New Jersey. For such concertgoers (and for many others) Perlman has become, in his championing of Israel and his refusal to be defeated by adversity, a symbol of the Jewish state itself. Indeed, his Tanglewood appearances are often accompanied by fêtes for Jewish or Israeli causes. For older listeners, who make up a large part of the audience, there probably is also an echo of Franklin Delano Roosevelt's confidence, even cockiness, in the face of polio's assaults.

How indeed can an audience resist? A Tanglewood audience can't, and year after year it happily pays premium ticket prices—$20 to $76 for the Shed in 1997—to hear Perlman in programs that fetch $6 to $11 less when noncelebrity artists play the same music. And not just orchestral programs. In 1995 nearly eleven thousand listeners paid those premium prices to hear Perlman and pianist Emanuel Ax play a sonata recital in the Shed. In the cavernous space no one beyond the first few rows of seats could hear more than a bare outline of the music. In Seiji Ozawa Hall, where such programs are ordinarily held, they go for half the price and every listener can hear every note. But Seiji Ozawa Hall does not seat five thousand as the Shed does, with room on the lawn for thousands more.

Whatever Perlman may feel in the lonely communion of the soul, the impression he leaves is of joy in everything he does. Joy is no small satisfaction or achievement. But in the 1980s a certain slickness or self-satisfaction crept into Perlman's playing, as if sumptuous tone and dazzling technique were enough. He tended to stick, more and more, to the same top-ten concertos. Critics accused him of going on automatic pilot—a recurring phrase in reviews—as he rushed around the country playing one-night stands. All those Beethoven, Brahms, Mendelssohn, Tchaikovsky, and Mozart concertos seemed to blur into one another, each layered under a rich coating of chocolate. Typically Perlman arrives at Tanglewood on the day before a concert, runs through his concerto in a BSO rehearsal, plays the concert, and leaves for the next festival, collecting a fee reported to be $45,000 per appearance in the mid-1990s—one of the highest in the soloist's trade. At one hundred appearances a year, that would put his income at $4.5 million, not counting record and television fees. Critics began asking whether all that money was good for art.

Perlman, who lives in an East Hampton, Long Island, house valued at between $3 million and $4 million, denies that he is wealthy or that his performances are merely copies of one another. In a 1996 interview with the *New York Times*, he said his tax bill and the costs of putting five children through school ate up much of his income. "Being wealthy and living well are two different things. If I wanted to stop playing next year and take a year to go around the world, I couldn't do it. I have to play."[2]

As for the artistic question, Perlman's standard interview response is that there is a danger in repetition—but not for him. In 1988 he conceded to the *Times* that he was recycling the same familiar masterpieces over and over, but said he constantly listened to and questioned his playing to keep it from becoming a "Xerox" of itself. He would like to play new works and had, in fact, premiered concertos by Earl Kim and Robert Starer, but audiences, conductors, and concert managers would not let him explore the outer reaches of the repertory. "That is simply a question of economics: it's always sure-fire to hear one play Tchaikovsky or Mendelssohn." Unless a music director makes his own programs and asks for a twentieth-century or other nonstandard work like the Berg concerto (which Perlman recorded in the early 1980s with the BSO under Ozawa), "you don't get asked to do that." Recitals gave him the opportunity to try out new repertory and bring variety to his musical life.

His appearances on television commercials and talk shows, Perlman said, built new audiences for good music. Television, in fact, was "*the* strongest way to bring more music to more people. My being on talk shows has familiarized countless people with fiddle playing. A lot of people come to my concerts who've never been to a concert before."[3]

Perlman's argument was essentially Lockhart's with the Pops and Luciano Pavarotti's with "The Three Tenors": get the people into the hall, give them a show, and they'll come back for more. Like the Pops and tenor mania, Tanglewood offered proof that the formula got listeners inside the gates. But the underlying question was, Were those crowds there to hear great music, or had they come for a show? In more basic terms, Would those listeners, initiated into the mysteries, return to hear thoughtful, provocative musicians like Gidon Kremer or pianist Alfred Brendel in more challenging repertory played in a more challenging style?

Perlman was right that audiences, managers, and conductors wanted the same old warhorses. Warhorses were essential to the system of top-forty masterworks, celebrity artists, and high fees and ticket prices that kept the concert business going. But at what price to musical vitality? Though still a fine instrumentalist, Perlman had become a less interesting musician than he was when younger, and no matter what his rationalizations about repertory and money, the change was etched in his playing. In the always intricate interplay between art and personality, personality emerged on top. The same fate was overtaking two other Tanglewood idols, Jessye Norman and Kathleen Battle, whose prima donna airs were turning them into caricatures of the fine singers they once had been. Yet for them, too, ticket prices bumped the ceiling and the crowds came to cheer, no matter how well or badly their goddesses sang.

Whatever the answers to the audience problem—and no one knew all of them—Tanglewood followed the law of supply and demand. Perlman might charge one of the highest soloist's fees in the world, and an audience of fifteen thousand might bring in $350,000 in a day. Yet those premium ticket prices and premium-size crowds helped to pay the costs of boarding a symphony orchestra in the country for two months and running a major school.

How could a right-thinking, up-to-date festival refuse? It couldn't, and in the trade-off between art and commerce, music survived but sometimes had to play the game by commerce's rules.

S OMEWHERE far from the sunny kingdom of Perlman, storm clouds roil the land of Brendel.

Such audience and Ozawa favorites as Perlman, Norman, and Battle are, often self-consciously, "stars." If Alfred Brendel is a star, it is precisely for his absence of star luster: for his awkward stage presence, his intellectuality, his refusal to play to the crowd. His struggles at the keyboard seem to mirror a fierce inner struggle to wrench the essence out of music's soul. At Tanglewood he commands only standard ticket prices and standard-size audiences. His followers are mainly cognoscenti.

The five Beethoven piano concertos in five days was the task Brendel had set for himself when he returned to Tanglewood in 1992. Even though he had been out of action for the previous two months with tendinitis of the elbow, the assignment held no terrors for him. Over the span of a forty-four-year career he had played the cycle about twelve times, mostly in the last two decades, and most recently with Simon Rattle in London and Birmingham. When he began a two-night cycle with the Chicago Symphony Orchestra in 1977 at Chicago's outdoor Ravinia Festival, the temperature stood at one hundred degrees and the humidity at 95 percent. The performances not only worked, he recalled, still half-amazed at the feat, but worked well. Compared to Chicago's heat wave, Tanglewood would be a breeze.

The Tanglewood cycle opened on a Tuesday night with the Fourth Concerto, which Brendel played with the Music Center Orchestra to give it a share in the experience. With the BSO he played the First and Third Concertos on Friday night and the Second and Fifth on Sunday afternoon. Seiji Ozawa conducted all three programs as part of a Beethoven week. In his Viennese-accented English, Brendel said the project was daunting, but not as daunting as a solo recital:

If you play a recital all by yourself, or two recitals or three recitals, you have to cope with even more music. In a way you do everything. You do the solo and the orchestra, and the voices if there are singing scenes. So I think the cycle is not quite as demanding in some ways. What is the complication is that one has to set up a performance with the conductor. But there I know that Mr. Ozawa has wide open ears, and when I have worked with him so far, there has never been a problem in our collaboration.

Alfred Brendel performs with the BSO in the Beethoven concerto cycle. (Walter H. Scott)

A transplant from Vienna to London, the lanky, owlish Brendel is sometimes called the thinking man's pianist. Although best known as a specialist in Beethoven and Schubert, he is also a champion of Liszt, in whom—contrary to the standard virtuoso view—he finds an intellectual soul mate. Among the moderns he favors the cerebral Busoni and Schoenberg. He leaves Chopin, Tchaikovsky, Rachmaninoff, and other heart-on-the-sleeve romantics to keyboard sluggers who enjoy such things. Unsympathetic critics have likened his concerts to lessons in musical analysis. In his Germanic intellectualism he follows in the tradition of Artur Schnabel and Rudolf Serkin.

Also a painter when young—a show of his paintings hung nearby when, in Graz, Austria, he made his piano debut—Brendel gave up formal piano studies at seventeen to find his own way as a musician. Despite early successes he did not gain an international reputation until he was in his forties. Even then he remained outside the musical establishment. He has no regular chamber music partners and, as he puts it, belongs to no club or school. Unlike Perlman-style soloists who play a hundred concerts a year, he takes time to study musical sources and read in other fields: novels, plays, poetry, architecture, philosophy. He collects kitsch art as a hobby and admits to self-doubt and physical difficulties in wrestling with finger-taxing pieces.

Brendel is also the author of two volumes of perceptive essays on music. In one of those books, *Music Sounded Out*, he writes that playing cycles of a composer's concertos or sonatas makes "the stature of a composer more clearly recognizable. They are especially appropriate to great composers like Beethoven, who constantly have something new to convey. The unmistakable character of each movement, when played in close succession with the rest of the cycle, shows its profile even more distinctly to performers and listeners alike."[4]

Brendel came to Tanglewood fresh from a rethinking of the Beethoven piano sonatas. He had taken the winter off to stay at home and restudy the thirty-two sonatas for a new round of cycle performances in Europe and the United States. He wanted to "sit in front of a clean page and try to be as naïve as possible and start a new chain of experiences with these pieces." His conception of the concertos also had evolved over the years. But looking back, he found "a kind of lifeline, a thread of character, of my character," connecting the performances. As a performer grows and gains in insights and experiences, he said, "one sifts these experiences and finds out what is more and what is less important."

Three passages in the first movement of the Fourth Concerto illustrated his sifting process. In each a new idea is stated for the only time, and then only in passing. "They are lyrical, like glimpses of a different world in a distance," Brendel said, "and they are very hard to incorporate in the flow of the whole. One of the hallmarks of a good performance of this movement, a happy performance, is if they fit in or they stick out."

Brendel considers himself inured to the hazards of outdoor music—not only heat and humidity but also, in urban settings like Ravinia, the roar of trains and screech of jets. In *Music Sounded Out* he recalls concerts "with screaming babies (Japan), a barking dog (New York), a mewing cat (Istanbul), somebody falling down in a faint, a maniac clapping in the most impossible places, and a power cut plunging us all into darkness." In Chicago he once had to stop during a recital and tell the audience, "I can hear you but you can't hear me."[5]

Except for the dog and cat the distractions could have happened at Tanglewood. But a Brendel audience is not a Perlman audience, just as a Brendel performance is not a Perlman performance. Brendel's Beethoven, lit by flashes of impish wit, had a monumentality born of formal, psychological, and metaphysical mysteries revealed; under Ozawa the accompaniments followed faithfully wherever the soloist led. In any case Beethoven's name on the program guaranteed an audience even if the soloist's didn't. The public, besotted by "Three Tenors" spectacles, chose Perlman. Tanglewood also made room for Brendel.

CELEBRITY SOLOISTS who inflamed a public's itch for idols were nothing new. Among violinists there had been Jascha Heifetz before Perlman, and Eugène Ysaÿe before Heifetz: a long line stretching back as far as the supposedly devil-possessed Paganini. Among pianists the flamboyant, lady-killing Liszt was the avatar. The vocal acrobats went back to the castrati of Handel's time. What was new in the twentieth century was the nexus of big money, fast travel, the recording studio, and the television camera, all of which—given an artist with the right potential—could turn a ripple into a tidal wave overnight.

Alongside the celebrity tradition exists another kind of soloist: the thoughtful musician involved in the music of his or her time, where the waves of public approbation seldom lap. When Bernard Haitink led the Tanglewood Music Center Orchestra in its final 1996 concert, the program was dedicated to the memory of one of those figures, Louis Krasner.

Krasner, a Tanglewood faculty member who died in 1995 at the age of ninety-one, earned a niche in history by commissioning and premiering Berg's Violin Concerto, the work that Perlman said conductors would not let him play. But Krasner was something more, as students who received the benefits of his coaching knew. He was a living link to the 1920s and 1930s Vienna of Berg, Anton Webern, and other twelve-tone composers following in Schoenberg's tracks. He also embodied the humane values of an earlier time—what Bernstein spoke of as "nobility."

The Berg concerto, one of the few works of its kind that seem certain to live on beyond their twentieth-century origin, mirrors the anguish of its times and its creator's soul, but rises above turbulence to end on an ethereal plane. Berg dedicated the work "to the memory of an angel." It thus became a requiem for Manon Gropius, the beautiful, talented daughter of architect Walter Gropius and Alma Mahler, dead of polio at eighteen. Krasner, who had a tart sense of humor, was no angel. But there was an echo of Berg's gesture when the Music Center dedicated its concert to Krasner's memory. The Violin Concerto, Berg's last completed work, became his own requiem when he died four months after finishing it. Now, as the centerpiece of the program in Ozawa Hall, it memorialized the man responsible for its birth. Joel Smirnoff, a former BSO violinist who had gone on to the Juilliard String

Quartet—he would become its first violinist the following year—was the soloist.

Wispy and only about five feet tall, Krasner looked like an elf as he presided in a classroom or crossed the lawn to a concert. (Indeed, BSO brats in the summer colony around Tanglewood had at one time called him and his equally diminutive wife, the former Adrienne Galimir of the Galimir family of string players, "the little people.") But the Berg concerto, other important premieres (including the Schoenberg Violin Concerto), his renown among violinists and followers of new music, and his influence as a teacher marked Krasner as a giant.

He wore his eminence lightly. Once, as head of the team that traveled around the country auditioning string players for the Music Center, he took special pains with a young man who clearly was not Tanglewood material. Krasner let the student play his allotted ten minutes: no cutting him off with the peremptory "thank you, that's all," common in this situation. Then he put the auditions behind schedule while he discussed the young man's hopes and studies with him. Why all the trouble over one unpromising student? Every applicant should get something out of the audition, Krasner explained afterward, and the least he could do was to make the experience helpful for the boy.

Krasner was born in Ukraine but brought up and trained in the United States. In the late 1920s he went to Europe as a young man aflame with passion for new music. In the Vienna coffeehouses he got to know Berg, Webern, and other members of the twelve-tone circle. The music, revolutionary in style but growing out of Viennese traditions, gripped his imagination. Yet on his concert tours he found that "twelve-tone music was rejected generally not only by concert audiences but almost as often by influential and successful performers."[6] He resolved to show the world the error of its ways.

The means suggested itself when, in 1931, he attended a New York performance of Berg's *Wozzeck* by Leopold Stokowski and the Philadelphia Orchestra. Overwhelmed by the opera, with its twelve-tone episodes and theme of the individual trampled by society, Krasner approached Berg with the idea of commissioning a violin concerto. Friends discouraged the idea, as did Berg. But Krasner persisted. After three years Berg, needing the money, gave in. He completed the concerto in 1935 and Krasner premiered it the next year in Barcelona. It became a staple in the twentieth-century repertory (as did *Wozzeck*), although most twelve-tone music has yet to find a nonspecialist audience.

Fleeing Europe as the Nazi menace spread, Krasner returned to the

Louis Krasner during a coaching session with students. (William Mercer)

United States. He became concertmaster of the Minneapolis (now Minnesota) Symphony Orchestra and then taught at Syracuse University until his retirement. In 1974 he moved to Boston and began teaching at the New England Conservatory and Tanglewood. In these positions he coached chamber music, passing along his knowledge of the works, personalities, and styles of Schoenberg's second Viennese school as well as a lifetime's experience with the standard repertory. In the late 1980s a degenerative spinal disease reduced him to using a walker and then confined him to a wheelchair. Even then he insisted on going to Tanglewood. The Music Center arranged special transportation and housing so he could continue to teach and go to concerts. The summer of 1994 was his last in the Berkshires, but almost until his death, two months before the 1995 season was to begin, he was still talking about going back.

Krasner was one of three grand old men on the Music Center faculty when the 1990s dawned. All had connections to the musical ferment of interwar Europe, and all had fled Hitler's grasp. Conductor Maurice Abravanel had worked with Kurt Weill in Berlin and later premiered many of Weill's stage works in New York. Violist Eugene Lehner had been a member of Vienna's celebrated Kolisch Quartet, which championed the works of Schoenberg, Berg, and Webern. When Krasner died, only Lehner, a retired

BSO violist who also coached chamber music with an emphasis on the second Viennese school, remained.

Just before leaving Tanglewood in 1993, Abravanel told friends he did not think he would be back the next year. Though he was ninety, he was not talking, at least publicly, about dying. He had already retired once, in 1979 as conductor of the Utah Symphony, he said. How long could he go on being a Tanglewood "presence"—as he was called, often in reverential tones—with no formal duties? He was outliving his usefulness, overstaying his welcome.

He didn't return. Already suffering a bronchial infection when he left for home in Salt Lake City, he died of pneumonia a month after his farewell.

More than a "presence," Abravanel held the title of artist in residence, an honor that only soprano Phyllis Curtin and, later, John Williams shared. He first came to Tanglewood in an official capacity as acting director of the Music Center in 1982 while Gunther Schuller took a sabbatical. The next year Schuller returned, but the BSO brought Abravanel back to give seminars, attend student rehearsals and concerts, evaluate them with faculty members, and generally act as an ombudsman and father confessor for students. He returned every summer afterward as a presence both at the Music Center and in the Shed. Nobody who promenaded across the Shed's main aisle during a BSO intermission could miss him and his wife, Caroline. A friendly gathering always clustered around their box. If there were attractive women in the group, so much the better: they received an Abravanel kiss, planted on the cheek with Gallic chivalry.

Born in Greece, Abravanel got his grounding as a conductor in European opera houses (still the customary place in Europe) and studied composition with Weill in Berlin. In New York, where both he and Weill landed after escaping Nazi hospitality, Abravanel conducted the Broadway productions of Weill's musicals, beginning with *Knickerbocker Holiday.* After short-lived tours of duty at the Metropolitan and Chicago operas, he went west in 1947 to Salt Lake City. There, like Rattle with his Birmingham ensemble a third of a century later, he built the lowly Utah Symphony into an orchestra of national repute with a history of pioneering recordings.

Also like Rattle, Abravanel was one of the last of the conductors who stayed in one place to devote their lives to an orchestra rather than jet around the globe to glamorous podiums. But there was nothing of the gray eminence about this tall, gangling figure, who could usually be found at lunchtime surrounded by a gaggle of students at a Tanglewood cafeteria table. He exuded Old World charm, and if he offered criticism to a student or professional, he did it with grandfatherly care. He once said he could not understand how he could help, "because all I do, really, is conversations— you know, presence, a little nod, a little question, a little discussion." When death ended the discussions after thirteen summers, Tanglewood did not replace him. There was no one who could do exactly what he did, undefined as the duties were, and do it with his special touch.

The BSO dedicated its opening program in 1994 to Abravanel's memory. Because Krasner died so soon before the 1995 season, his memorial had to wait a year until it could be fitted into the schedule. And because his association was primarily with the Music Center rather than the world embodied in the Shed, the student orchestra would play the Berg concerto under Haitink in his first public appearance with the group. Haitink said the students caught on quickly to Berg's style; they "reacted wonderfully," in fact, in both the concerto and Brahms's "Haydn" Variations, which he also conducted. The response was audible in the solo and orchestral playing. The lyrical, romantic spirit that suffused Berg's tormented music would have brought a twinkle to Krasner's ever-vigilant eye.

Although Abravanel maintained an outpost in the Shed's boxes, Krasner, like most Tanglewood teachers, was largely invisible to the public. But in 1985 he spoke to a luncheon meeting of patrons about his experiences. He discussed many people and events, including the Berg concerto, but always he returned to his central concern: music as an expression of spirit. He quoted Saint Augustine: "Man's profoundest expression is eloquent silence. But how can one know God and commit the concept of God to silence? Next to silence man's deepest expression is music. Therefore sing to God."

"In truth," Krasner said, "all great music sings to God." Melody, rhythm, and harmony "are only the wings to spiritual and divine regions." The musics of past and present flow into and feed one another:

Bach needed Beethoven, Beethoven needed Brahms, Brahms needed Schoenberg for continued life. Conversely, Beethoven was nourished by Bach, Brahms by Beethoven, and Schoenberg by Brahms. Art, as [is] all life, is constantly reborn and recreated. Styles change, but not substance. All great masters, each in the language of his own time, address themselves innerly to man and his universe.

Innerly to man and his universe! Even the language seems out of date. Yet in figures like Abravanel, Krasner, Haitink, Brendel, and Rattle the values endured. The crowds might flock to entertainments and spectacles, but music has a spiritual basis that goes beyond the merely ephemeral or communal. Indeed, from the time of ancient Greece through Bach, music was primarily a form of religious observance or expression. Out of this heritage arose Koussevitzky's "central line," the tradition that sustained three centuries of music and civilization until a new generation ordered Beethoven to roll over and declared art of no utility, an irrelevancy in a pleasure-oriented society. The overthrow of values mirrored the deeper divisions in American life as commercial and social forces, including some within the music industry itself, sought to transform the symphony orchestra into an engine of entertainment.

Like Bernstein, Abravanel and Krasner took a part of the past with them when they died. Lehner taught for another year before his death, in 1997, and other Tanglewood teachers dedicated to the performance of both old music and new, such as Yo-Yo Ma, Joel Smirnoff, cellist Joel Krosnick, and pianists Gilbert Kalish and Peter Serkin, also carried on the tradition. Each, like Krasner, devoted himself to masters of all periods who addressed humanity's deepest emotional needs. Each looked not for wealth or celebrity, though those things were not necessarily evil, but for the opportunity to nourish themselves and the public through music whose values transcended mere ingenuity and fashion. But musicians of the late twentieth century bore a burden that earlier generations hadn't. They had to initiate audiences steeped in pop, television, film, and the cult of celebrity into the pleasures of a half-forgotten tradition. There were no more Bernsteins, Abravanels, and Krasners to do it.

5

Intruders in the Temple

OLIVER KNUSSEN did everything but knock down the walls for his farewell concert. Departing Tanglewood in 1993 after seven years as its new-music czar, he ripped out a quarter of the seats in the front of the Theater–Concert Hall, installed three orchestras on the expanded stage, and, as one of the three conductors, led the student assemblage in Karlheinz Stockhausen's *Gruppen*.

The 1957 work is more often written about than performed because of its logistical demands, difficulty of execution, and cataclysmic eruptions of sound. Following Stockhausen's plan, Knussen arrayed the orchestras in an inverted V, with part of the audience wedged between the legs of the V. To demonstrate the spatial differences in the wraparound sound, he took a short break after the performance and had the audience exchange seats—those in the front to the back, those on the sides to the middle, and so on. Then Knussen repeated the twenty-four-minute exercise. From any position the three percussion-heavy orchestras going at it at once were like three jackhammer-equipped wrecking crews tearing up a city block. *Gruppen* (German for "groups," referring to the clusters of sound) is not so much music as organized noise. It is not meant to be enjoyed. It is experienced, for better or worse.

The concert culminated Tanglewood's Festival of Contemporary Music, a weeklong festival within a festival, and was the Music Center Orchestra's farewell to the Theater–Concert Hall, its home since 1941. A performance of Peter Lieberson's *King Gesar* by Yo-Yo Ma and pianists Peter Serkin and Emanuel Ax the next night concluded the new-music festival and sent the old hall into retirement. The next year Seiji Ozawa Hall would replace it.

Also the next year a new festival director, Reinbert de Leeuw, would take over, bringing new programming ideas and composers. Conspicuous among them would be the loose grouping called postmodernists, who, with their hip, cutting-edge posture, much of it coming out of rock, had not found a Tanglewood welcome before. Not one but two eras were ending.

The Festival of Contemporary Music attracts minuscule audiences, usually of only a few hundred per concert, compared with the BSO's thousands in the Shed. The performances are given by Music Center students and by guest artists and ensembles that specialize in twentieth-century music. In both cases the performers are able to prepare the often difficult works without the rehearsal and programming pressures that go with concerts for a large general audience. The trade-off is that by confining new music to a ghetto, the separate festival deepens the estrangement between the public and the music of its time. A vicious circle takes hold, nowhere more visibly than at Tanglewood. Ordinary concertgoers don't listen to new music because it sounds strange to them, and it remains strange because they don't listen to it.

Tanglewood's contemporary series dates from 1956, when Paul Fromm, a Chicago wine importer, began underwriting new-music concerts at the Music Center. The programs were formalized into a festival in 1964 under Gunther Schuller, a Music Center force for two decades. When Schuller resigned in 1984, Knussen, a protégé who had gone on to become a major composer and new-music conductor in England, succeeded him as festival director. (At the same time Leon Fleisher succeeded Schuller as the overall Music Center head.) When Knussen in turn resigned, pleading a need for more time to compose, he recommended his friend and fellow *Gruppen* conductor, de Leeuw, as his successor. (BSO assistant conductor Robert Spano, later to become a Tanglewood fixture both in new-music activities and with the BSO, took the third *Gruppen* orchestra.) Accelerating a trend begun under Knussen, de Leeuw steered the programming more toward composers who had been anathema to Schuller, particularly the postmodernists and the minimalists who had preceded them.

A Dutchman with a long record of service to twentieth-century music, de Leeuw stated his credo in the 1995 festival program book:

As we approach the turn of the century, views on both the musical past and musical present are changing in a striking way. The simplicity and purported self-evidence in the 1960s and '70s of looking at musical history as a logical developmental progression has now proved to be at least very one-sided. The ambition of approaching music with a universal language comparable to the language of tonal-

ity has failed; no longer is distinguishing between "musically correct" and "musically incorrect," or believing in one musical truth, in any way helpful to understanding the complexity and variety of the music of our century.

The new diversity mirrored trends in other areas of American life, ranging from novels and painting to fashion and college curricula. Minimalism, with its pulsing figures and trancelike states, and postmodernism, with its punk or over-the-top gestures akin to those in cutting-edge pop, came out of the youth-oriented revolutions of the 1960s. Both styles, and the many variants that developed after or from them, rejected the established order as embodied in the so-called uptown music dominant in the 1960s and 1970s, whose "one-sided" sway over composition de Leeuw termed out of date. The uptown composers, epitomized by Elliott Carter and Milton Babbitt, emphasized complexity and post-Schoenbergian rigor, much of it coming out of academia. By the 1990s "downtown" music—the distinction arose from concert scenes in New York—reigned in the slimmed-down, simplified styles of such composers as Philip Glass, Steve Reich, and a variety of younger followers.

Pastiche, parody, camp, rock licks, synthesizers, amplification, a streetwise stance: the urban voices of these composers come out of a society that has jettisoned its intellectual baggage and takes refuge in easy pleasures and sensations. The music has a vitality, an immediacy, and often a sense of fun lacking in other contemporary works. But the price is a two-dimensionality arising from rejection of the traditions and values that figures like Louis Krasner stood for.

Back home in Amsterdam, de Leeuw (pronounced duh *Layoo*) is director of the Schoenberg Ensemble, a leading European new-music group. He first came to Tanglewood at Knussen's invitation for three weeks in 1993 to help with rehearsals and conduct in the contemporary festival. Like John Williams and countless others, he was enchanted by the place. So when Tanglewood offered, he accepted the opportunity to plan and oversee the new-music week. He proved as indefatigable as both of his predecessors, creating marathon concerts that defied playing and listening capacities yet somehow drew the best from Tanglewood's students, who perform all but two or three of the daily (and sometimes twice daily) events.

De Leeuw, who was fifty-five in 1994, is nothing if not catholic. In addition to the new generation of composers, his programming took in a generous sampling of figures representing other countries and styles, including the uptown group. These composers included some familiar to Tanglewood and the United States, such as Elliott Carter and Olivier Messiaen, but oth-

Reinbert de Leeuw leads a student ensemble in the Festival of Contemporary Music. (Walter H. Scott)

ers—particularly Europeans like Henri Dutilleux and Mauricio Kagel—known by name if known at all.

The divisions between uptown and downtown, and the linkage between the United States and Europe, were personified in the 1994 composers in residence, Mario Davidovsky and Louis Andriessen. Davidovsky, who was in residence in July, is an American (born in Argentina) who writes in the structured European tradition. Andriessen, who succeeded him in August, is a European (and friend of de Leeuw's) who adopted and expanded upon the more open American styles. De Leeuw said the paradox summed up the interchange by which, since the 1960s, European and American composers' ideas had flown back and forth across the Atlantic. To complete the irony, de Leeuw pointed out, a younger generation of American composers like David Lang and Michael Torke—both on the 1994 festival schedule and both Tanglewood graduates—looked up to Andriessen as a model.

De Leeuw launched the new era with the Tanglewood debut of the Bang on a Can All-Stars, a six-member ensemble from the collective of composers and performers, primarily downtown and postmodern, who annually stage the Bang on a Can Festival in New York. Bang on a Can, as the irreverent name might suggest, was the epitome of everything Tanglewood had once barred the gates against. Yet here it was, presenting a concert as the 1994 festival's opening event. Lang and Julia Wolfe, two of the group's founders, were on the program, as were both Davidovsky, with his *Synchronism No. 6*, and Andriessen, with his *Hout* (Wood). Except for the Davidovsky piece the program was a postmodern dance on academia's grave, as orthodox in its high energy and decibel levels as the cerebral orthodoxy it sought to supplant. Wolfe's description of her *Lick*, a pop-driven riff for piano, percussion, electric guitar, saxophone, cello, and string bass, could have served as a motto for the evening's eight works. In the program notes she wrote: "The last piece I wrote, a work for six pianos, cracked something open, broke further away from the Western classical tradition. The body energy of pop music came into my music and it's still here and definitely in *Lick*. I'm totally excited about it."

A four-hour marathon concert given by students two days later began with a Charles Ives classic, *The Unanswered Question*, ranged through works by John Adams, Edgard Varèse, Silvestre Revueltas, John Cage, Wolfe, Torke, and Lang, and ended with the American premiere of Andriessen's *Hadewijch*, a half-hour vocal-instrumental work that forms part of an evening-length music-theater piece. For its contribution to the festival, the BSO performed a sumptuous new cello concerto it had commissioned from former composer in residence John Harbison; Yo-Yo Ma, for whom it was written, was the soloist. A whole evening was devoted to Messiaen's *Des Canyons aux étoiles*, with de Leeuw conducting a student orchestra and Peter Serkin playing the seemingly unplayable solo piano part. Another evening was given over to knotty chamber works by four senior Americans: Leon Kirchner, Ralph Shapey, Carter, and Davidovsky. The next night brought three enigmatic, often theatrical works by Kagel, whose quirky effects de Leeuw likened to the dream world of Luis Buñuel's films but whose aim seemed more like Dadaist jokes with sonic effects and unusual configurations of players. The final orchestral concert, also conducted by de Leeuw, ambitiously included Ives's *Orchestral Set No. 2* and Alexander Mossolov's once-popular *Iron Foundry* along with Davidovsky's *Shulamit's Dream*, Knussen's *Symphony No. 3*, Andriessen's *De Snelheid* (Velocity), and the world premiere of a commissioned work, Eric Zivian's *Quincunx*.

Whatever orthodoxy there might have been in the Theater-Concert Hall days, the doors were open wide in Ozawa Hall. Yet Bang on a Can's thunderously amplified arrival on opening night was like the fall of the Bastille. Haitink's warning about an "ego trip" by his countryman seemed misplaced, at least in terms of self-promotion. Rather, de Leeuw was intent on breaking down old barriers with new composers, new performers, new sounds. As he promised, "correct" and "incorrect" no longer applied. In the new democracy of tastes, one thing was as good as another, and each had an equal right to be heard.

Something was gained but something was missing. Schuller, a Pulitzer Prize–winning composer himself, put his finger on it as well as anyone could. In *Musings*, a collection of essays, he described it as "that fullness, that richness of experience we associate with the great music of the past, an experience in which all of our listening and feeling faculties are involved." Calling for a "new classicism" in composition, he proposed

a turning back to those profound verities—and, dare I say, human truths—that are common to all great music, whether of the baroque or the romantic or the modern era. In other words, it is not so much a "return to" as an "analogy to." I dream of finding contemporary analogies to that glorious past from which we still have much to learn and which we should not merely discard. Nor is my new classicism merely a new form of conservatism. It is in fact the opposite: a daring confrontation with certain rather disturbing realities and a radical move to gain back much of what we lost.[1]

Krasner called it spirituality, Bernstein nobility, Koussevitzky the central line. By any name it was in danger of being drowned out by music that made up its rules as it went along, creating a 1990s brand of radical chic.

THE BAD-BOY, BAD-GIRL STANCE was not original with composers of the 1980s and 1990s. They were descended from a line of American pioneers and tinkerers going back to Ives, Henry Cowell, and John Cage. During the same period in Europe, Satie, Poulenc, and Prokofiev poked fingers into the bourgeoisie's eye. Tanglewood had an enfant terrible of its own in Lukas Foss. But when he returned in 1989 for the first of two consecutive summers as composer in residence, he was more like an elder statesman and tabby.

Seated in the Hawthorne Cottage, a replica of the house where Nathaniel Hawthorne had lived and written on the Tanglewood grounds during 1850 and 1851, Foss listened to his seven composition students carry out the day's assignment: to play recordings of works they loved and tell what they loved about them. The young woman who went first played an acidic, angular piece for soprano and chamber ensemble by Brian Ferneyhough, a contemporary Englishman. Standing at the piano in the wood-paneled studio, she said she liked the relationship of long to short notes.

Foss, in Tanglewood garb of battered jeans, a blue jacket, and a plaid blue shirt, gently chided her for her analysis. "It's all very cerebral," he said.

The woman denied being cerebral. She said she was trying "to describe something very sensual."

With an easy laugh Foss said she was still describing a technical process, not an emotional response. Turning defensive, she replied that she found a certain gesture in the music "like a thought that begins to have doubts about itself."

"That's good," Foss replied soothingly. "We want to know what you love, and why." But when a young man played some of Mozart's *Figaro* a few minutes later, he found an instant ally in his teacher. Foss, the composer of doomsday works like *Exeunt,* loved the classics.

A composer in residence's only prescribed duty is to meet with the composition fellows, who usually number between six and twelve, and offer suggestions on their work. Some of these senior composers also conduct, usually their own works; all receive a garland of performances in the contemporary festival. Beyond that, they are free to work on their own pieces or just go sailing or golfing if they hear the siren call of summer in vacation country. Forty-nine years after his first of two student summers at Tanglewood, which were also the Music Center's first two seasons, Foss was loving being back, even though he usually spent his summers composing at a home in Bridgehampton, New York. For excitement, he said on the terrace at Seranak, Koussevitzky's former mansion, "nothing can equal those student days." But "for me it is wonderful to have come full circle, to be Paul Hindemith," the 1940 composer-teacher who, after three hours in the classroom, would hit the water belly-first with a smack and lead Foss and his fellow students on a hard swim in Stockbridge Bowl.

Foss is a triple-threat composer, conductor, and pianist, as was his 1940–41 classmate Leonard Bernstein. After two student summers each became a Tanglewood assistant to Koussevitzky, beginning an extended BSO association. Always Bernstein's star shone more brightly. If Foss felt any envy beneath the blue-eyed twinkle he turned on the world in 1989 from his rumpled face, he didn't show it. In fact, he spoke of Bernstein as an "older brother" to him at Tanglewood, just as Koussevitzky had been a "father."

Unlike Bernstein, who was gifted from the start but not a prodigy, Foss was composing as well as playing music by the age of seven. He tried his hand at an opera at eight. Three decades later that early effort blossomed into *Griffelkin,* his only full-length opera. (A short earlier opera, *The Jumping Frog of Calaveras County,* is probably his best-known work.) *Griffelkin* retells a German fairy tale, "The Devil's Birthday," which Foss said is "about a little devil who discovers what's beautiful about the world, falls in love

Lukas Foss conducts the BSO during his 1989 residency. (Walter H. Scott)

with the world, and commits a good deed for which he's banished from hell and ends up as a young human." As a boy Foss loved the story so much that his mother wrote a libretto based on it for him. When his mother died, he was thirty-five and had Alastair Reid adapt her libretto. Foss then rewrote the opera and dedicated it to her memory. The work had an early performance at Tanglewood with Foss conducting and Boris Goldovsky directing. A handful of other performances followed, but only recently had it occurred to Foss to have the piece published.

"I was so dumb," he said, shaking his head. "I had this property that could be my children's estate, that could be like *Hansel and Gretel*. It's really more like *The Magic Flute*—that kind of thing. I just wrote it, had it performed, and then wrote the next piece: forgot about it."

A march from *Griffelkin*, newly arranged by Foss for wind band, provided the opening fanfare for both the 1989 contemporary festival and the Tanglewood on Parade gala later in the season. Three longer Foss works, all E-titled—*Embros*, *Echoi*, and *Exeunt*—followed in the new-music series. Performed by the Boston Musica Viva, the 1984–85 *Embros* is a jest for a chamber ensemble with an electronic instrument of the performers' choice (here, a synthesizer). With its thumping ostinato rhythms and scraps of melody tossed back and forth, the piece suggests a march gone awry. In the 1980–82 *Exeunt*, which Foss conducted with the Music Center Orchestra, brief quotations from T. S. Eliot's "Waste Land" title the five interlocking sections. The piece begins in what Foss describes as a "maze": strings divided into twenty-eight parts, each playing a separate, eerie glissando. Stark and angry, or bare as a denuded forest (Eliot's "withered stumps of time"), succeeding passages lead to a repeat of an earlier section in reverse and a final fade-out with an apocalyptic thwack on a drum.

Echoi, from 1960–63, plunges even deeper into the doomsday chasm. Foss likened the thirty-five-minute piece, which is in four movements for four instrumentalists, to "a scaffold which in the process of composition is gradually eliminated, destroyed." Echoes of many kinds appear: pitches, motives, sonorities, even tape loops. Passages of massive, sometimes obsessive complexity alternate with moments of glancing beauty and reach a climax that is not for the tender of ear. The cacophony ceases only when a percussionist "invades the innards of the piano" (in the program notes' demure phrase) and throttles it.

Though most of his music is cheerful, Foss confessed, *Exeunt* is "about the end of the world. It's the most pessimistic piece I've ever written, the most tragic." It doesn't, he said, predict or warn about any specific threat, such as the bomb, because only propaganda can do that. He merely wanted "to make some kind of statement without being pompous about it."

None of his music, however, cost him as much grief as *Echoi*. To Foss it "is a wildly experimental piece in which I really found myself as an avant-gardist." Nearly half an hour long, it

took three years out of my life. I thought I was going crazy. It turned out to be the most difficult chamber piece I have ever written. I thought I was going insane. I began to have blurred vision. I thought I'd never finish it. And when my friend Lenny Bernstein saw the score, he said, "Lukas, it looks like your last will."

Foss laughed. "Maybe it is."

A former director of the Buffalo, Brooklyn, and Milwaukee orchestras, Foss also conducted the BSO in a Sunday afternoon program during his 1989 return. One of the pieces was Tchaikovsky's *Francesca da Rimini*, a favorite of Foss's, once popular for its romantic furies but now out of fashion for the same reason. Beethoven's *Leonore* Overture No. 3 opened the program, and Copland's *Lincoln Portrait* closed it. In the middle came Foss's own *Renaissance* Concerto for flute and orchestra, with James Galway as the soloist. With its quotation of Orpheus's lament for the dead Eurydice from Monteverdi's *Orfeo*, and with other references to the past, the work is, in Foss's words, "a handshake across the centuries."

So, in a sense, was the entire BSO program. Amid bright summer sunlight three of history's great pairs of lovers were there: Beethoven's Leonore and Florestan, Tchaikovsky's (and Dante's) Francesca and Paolo, and Monteverdi's (and mythology's) Orpheus and Eurydice. In spirit Abraham Lincoln was there, invoked by Copland's musical portrait. Martin Luther King Jr. was likewise present, in the person of his daughter, Yolanda King, who narrated the lines from Lincoln. Copland—one of Tanglewood's seminal figures, now too frail to travel and only a year from death—was there in the ringing affirmations of his music. And, of course, Foss himself was there as a representative of Tanglewood's beginnings.

As a conductor, Foss confessed, he would rather do the classics than modern pieces.

When I do the classics, I do the music that made me become a musician. I pour my whole love into it. And, actually, why did I begin to conduct? Because since as an avant-garde composer I left the classics, I wanted still to have an outlet towards the thing I loved. So, in other words, I turned to the future as a composer, and I was able to make love to the past as a conductor.

In both his conducting and his compositions, there was still something boyish and almost naive about this elder statesman; even his doomsday proclamations had a touch of the innocent. Yet when Yolanda King spoke Lincoln's burning lines about a divided nation's need to come together in brotherhood and equality, the present made connection with the past in a more than musical way. Music at its best invokes truths that are larger than either words or music. Foss, the avant-gardist, found truths for the present in the great figures and traditions of the past.

A LSO A LOVER of the classics, John Harbison confronted the sometimes noisy present in a different way. He decided that rock music was a weed that had taken over too much of the garden to be ripped out. It was better to see if he could make it blossom.

As a composer and teacher Harbison had thought long and hard about the problems of art music in an age dominated by rock. In the 1980s he wrote a series of articles worrying that America was impoverishing its composers and musical heritage by heaping money and adulation on entertainers. Rock was still foreign to Harbison when, at the age of fifty-three, he returned to Tanglewood in 1992 for a second stint as composer in residence. But he no longer held a "prophetic, Old Testament vision" of the affair. Rock is the music that today's young grew up on, he said, and "in this society, driven as it is by very powerful capitalistic forces," it is here to stay. The teacher must help the student turn this legacy to his advantage in an art medium.

Steven Mackey was a case in point. During Harbison's first Tanglewood residency, in 1984, he had Mackey as a student. Though Mackey had been a rock musician, his compositions, Harbison found, "bore almost no trace of that experience." Harbison suggested ways to put it to use while preserving a larger sense of craft.

As with the individual, so with society. "It's impossible to cut music off from our experience," Harbison said. "A culture will get exactly what it nurtures. The quality of the concert music and the rock music is going to be exactly equivalent to what the fertilizer is."

Harbison is a Bostonian: a Harvard man and, since 1969, a faculty member at the Massachusetts Institute of Technology. Unlike most composers in residence he brought extensive programming, conducting, and administrative experience to the Tanglewood assignment. In Boston he had directed the Cantata Singers, one of the city's many fine choral ensembles, which performs everything from the seventeenth-century sacred music of Schutz, a Harbison favorite, to premieres and commissions. As the Los Angeles Philharmonic's composer in residence from 1986 to 1989, he had directed the orchestra's new-music group and helped to pick new works for the Philharmonic itself to play. So when he came to Tanglewood in 1992 to teach, he was also equipped to run the contemporary festival while Knussen took a sabbatical to do more composing. As a result of his West Coast experience, he brought a California air to concerts that, under Schuller and Knussen, had looked primarily toward the East Coast and Europe.

Harbison liked everything about Los Angeles, including the city itself, but found the music being composed there a world apart from new music that he heard in Boston and other East Coast cities. The influence of Asia, pervasive on a broad artistic front during the counterculture days of the 1960s and 1970s, retained its grip on California composers. "The tradition on the West Coast that seems to persist is one of an almost anti-European stand," Harbison said, "or at least a stand that says, 'We don't have any sort of across-the-board criteria.'"

Californians Frederic Rzewski, Roger Reynolds, Art Jarvinen, Rand Steiger, Morton Subotnick, Terry Riley, and Mackey were on the contemporary festival's programs, most of them for the first time. They were played by the California EAR ("experimental and recent") Unit and the California-based Kronos Quartet. The Kronos, which performs everything from Bartók to Jimi Hendrix and beyond, had brought its funky twentieth-century repertory to Tanglewood before. Harbison, who got to know the EAR Unit in Los Angeles, invited it for a debut.

Among younger composers Harbison continued the tradition of presenting Tanglewood alumni, such as Mackey and another from the class of '84, James Primosch. Among older Americans he programmed works by two guest teachers that summer, Subotnick and George Perle. Two major European figures, Hans Werner Henze and Peter Maxwell Davies, and a leading American, Jacob Druckman, shared a program in which each was represented by a memorial piece. The climactic orchestral concert included Schoenberg's Violin Concerto, which Harbison conducted with his wife, Rose Mary, as the soloist, along with *Un Vitrail et des oiseaux* by Olivier Messiaen, a former composer in residence who had died in 1992, and *The World in the Evening* by Nicholas Maw, an Englishman whose work Harbison esteemed for its "largeness of spirit and boldness of gesture."

Other composers heard during the week were Peter Sculthorpe of Australia, Henryk Górecki and Andrzej Panufnik of Poland, Luigi Dallapiccola of Italy, and Americans Yehudi Wyner (a Tanglewood faculty member) and Shulamit Ran, winner of the 1991 Pulitzer Prize in music. Program building, Harbison said in the festival program book, is "a brave kind of roulette":

For a composer to present a piece he or she has composed is a natural, sometimes nerve-wracking part of a basic artistic transaction we signed for early. But presenting other people's music is different. It is a little like asking people over and hoping they like the food, the house, and the climate. The concerts must say: "I love these pieces," or "I think these are all worth hearing," or at least "I'm sure you'll find at least one thing here you like."

The Californians' laid-back, anything-goes styles were a harbinger of things to come under de Leeuw. Otherwise the programming still centered on the European and East Coast establishment composers favored by Schuller and Knussen.

Harbison is, in his way, a member of that establishment. At Harvard he studied under the well-known Walter Piston, who told him he would never amount to anything as a composer. Undaunted, Harbison kept at it, meanwhile playing jazz and getting experience as a conductor. He spent the summer of 1959 at Tanglewood as a composition student and returned to Har-

John Harbison. (Boston Symphony Orchestra)

vard in 1963 as a junior fellow. Both the Los Angeles Philharmonic residency and a two-year residency with the Pittsburgh Orchestra earlier in the 1980s were at the invitation of André Previn, the director of first one and then the other orchestra. While commuting to the other cities, he remained based at MIT.

In 1987 Harbison won the Pulitzer Prize for his cantata *The Flight into Egypt*. Characteristically for him, it tells the biblical story not from a conventionally pious perspective but, according to his program note, as a portrayal of "the darker side of Christmas . . . as the distance widens between the privileged and the less fortunate." Further recognition came in a MacArthur Fellowship in 1989 and a 1996 commission from the Metropolitan Opera for an opera based on *The Great Gatsby*.

Harbison has composed in every form from symphony and opera through chamber music and song cycles, and works of his in nearly every genre, including the chamber opera *Full Moon in March*, have had a Tanglewood hearing. For his 1984 return the BSO honored him with a performance of his First Symphony, a BSO centennial commission. In 1992 the BSO played his Concerto for Double Brass Choir and Orchestra, a set of fanfares written for the brass section of the Los Angeles Philharmonic. He allowed only one other work of his, *Due Libri*, for mezzo-soprano and chamber ensemble, to be played during the 1992 contemporary festival. He wanted the spotlight on other composers.

A distinctive feature of Harbison's music is the sensuous sound it layers over ambiguous shapes and gestures. This quality draws a listener in even as it sometimes keeps him at a distance. Critic Lloyd Schwartz has described the appeal this way:

> *By refusing the demands of the marketplace for an easily identifiable style, and by concentrating on the work itself, Harbison has discovered the voice he wasn't looking for: humane, poetic, flexible, guardedly optimistic, but with a pervasive resignation to the inevitability of pain and disappointment. The pieces since the Violin Concerto [completed in 1980 for his wife] have had more and more complex musical and emotional identities, binding together lyricism and irony, humor and sadness, classical and popular procedures, and a mysterious intimacy—all within large-scale structures that have become, if anything, increasingly lucid and accessible.*[2]

The openness to a variety of emotional states comes from the same humane source that sees the darker side of Christmas and places other composers' work ahead of one's own. Cut off from the humane tradition, younger composers must work with the materials at hand—in many cases rock. The absorption and reconfiguration of rock, Harbison said, becomes "a part of their task, and in some cases a very large part of it." Throughout history "the use of popular culture in so-called art music is always an essential. It has to be dealt with, and it has almost nothing to do with the intrinsic original quality of that music." This lover of Schütz, Schubert, and other early masters had "to place a lot of trust in the ears of the coming generation of composers to find gold where some of us hear nothing but plastic."

THE THEME RECURS in the music and thought of other recent Tanglewood composers, as in the work of performers like Haitink and Brendel: largeness of spirit, engagement with the past and present, and a quest for meaning beyond fashions and trends.

In 1988 Hans Werner Henze, the 1983 composer in residence, returned for a second residency. Born in Germany but living in Italy out of a rejection of the Nazi past and the postwar avant-garde of Pierre Boulez and Stockhausen, he came trailing a history of radicalism. In 1969 he had written a requiem for Ché Guevara, the Cuban revolutionary. The police invaded the hall during its Hamburg premiere and arrested student agitators and the librettist, Ernst Schnabel. In response Henze composed *An Essay on Pigs*, a declamatory work that proclaimed "the necessity to revolt." A composer's aim, he wrote in an essay around the same time, must be "provocation."

Three major Henze works were performed in his honor in 1988: the Seventh Symphony, the cello concerto *Sieben Liebeslieder*, and the chamber op era *Elegy for Young Lovers*. The symphony was played by the BSO under Seiji Ozawa. Music Center students did the other works; Yo-Yo Ma—indefatigable in the cause of new music—was the soloist in the concerto, which received its American premiere.

Henze said in a program note that the Seventh Symphony, completed in 1984, offered "my own interpretation of our conflict-ridden time" but could best be understood as arising from the traditional German symphonic style and "our classical canon of beauty." In the secluded house that Tanglewood found for him across the mountain to its west, he said that revealing his specific concerns in the work "would spoil it" for listeners. Yet in his fluent English he made no secret of his fears over the greenhouse effect, the Chernobyl nuclear disaster, and other man-made threats to survival. If some of this anxiety rubbed off in the symphony, he said, "people can identify without quite knowing what it is that makes this identification."

Sometimes apocalyptic in incident, the symphony follows in the Mahler tradition of embracing the universe. *Sieben Liebeslieder*, on the other hand, recasts seven love songs for the solo cello, which becomes a lyrical but wordless singer. The original songs are so transformed as to be unidentifiable, and Henze, believing that the music now stands apart from the words, leaves them that way. *Elegy for Young Lovers*, which Gustav Meier conducted with a student cast and orchestra, is an unromantic look at the romantic figure of the artist as hero, whom Henze portrays as still inflicting a ravenous ego upon others in the twentieth century.

By 1988 Henze's most radical activity consisted of attending city council meetings to thrash out festival budgets with politicians. Received cordially by the BSO, he went home with a commission to write a new symphony for it. The Eighth had a 1993 premiere under Ozawa in Boston and a repeat performance in Henze's presence that summer at Tanglewood. The former revolutionary had written a symphony based on scenes from Shakespeare's *Midsummer Night's Dream*.

During his 1988 visit, when he was sixty-two years of age, Henze said he had moved to Italy in 1953 "to build up my own life, develop my own school of thought, and to write the sort of music that I wanted to write without being influenced or discouraged by my colleagues who wrote different music." He was "beginning to pull together the experiences of my life to come to an essence and to a kind of harmony." The process had "something to do with aging, I suppose, and also with success, I suppose. When time passes and events get more distant, you are also better able to judge them with that distance."[4]

That sense of perspective, of independence yet involvement in the world, produced both the apocalyptic concerns of the Seventh Symphony and the tender allusiveness of the Eighth. Like Foss and Harbison, Henze confronted the present and future while remaining connected to the past.

In 1993 Alexander Goehr of England held the composer's chair. Asked by a Tanglewood patron at a lunch why he didn't write music like Beethoven's, he quickly replied that he would gladly write like Beethoven if he were as good a composer as Beethoven. So much for one of the hardy put-downs of living composers.

The BSO played Goehr's *Colossos or Panic*, a commissioned work based on the Goya painting known as *The Colossus*. In the picture a colossus sits impassively amid a swirl of people, horses, mules, and carriages in an apparent panic. Only a solitary donkey seems calm. Goehr said his intent in the dense, multilayered music was not pictorial or programmatic. "When you deal with a human being in some sort of imaginary or real catastrophic circumstances, the description of terrible events doesn't seem to me as interesting as what goes on in the mind of the person at the center."

Goehr (pronounced *Gur*) was sixty when Oliver Knussen, a friend, lured him away from Cambridge University for the summer. Long interested in characters placed in hostile or destructive environments, he began early, like Henze (but without Henze's activism), to write vocal works and theater pieces with political themes. He was attracted to Goya's *Colossus* because of the enormous, enigmatic figure—"neither threatening nor benevolent, nor seemingly aware of the effect of his unexpected appearance," he said in a program note.

Less menacing, Goehr's other major work in the contemporary festival was *Sing, Ariel*, a fifty-minute song cycle performed by soprano Lucy Shelton with the Boston Symphony Chamber Players under Knussen. Goehr said the assemblage of texts by Auden, Pound, Milton, Yeats, Coleridge, and other poets writing in English, made for him by the English literary critic Frank Kermode, was a "construction" in its own right, with a private meaning embedded in it. He suspected that Kermode's subtext was "an autobiographical poem about aging." The poetry met Goehr's primary requirement for a text: it must "seem somehow relevant to the conditions of the world which one is concerned with as a human being."

In 1995 the seventy-nine-year-old Henri Dutilleux came from France. He was happy about everything at Tanglewood—he didn't even mind the heat wave—but he was unhappy with himself. He was afraid he had let Seiji Ozawa down by not completing a work commissioned by the BSO. It was to have been premiered under Ozawa in Boston the preceding February.

Since there was no new work, the BSO, under André Previn, played Dutilleux's Symphony No. 2. Commissioned by the BSO for its seventy-fifth anniversary, the Second had its premiere in 1959 under Charles Munch. Like many of Dutilleux's works it has a subtitle: *Le Double.* The subtitle refers first to a twelve-piece second orchestra placed between the conductor and the main orchestra, giving something of a concerto grosso effect. In a piquant mixture of English and French, Dutilleux described the interplay as "a kind of *jeu de miroirs,* a play of mirrors . . . a reflection from one orchestra on the other." The psychological sense of a double is also intended. In a program note Dutilleux explained: as the two orchestras mirror, collide, and become fused or confused with each other, they "are indeed two personalities within one."

Performed by Music Center students in the festival, two other Dutilleux works offered mystically charged visions. *Timbres, espace, mouvement, ou La Nuit étoilée* reproduces in sound the cosmic wonder of Van Gogh's *The Starry Night,* with a second orchestra of twelve cellos singing rhapsodically against the main orchestra's evocations of musical and psychic space. *Mystère de l'instant,* for twenty-four strings, cymbalom, and percussion, is a series of short, independent movements, each with its mysterious instant of arrival. The "mystery," according to a commentary in the published score, "must be understood in its broadest sense, not excluding its possible spiritual resonances. As Henri Dutilleux has declared several times, the act of writing music is related for him with a religious ceremony, 'with its portion of mystery and magic.'"

Like Henze, Dutilleux steered clear of the Boulez-versus-Stockhausen isms and schisms that dogged the avant-garde in postwar Europe. His elusive yet evocative musical language follows in the tradition of Debussy, Ravel, and Roussel. And, yes, he said, he knew he had a reputation for taking several years to complete a piece and being late with commissions. (Dissatisfied with his early work, he destroyed much of it.) "It is a problem of the organization of my life, and also I am very *perméable*—interested in many things in the world." The commissioned work had its premiere under Ozawa's direction in October 1997. Titled *The shadows of time,* it evoked the spirit of Anne Frank and other innocents of the world in one of its five movements.

In 1996 Bernard Rands, a transplanted Englishman living in Boston and teaching at Harvard, shared the chair with William Bolcom, an American. Bolcom stayed only two weeks, filling in until Rands could arrive for the rest of the season from the Aspen Festival in Colorado, where he is the composer in residence every June and early July. In Rands's honor the BSO performed his *Le Tambourin Suite No. 2*, and the Music Center Orchestra played his Symphony.

Rands, who was sixty-one that summer, shares with Dutilleux an interest in Van Gogh. Taken from an unfinished opera on the painter's life, Rands's two *Tambourin* suites are a representation of Van Gogh's methods and techniques—but not his actual subjects—in sound. The symphony (it has no further name or number) borrows from and transforms music from other works by Rands. Both compositions performed in the festival use color, textures, and transformations to create what he described as "a complex network of relationships." A Pulitzer Prize winner in 1984 for his song cycle for tenor and orchestra *Canti del Sole*, Rands said he was content to compose in his own way, even if it meant a degree of bafflement for listeners and reaching a smaller audience than pop-oriented composers get. "In the end I am happy that music is what it is, and just in order to define who I am and know who I am, I work in a little garden here."

The echo of *Candide* referred to his country home near Tanglewood. The credo was one that even an old revolutionary like Henze could embrace.

THERE WERE THOSE WHO felt otherwise.

When American composers try to follow in the European classical tradition, David Lang, one of Bang on a Can's three founder-directors, said in a 1991 *New York Times* interview, they are "not writing a piece of music but worshiping at a shrine." Rather than adding to history, they are trying to prove they "belong to history. That's a wonderful idea, but it's a paralyzing idea, and ultimately it's one that Americans have no business believing."

If the past is of no concern, what then should they believe?

"There isn't another place that has the dirt and grime and diversity that we have, and I think that chaos is incredibly provocative." Rock, Lang said, is the common language of composers today. When rock, Asian-influenced music from the West Coast, and inner-city black music "hit someplace, when all those cultures speak the same language, I think the earth will shift one degree off its axis."[5]

The All-Stars' Tanglewood program didn't move the earth, but not for lack of shoving and hauling. Except for Davidovsky's *Synchronism No. 6*, an elegant dialogue between a synthesized tape and a live pianist, and Tom Johnson's *Failing*, an extended joke for a lone double bass, each piece took a simple idea and played with it long after it had exhausted its expressive possibilities. Each piece except Lang's *The Anvil Chorus*, which didn't need the help, was amplified—often to the threshold of pain. Each was as indebted to pop, rock, street noises, industrial sounds, electronic gadgetry, in-jokes, camp, or Julia Wolfe's "body energy" as the old orthodoxy was to its schematic designs. Each proclaimed, in the way of the young, that the old ways of thinking and feeling and doing were dead. In the program notes Wolfe, another founding director, explained that when Lang, Michael Gordon, and she staged the First Annual Bang on a Can Festival in New York in 1986,

we wanted to provide a place for new music in society. It wasn't like other art. People knew who the new painters were, the writers, the filmmakers. But music was perceived as this really elitist [thing]—academic, clever, scientific, inaccessible. Nobody cared if people came to the concerts. And the music reflected that. It got so removed from life. It was important to us to find a new audience.

In a symbolic sense the pivotal work at Tanglewood was Johnson's *Failing*, a 1970s-style happening in which a string bassist must play and speak often simultaneously—an increasingly difficult solo part. By the rules of the game, he succeeds in carrying out the almost impossible assignment. Conversely, if he fails at the assignment, he succeeds in the aim of the piece.

Failing is a sendup of the uptown school's complexities. In pieces from the 1980s and 1990s other composers made the same point through sledgehammer attacks on the nerve centers. In *The Anvil Chorus* Lang had a solo percussionist hammer out a "rhythmic melody" on "junk metals" of his choice. Andriessen's *Hout* was a speeded-up canon that, thanks in part to the amplification, turned into a sonic hash. Hermeto Pascoal's *Arapua*, a Brazilian jam session transported to a New York club, suffered the same fate. Gordon's *Industry*, for a solo cello electronically distorted, realized "a vision of a hundred-foot cello made out of steel suspended from the sky." Steve Martland's *Horses of Instruction*, a world premiere, drove a pianist, cellist, percussionist, saxophonist, and banjoist into hyperactive frenzies. Martland described his music as "a weapon against despair."

It was fitting that Andriessen, de Leeuw's countryman, collaborator, and

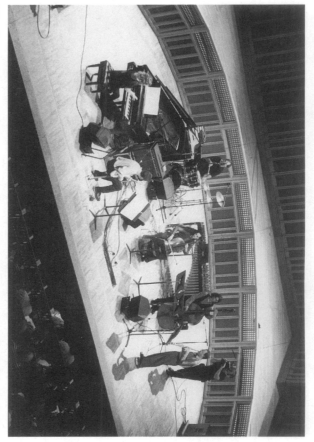

The Bang on a Can All-Stars are wired up for their appearance in the Festival of Contemporary Music. (Walter H. Scott)

friend, was in residence that summer. He was a guru to Bang on a Can and especially to composers like Wolfe and Martland, who made pilgrimages to the Netherlands to study with the master. To show their debt, the All-Stars called Andriessen to the Ozawa Hall stage to take a bow with them.

Born in 1939, Andriessen started out as a Marxist, turned anarchist, and marched with the student demonstrators of the 1960s. Among other things, he sought to overthrow symphony orchestras, which he considered tools of capitalists and record companies. (Leonard Bernstein, by contrast, considered orchestras "museums" but continued to compose for, conduct, and record with them.) Andriessen formed his own performing ensembles, set out to revolutionize musical language, and forced a shotgun marriage between high and low culture in his compositions. Elements from American minimalism, jazz, and rock as well as standard European modernism, all glued together with Stravinsky's motor rhythms and dry sonorities, and with unconventional groupings of instruments (often amplified), were the weapons of revolution.

Hadewijch, the principal Andriessen work performed at Tanglewood, is one of four sections in a large-scale music-theater piece titled *De Materie* (Matter). Hadewijch herself was a nun and poetess from the medieval duchy of Brabant in northern Europe, and a soprano sings one of her mystical visions of a union with God. The structure of the half-hour work is based on the architectural plan of the Rheims Cathedral. Although the theme of *De Materie* is the relationship between matter and spirit, the music itself is as hard, bright, and impersonal as surgical steel. Barren of vibrato, much of the vocal writing is disembodied and dehumanized; the instrumental parts incorporate elements from boogie-woogie, rap, Stravinsky's Symphony in Three Movements, and even an extended duet for two hammers, which represent a seventeenth-century Dutch shipyard. Despite its intellectual scaffolding, the music has nothing of the quest for transcendence in Henze or Dutilleux, nor of their evocative language. It exists in a world without love, sorrow, or pity.

There was something admirable about the energy and virtuosity with which the six punk-clad All-Stars threw themselves into their work. But clearly the age of fifty was a line drawn in the sand. In the first contemporary festival program under the new director in the new hall, a rock generation was declaring the Fosses, Harbisons, Henzes, and Dutilleuxes, with their connectedness to the past and love of the classical canon of beauty, relics of an alien time. Just as the generals had said that Vietnam had to be destroyed in order to save it, banality was to lead music into the glorious new age.

ℕ EW MUSIC has been a driving force at Tanglewood since the founding of the Music Center in 1940, but not primarily in BSO performances. Despite Koussevitzky's championing of living composers, the BSO's schedule of three Tanglewood programs a week and its need to appeal to a popular audience limited its new-music activity from the start. Instead, Koussevitzky assigned the primary responsibility to the school and its composer-teachers.

Although the BSO plays at least one work in the contemporary festival, the one-week concentration of new music performed by students and specialist artists forces the repertory into a ghetto where only a few hardy souls—mostly fellow composers and performers, teachers, students, critics, and publishers—venture. In this, of course, Tanglewood is not alone. Concert givers across the country have regularly limited dosages of the new or quarantined it in special series where it would not unduly disturb conservative patrons. The budget crunches of the 1990s heightened the skittishness about anything that might offend. In 1996, for example, the Philadelphia Orchestra, needing to cut costs, chose to abolish the position of composer in residence when Rands left it after seven years' service.

The resident-composer tradition at the Music Center began with the founding, when Aaron Copland and Hindemith jointly headed the composition department. Both returned in 1941, Copland staying on for a quarter-century as a teacher and chairman of the faculty. Other notable figures during the Koussevitzky era of the 1940s were Bohuslav Martinů, Arthur Honegger, Samuel Barber, Darius Milhaud, Olivier Messiaen (who returned in 1975), and Jacques Ibert. Recent occupants of the chair are an international array that has included Luciano Berio, Ralph Shapey, George Crumb, Toru Takemitsu, Jacob Druckman, Leon Kirchner, and George Perle in addition to Harbison, Henze, Goehr, Dutilleux, and Rands. A long string of visiting teachers has ranged from John Adams, David Del Tredici, and Tod Machover on the vernacular side to the more cerebral Elliott Carter.

Much of the music played in the festival has gone to a natural death. But the programs, designed by the festival director in consultation with the Music Center director (until 1998 Leon Fleisher), the BSO's artistic administrator (Anthony Fogg), and other faculty members, have offered landmark compositions and notable premieres, nearly always in meticulously prepared, strongly committed performances. In 1975, for example, Schuller conducted an orchestral extravaganza featuring Messiaen's *L'Ascension* (in honor of his residency), the world premiere of Stephen Albert's *Voices Within* (a Music Center commission), Boulez's *Rituel* (in honor of his fiftieth birthday), and Copland's *Connotations* (for his seventy-fifth birthday). Copland and other Americans, including Tanglewood graduates, have been generously represented over the years, but so have Europeans both celebrated and unknown.

Under both Schuller and Knussen, Tanglewood had its flirtations with the avant-garde, including an experimental Music Theater Project from 1971 to 1973. There were sporadic other music-theater productions in the late 1970s and early 1980s, offering works by such fringe figures as H. K. Gruber. But until 1994 the emphasis was on composers—often from academia—working within the Western canon. Adams, Del Tredici, and Machover might use vernacular elements in their music, but each enjoys the cachet of respectability in uptown or academic circles. Even Shapey, whose music is as anarchic in its way as Bang on a Can's, has the authority of the University of Chicago music department behind him. Tanglewood might have been behind New York and Los Angeles in arriving at the cutting edge, but in the broad picture of things it has accurately tracked the main currents of new music in the United States.

The change in 1994 was not a wrong turn. In repertory as in concert facilities, Tanglewood had to catch up with the outer world. De Leeuw was correct. This was music that was attracting a new kind of listener, especially among the rock-oriented young, to the "classical" concert hall. It had to be heard at Tanglewood along with other emerging styles.

Although American composers sometimes complain that Europeans are too heavily represented in what should be an American festival, de Leeuw has maintained balance in the programming. He said he was particularly interested in the experimental strain represented by Ives, who gave him one of the greatest shocks of his life when he first encountered the American's music in 1965. In that tradition he programmed such European figures as György Ligeti and György Kurtag along with the younger Americans. As a sequel to Bang on a Can, Steve Reich and his ensemble came from New York in a 1995 debut to perform an evening of his minimalist and rhythmically repetitive music. In 1996 the Netherlands Wind Ensemble played a program of postmodern pieces from Europe, proving that the New World didn't hold a patent on trivia. De Leeuw also brought a strong representation of unknowns (at least to Americans). Among the most striking of these was Claude Vivier, a Canadian whose *Lonely Child*, for soprano and orchestra, evoked the feelings and even the nonsense-syllable private language of an abused child (clearly Vivier himself). Many younger composers on the programs wrote in styles that depended heavily on color, texture, or atmosphere.

Still, most of this music was far from the "nobility" whose disappearance Bernstein had lamented or the "profound verities" whose rediscovery Schuller espoused. (Bernstein's 1970 words carry the ring of prophecy: "Some of it is fascinating, some is titillating, some of it is touching and even beautiful, and some merely opportunistic—but one thing it almost never is is noble.") The spirituality that Louis Krasner had heard ("in truth all great music sings to God") seemed even more remote.

Nobility was not in fashion at the end of the twentieth century. It smacked of elitism, the ultimate cultural crime. But great art in all times is elitist—that is, it is open to all but it avoids the black-and-white simplicities of popular forms in favor of ambiguity and a vision of life in all its infinite guises. Gunther Schuller and Peter Schickele are only two of many musicians who have promulgated the dictum that "all musics are created equal." True. But not all musics have equal expressive capacities, just as not all individuals have equal capacities for responding to deeply expressive music. Rock, born in rebellion against the rights as well as wrongs of established society, spawned the belief that the Beatles were the equals of Mozart and, in fact, made Mozart unnecessary. The underlying stance is anti-intellectual. Neither the past nor the future matters: only the amplified, strobe-lit here and now.

The issue isn't pop versus art, any more than it is uptown versus downtown. In all ages there has been popular music—some good, some bad—and in all ages, as John Harbison said, some of it has found its way, reworked and transfigured, into art music. In today's babel of styles, moreover, there are probably more composers who are neither uptown nor downtown than there are in the two groupings together. Yet from its start in the medieval church until the twentieth century, Western art music had a basis in religious or at least transcendental states. When music came out of the church and into the concert hall in the eighteenth century, it retained that connection through a concern with formal and expressive breadth. Beethoven's "Heiliger Dankgesang eines Genesenen an die Gottheit" (Sacred song of thanksgiving of a convalescent to the deity) in the A Minor Quartet, op. 132, has no text linking it to the Almighty, but any sensitive listener can recognize in it a state of spiritual grace. A reverence for the forces that magnify everyday life informs even the profane love of Wagner's *Tristan and Isolde* and the naked barbarism of Stravinsky's *Sacre du printemps*.

Music with transcendental qualities was still being written in the late twentieth century, as Tanglewood's Harbisons and Henzes attested. To conclude the 1995 festival, de Leeuw led the Music Center Orchestra in another of those unblinking confrontations with the age's complexities, Sofia Gubaidulina's *Stimmen . . . verstummen* (Voices . . . silenced). Over its thirty-eight-minute span the Russian-German composer's work ranges from the ethereal to the cataclysmic in its sonorities. There are electronic whines (from an organ), rumbles from the bowels of the orchestra, eruptions from the brasses, spectral whispers, otherworldly tremors.

All tend toward silence. The most astonishing moment comes, in fact, when for a full minute toward the end the conductor beats nothing but silence. (The actual gestures are notated in the score.) The idea sounds absurd, impossible. The effect in performance proved overwhelming. Nobody in Ozawa Hall dared to stir. With the hall's big back door open to the lawn and its audience, the nocturnal crickets rasping outside sounded like agents of creation.

Three more of the twelve movements followed, apocalyptic, struggling toward completion, finally drifting into silence. For good reason de Leeuw chose to end the program and festival with the piece. It stood in awe, and put its audience in awe, of the surrounding forces of heaven and earth.

Something more than stylistic change happened to music in the twentieth century when Schoenberg led it into atonality and, in reaction, the minimalists and postmodernists led it into the streets. Audiences sense the loss. Except for specialists—performers, composers, critics, scholars, and the like—they still, after nearly a century, have not accepted Schoenberg, much less his more cerebral followers. At the other extreme Bang on a Can-style music offers the licks and kicks of pop blown up beyond pop proportions. Both extremes propose a kind of nihilism: logic without feeling or feeling without reason. Yet it is impossible, as the older generation of moderns like Foss, Harbison, Henze, and Dutilleux recognizes, to remove the traditional elements of transcendence and awe without losing music's most redemptive, most human qualities. It is those qualities that all peoples in all times have sought in art, whether cave dwellers with their wall drawings, ancient Greeks with their ritual dramas, or medieval worshipers with their cathedrals.

In the late 1960s and early 1970s Tanglewood experimented with rock concerts, presenting such attractions as B. B. King, the Who, and Jefferson Airplane (all on one bill in 1968). Attendance broke records and swelled coffers, but the series had to be dropped after a few years because of the problems of noise, litter, and stoned youths staggering along quiet country roads. Two decades later the descendants of the rock rebellion came to Tanglewood not through the main gate, as earlier generations of composers had, but by the newly erected back gates leading to Seiji Ozawa Hall. The wrong turn—if that is what it was—was not Tanglewood's. In embracing the new fashions, Tanglewood only mirrored the world outside. Those concerned with the future of a cultural heritage had to trust, with Harbison, that the ears of the coming generation could find gold where other ears heard only plastic.

6

Grasping
an
Octopus

Opera is an octopus," sighed Music Center administrator Richard Ort- ner as he contemplated the 1996 season—his last, as it happened, before Seiji Ozawa deposed him.

Ortner had reason to invoke the old saw. The school was embarking on its most ambitious project in three decades: a revival of Benjamin Britten's *Peter Grimes* in celebration of the fiftieth anniversary of its American pre- miere, which took place at Tanglewood in the composer's presence. As in 1946, a student cast and orchestra would present a fully staged production in the Theater-Concert Hall. But now, instead of Bernstein, Ozawa would conduct. Besides providing a centerpiece for the season, the two perfor- mances would serve as a trial run for the return of a student opera program, missing since the dismantling of Boris Goldovsky's opera department in 1962.

For a festival devoted primarily to symphonic and chamber music, an opera training program, when it arrived—there seemed no question of if— would be a step more far-reaching than an embrace of new composers. It would also realize a dream of Ozawa's. Virtually from the day of his ascent to the BSO podium in 1973, he had talked about a return of student opera. Over the years there had been sporadic student performances under vari- ous conductors: the experimental music theater productions of the 1970s and 1980s, partially staged scenes from standard operas, and—most ambi- tiously—the staging of Hans Werner Henze's *Elegy for Young Lovers* during his 1988 residency. In the Shed Ozawa himself had led the BSO in its annual semistaged productions from 1980 until 1991, using professional singers, often of celebrity caliber.

But always the productions ran up against logistical and financial prob- lems. The Shed's lack of a fly loft, a pit, and backstage support facilities put opera in a vise, and the BSO had to give up its attempts in any case during the budget cutting of the early 1990s. A training program posed even greater problems of staffing, expense, and equipment. Opera—even of the student variety—requires singers, a pit orchestra, a chorus, and generous rehearsal schedules. It also requires sets, costumes, lighting, a stage director, design-ers, rehearsal assistants, stagehands. All these things cost money, which, for a symphonic festival that operates only two months out of the year, a board of trustees will be chary of spending. And at Tanglewood they all must be fitted into a rehearsal and performance schedule that is already squeezed tight from breakfast till midnight.

Among other things, opera requires a working opera house. A working opera house was one thing that Tanglewood lost during the three decades of operatic drought. The Theater-Concert Hall pit had been filled in, the rigging abandoned, and an acoustical shell for concert performances in-stalled across the back of the stage. Even if a pit and the other necessities had been available, the Theater-Concert Hall was in constant use for stu-dent rehearsals and performances and for the professional chamber and re-cital series. There was no place for stage work.

With the opening of Ozawa Hall, suddenly the old hall was dark. It was as if nature had created a vacuum and opera had to fill it. In 1996 there was a special incentive to bring opera back: the *Grimes* jubilee, which would provide an opportunity for a look back at one of Koussevitzky's and Tangle-wood's greatest triumphs.

Grimes, which requires a cast of twelve (plus chorus), was big for a maiden effort, but so was Tanglewood's appetite. A student cast—two casts actually, for each performance was to have its own singers—was assembled. The Theater-Concert Hall was patched up, its pit reopened. Sets, costumes, wigs, lighting—all the necessary accoutrements were requisitioned. Ozawa's BSO schedule was lightened to give him more time with the student singers and players. Guest conductors were engaged to replace him with the BSO. The team of David Kneuss, John Michael Deegan, and Sarah G. Conly, who had staged and designed most of the BSO's Shed productions, was recruited for the student project. The Tanglewood Festival Chorus, the BSO's year-round choral arm, was assigned the all-important part of the villagers who drive Grimes to his death. The octopus spread its tentacles into green rooms, studios, and offices on the new and old campuses alike.

THE 1946 *Grimes* premiere holds a special place in Tanglewood's new-music legacy. It was not only a coup in its own right but demonstrated Kous-

Anna-Maria Bogner and Thomas Doherty appear as Ellen Orford and Grimes in the 1996 performance of Peter Grimes. (Walter H. Scott)

sevitzky's acumen in choosing composers to perform and support. With Berg's *Wozzeck* and Stravinsky's *Rake's Progress*, *Grimes* ranks as one of the three twentieth-century operas that seem most likely to endure.

An earlier new-music coup at the Music Center set the stage for *Grimes*. In 1942, although World War II forced cancelation of the BSO's Tanglewood season, Koussevitzky led the Music Center Orchestra in the American concert premiere of Shostakovich's *Leningrad* Symphony.[1] The timing was superb. A native of Leningrad (now Saint Petersburg), Shostakovich had composed most of the epic-length symphony the year before, while living under the Nazi siege, and the music tells the city's anguish. With the premiere Koussevitzky unerringly drew war-troubled America's gaze to his cherished academy of musical arts.

In 1944 and 1945 the war limited Tanglewood to small-orchestra concerts by BSO members, but in 1946 the festival was back in full operation. Many veterans, attending on the G.I. Bill and eager to get on with their lives, were among the four hundred students who thronged to Koussevitzky's already-famous music festival and school. With the end of wartime gas rationing, concertgoers could travel freely again to the Berkshires.

Into this heady mix Koussevitzky dropped the *Grimes* premiere. Commissioned by Koussevitzky through his music foundation, the opera had scored a triumph in London in its world premiere a year before. Britten and his stage director for the London production, Eric Crozier, would come to observe and work with the Tanglewood cast. Crozier would direct and Leonard Bernstein, promoted from Koussevitzky's protégé to his assistant, would conduct. To advertise his feat, the canny Koussevitzky performed the Passacaglia and Four Sea Interludes from *Grimes* with the BSO in Boston and New York during the winter before the Tanglewood production. Critics paid attention. Interest ran high.

"It was a brand-new opera, it was a brand-new opera in America, and there was something about entrusting that to such young people which was pretty stimulating," recalled Phyllis Curtin, who sang in the 1946 cast, returned as the star teacher in Tanglewood's vocal program, and helped to coach the 1996 production. "I just remember it as an exhilarating time. I think that was pretty much the attitude of those of us who sang in the opera."

Peter Grimes takes place around 1830 in the North Sea fishing village of Aldeburgh, where Britten spent most of his adult life. Grimes is a fisherman, a loner, and something of a visionary. When his two apprentices die in separate fishing accidents, the insular villagers, smelling murder, become a lynch mob. Hounded down, Grimes drowns himself at sea.

As a conscientious objector and homosexual, Britten was an outsider in England himself (hence the strong sympathy for Grimes in the opera). When war in Europe broke out, the twenty-six-year-old composer went into self-exile in the United States. In 1941 he approached Koussevitzky with the idea of writing an opera. Koussevitzky, who had performed Britten's *Sinfonia da Requiem* with the BSO, responded with a $1,000 commission in memory of his first wife, Natalie, who had just died. Homesick, Britten returned in 1942 to England, where he worked on the opera for the next three years. Because Tanglewood was still closed in 1945, Koussevitzky yielded the world premiere to the Sadler's Wells Company (now the English National Opera) in London, which gave the first performances just a month after VE Day. In the headiness of victory and peace, *Grimes* was acclaimed not only for its musical and dramatic power but also as heralding a new era of greatness for opera in England.

Despite the Tanglewood cast's enthusiasm, the reception in America was less than triumphant. In his memoir, *My Road to Opera*, Goldovsky recalls the production as a success but says Bernstein drove everybody so hard in rehearsals that by the time of the performances, the two Grimeses "could hardly croak their topmost notes."[2] Britten, according to his biographer Humphrey Carpenter, "politely described the production as a 'lively student performance.'" Crozier, Carpenter says, "was so depressed by the standard of performance that he telegraphed Britten not to come." W. H. Auden, a friend of Britten's who was also living in America, said, "The performance was terrible but the work made an impression just the same." It didn't help Britten's spirits that he had to share a room in the Berkshires with Auden, who, according to Carpenter, "infuriated him by smoking in bed."[3]

In the *New York Times* Olin Downes, one of fifty critics gathered for the event, found the music "astonishing" in structure and effect, but termed the opera itself "nearer a dramatic oratorio with stage settings than it is to a living, breathing music drama."[4] In the *New York Post* John Briggs fumed over "a violent explosion of raw emotion, false and melodramatic for the most part, lumped into an incoherent mass and flung in the face of the audience."[5] No such doubts troubled Koussevitzky, who declared in a curtain talk on opening night that Grimes was "first after *Carmen*"—meaning, second best only to *Carmen*, his ideal opera. If Koussevitzky, in his pride, exaggerated somewhat, he was closer to posterity's verdict than the critics were.

Most of those in the double-cast production have been forgotten, but some of the singers and orchestra members went on to renown. Most renowned of all was Curtin, who was taking her first role in an opera. One of the bawdy "nieces" in 1946, she became a leading Ellen Orford (the principal female role) at the Metropolitan Opera and other major American and European houses and began her acclaimed series of Tanglewood master classes in 1962. Other singers who established careers were Mildred Mueller (later known as Mildred Miller), Frances Yeend, and James Pease. Sitting in the pit were concertmaster Norman Carol and principal trumpeter Adolph S. Herseth, who later held the same positions in the Philadelphia and Chicago orchestras, respectively. And, of course, leading the charge as Koussevitzky's lieutenant and their apparent was Bernstein. Curtin remembers him as a fountain of vitality in the pit, making light of the difficulties in the 7/4 meter in the chantey "Old Joe Has Gone Fishing" and having "such a good time doing it" that he had the singers rollicking along with him.

If Britten was unhappy with the production, Curtin saw no evidence of it. She recalled him as a quiet man who signed her score "very charmingly." Crozier was a different story. He was, Curtin said, "a very slight, proper Englishman" who was probably overwhelmed by so many young people "having such a gay and giddy time" and not behaving like a dignified opera company.

André Speyer, who played French horn in the orchestra and went on to a career in the Minneapolis (now Minnesota) orchestra, had taken part in the *Leningrad Symphony* premiere as a student in 1942 and then served in the army. His 1942 summer was exciting enough, he said. But in 1946 the veterans and other students eager to get on with their careers brought an "immense energy" to Tanglewood, and Koussevitzky, Britten, Crozier, Bernstein, and *Grimes* made the summer "almost electric—the whole thing geared to this immense, wonderful experience."

The late Thomas D. Perry Jr., then beginning a BSO management career that led to the executive directorship, recalled a rush for *Grimes* tickets that overwhelmed the "shoebox on a counter" box office he ran. The concertgoers' frustration was nothing, however, to what one of the two casts felt. When word got out that *Life* magazine was coming to photograph the first performance, Perry said, there was a scramble to get into the opening-night cast. Only half, of course, made it.

In the 1996 *Grimes* program book Steven Ledbetter, the BSO's musicologist and program annotator, wrote that the 1946 performance, "more than any other single event in Tanglewood's early history," established Tanglewood and its Music Center as a world center for music:

European musicians, who can hardly have heard of the summer festival during the preceding years of war, now learned that there was a place in the United States where a challenging modern opera could be credibly mounted by an ensemble of students (though, to be sure, advanced students on the verge of professional careers). Many of the participants in Peter Grimes—singers, conductors, and assistants, staging and directing personnel—went on to substantial careers, glowing with the memory of this special performance. The Koussevitzky Music Foundation demonstrated the value of taking a risk on a young composer of evident talent. And Tanglewood became firmly established as the premier location for advanced studies in music.

MUCH MUSIC has rolled across the lawn since Erich Leinsdorf, on becoming BSO director in 1962, abolished Goldovsky's opera department in a reorganization of the Music Center and began to conduct opera himself with both the BSO and students. Leinsdorf's aims were worthy. He wanted to reinvigorate the school after its thirteen years under the laissez-faire stewardship of Charles Munch, and he felt that Goldovsky was running a fiefdom independent of the rest of the Music Center operation. The BSO trustees, for whose purse the opera program was always a bit rich, were happy to go along with the change.

At the beginning Tanglewood had the only professional opera training program in the United States outside the music conservatories. Today nearly every major opera company, from the Met on down, has a young artists' program offering training and professional experience, as do three major spring and summer opera festivals: Saint Louis, Santa Fe, and Glimmerglass, in Cooperstown, New York. The Aspen Music Festival, in Colorado, runs an opera center that offers about ninety students each summer experience in one or more of three productions, as well as opportunities in the song literature. To attract the most promising participants to a revived training program, Tanglewood would have to offer something the competition didn't.

As it happened, that something extra was already in hand—thanks, paradoxically, to opera's self-immolation at Tanglewood. When Leinsdorf threw opera out, he left a void for the vocal students who had shown up expecting summer studies. More or less in desperation, the BSO management turned to Curtin. Would she, as a Tanglewood alumna and celebrated opera singer, give a *summer of master classes?*

Curtin became the guest who never left. Year after year her classes, dealing primarily with vocal technique and the art song but also with the essentials of opera, became not merely a stopgap but a major attraction in their own right. They were, in fact, as unique for a summer program as Goldovsky's opera department once had been, although similar programs were instituted later at Chicago's Ravinia and other festivals. Just as the original program had turned out a generation of leading opera singers such as Leontyne Price,[6] Shirley Verrett, Sherrill Milnes, and Curtin herself, Curtin's classes turned out a younger generation, including Dawn Upshaw, Cheryl Studer, and Sanford Sylvan, at home in both the opera house and recital hall. In time the Phyllis Curtin Seminars, as they came to be known, also became a sightseers' attraction. At most classes today the back of the studio will be filled with auditors ranging from hardcore opera fans to camera-toting tourists passing the time of day.

Whatever shape a future program took, it seemed likely that opera would be an enhancement of, not a replacement for, the program of lieder and contemporary music that centered on Curtin's classes. Indeed, BSO leaders from Ozawa down emphasized that Tanglewood had to build on its strength rather than dilute it. As head vocal coach Dennis Helmrich, who was in charge of the singers' preparation, said in the midst of the *Grimes* rehearsals: "We're not interested in just opera singers. We didn't want the opera to eat up the rest of the program, because it's too unusual. There aren't any other places that have what we have, and we didn't want to throw that out."

Opera was part of Koussevitzky's founding vision for Tanglewood. A friend of the Russian stage director Constantin Stanislavsky and a believer in the populist spirit of the age, he wanted to make both opera and the symphony accessible to a wide general audience. He envisioned an amphitheater sloping down toward Stockbridge Bowl, the lake overlooked by Tanglewood's lawn, and seating twenty-five thousand. But when the Music Center opened in 1940, he had to settle for a production of Handel's chamber-sized *Acis and Galatea* in the formal gardens of the Tanglewood estate. The Theater-Concert Hall would not be ready until the following summer.

Koussevitzky installed Herbert Graf as head of the opera department, with Goldovsky as his assistant. As preparations began for the 1946 season after the wartime shutdown, Graf and Koussevitzky came to a parting of the ways, apparently over Koussevitzky's wish for a more adventurous repertory (including *Grimes*) than Graf was willing to accept. Koussevitzky promoted his fellow Russian émigré Goldovsky to the top position, and thus began a fifteen-year record of pioneering productions that included the American premieres of Mozart's *Idomeneo* and Britten's *Albert Herring* as well as *Grimes*. Stressing theater as well as music, Goldovsky performed in English and used his singers as ensembles rather than potential stars. His methods set a standard that lives on in the training programs of large opera companies like the Met and San Francisco and festival companies like Saint Louis and Glimmerglass. In time they also created a rival for Goldovsky: Sarah Caldwell, who served five years as his Tanglewood assistant and went on to found her own opera company, in competition with his, in Boston.

Opera under Leinsdorf was an on again, off again affair. His most notable projects were a concert-style *Lohengrin* spread over an entire weekend in 1965 with the BSO—even he conceded it was a "disaster"[7]—and a well-received *Wozzeck* with students in 1969, his final year. In the early 1970s the foundation-supported Music Theater Project put on small-scale, experimental productions of works by Weill, Satie, and others, including a futuristic treatment of Monteverdi's *Coronation of Poppea*. Because the Theater-Concert Hall's stage facilities were already in disrepair, the performances took place in a barn. After three years the foundation money ran out, and the series died. Soon afterward the BSO announced plans to resume a student program under the direction of Nathaniel Merrill of the Metropolitan Opera. The money for that project never appeared.

When those efforts faltered, Ozawa in 1980 began his annual semistaged productions with the BSO in the Shed. They continued through 1991, when the limitations of the Shed, the extra expenses for soloists and stagings, and an inability to attract enough listeners for more than one performance shut down the series. After a debut with Puccini's *Tosca*, the productions went on to such works as Beethoven's *Fidelio*, Mussorgsky's *Boris Godunov* (heavily cut), Stravinsky's *Oedipus Rex*, Gluck's *Orfeo ed Euridice*, Berlioz's *Béatrice et Bénédict*, Honegger's *Jeanne d'Arc au bûcher*, Strauss's *Elektra*, and even a lightly staged version of Bach's *Saint Matthew Passion* before culminating in Mozart's *Idomeneo* in 1991. The critical reception was generally tepid, on grounds that the requirements of a stage without a pit, flies, or other opera house amenities compromised the productions beyond repair. But Ozawa insisted. He said that Tanglewood could not be a complete festival without opera, nor he a complete conductor. "For instance," he said in one of his many utterances on the subject, "if I don't know Mozart operas—if I don't know *Fidelio*, if I didn't know any Verdi opera, or if I didn't know Puccini, or if I didn't touch Wagner operas—it would be one big side of a great composer's work I never touched." [8]

Student opera was still on Ozawa's mind in the midst of his BSO productions. To recall the Music Center's operatic glories, he opened the season in 1990, the school's jubilee year, with a BSO program of arias and scenes sung by alumni, some going back as far as soprano Rosalind Elias (classes of '50, '51, and '53), others as recent as baritone Haijing Fu (class of '88).

The evening was a sentimental and symbolic one on several counts. Goldovsky, now eighty-two, was in the Shed audience as guest of honor and received an ovation when Curtin, speaking from the stage, asked him to stand. The return to Tanglewood was his first since 1962. In her remarks to the audience Curtin recalled her own start under Goldovsky at Tanglewood in the 1940s and early 1950s. In particular she mentioned her parts in the 1946 *Grimes* and, in 1951, in *Pique Dame*, which Ozawa and the BSO would bring back a week later with Mirelli Freni, Vladimir Popov, and Maureen Forrester in the principal roles. Speaking for herself and "many hundreds" of other students, she described Tanglewood as "a most demanding and most inspiriting place for people who want to have a career in music."

In the first half of the program, Shirley Verrett and Sherrill Milnes reprised their performances as Tosca and Scarpia in the final scene from act 1 of *Tosca*, the inaugural opera in the Shed series. A final bit of symbolism

Marthe Keller is Joan and Georges Wilson is Brother Dominic in the 1989 production of Arthur Honegger's Jeanne d'Arc au bûcher, one in the annual series of operas staged by the BSO. (Walter H. Scott)

came in the evening's pièce de résistance, the last act of Verdi's *Falstaff*. On and off for fifteen years Ozawa had talked of a revival of student opera with *Falstaff* as the inaugural production. If he couldn't yet have a student *Falstaff*, he had a cast made up of alumni, including Thomas Stewart as the portly knight, John Aler as Fenton, Hajing Fu as Ford, Dawn Upshaw as Nannetta, Margaret Cusack as Alice Ford, D'Anna Fortunato as Meg Page, and Rosalind Elias as Mistress Quickly.

Ozawa matured steadily as an opera conductor. Having sometimes misgauged the text, pacing, and his singers in the early productions, he developed a mastery of the craft by the 1990s. The feat was especially remarkable for a Japanese who still had difficulty reading English, his second language, and knew even less of the other standard operatic languages. (He works from translations into Japanese in his scores and is gifted with a photographic memory.) He favored certain singers, chiefly women: Hildegard Behrens, Jessye Norman, Kathleen Battle, and—increasingly in the 1990s—Barbara Bonney. He conducted regularly at La Scala in Milan and the Vienna State Opera, with occasional forays into other major European houses. In 1995 he did *The Rake's Progress*, first at his Saito Kinen Festival in Japan (where he also recorded it) and then, showing a fine sense of Stravinsky's dry wit and sonorities, with the BSO in Boston. But it was not until he conducted *Grimes* for the first time the following summer that student opera, after thirty-five years, returned to Tanglewood.

EVERYTHING ABOUT *Peter Grimes* argued against a youthful cast. It is a complex full-length opera, the three principal characters—Grimes, the widowed schoolmistress Ellen, and the retired sea captain Balstrode—are people in their middle or later years, and their parts require seasoned voices. Most of the other villagers portrayed in the story have also been absorbing small-town morality for many years. Done right, the production would also require four sets, the two casts of twelve singers each, a chorus of fifty, and the refitting of the Theater-Concert Hall: a tall order for an organization that had had no experience with an opera program in three decades.

For two decades the faculty and staff had been urging Ozawa to resume student opera but could not get a commitment from him despite his pronouncements on the subject. Finally the lure of the *Grimes* jubilee proved irresistible, and in the early 1990s he gave his consent for planning to proceed. Preparations for the production itself began soon after the BSO trustees approved the project in the fall of 1995. Dennis Helmrich and other staff members, including Curtin and Margo Garrett, head of the vocal department, traveled to New York, Boston, Cleveland, Los Angeles, Toronto, and London in December and January, auditioning hundreds of applicants. All knew that they would have a shot at *Grimes* as well as the Curtin seminars.

The twenty-four singers who were chosen ranged in age from twenty-one to thirty-five; all came with some operatic experience, some only in schools but others with professional companies. An "unfortunate by-product" of having to cast an opera, Helmrich said, was that some otherwise attractive candidates had to be turned away because there were no roles for which their voices were suited. They were urged to reapply the next year. But the double casting also provided cover singers (not needed, as it turned out) in case of sickness or emergency.

Though auditions matched singers to roles, the first- and second-performance casts were chosen by toss of a coin and designated X and Y rather than A and B to avoid any hint that one was ranked ahead of the other. The two Grimeses were Thomas Doherty, thirty-five, and Anthony Dean Griffey, twenty-nine. Doherty, a former Methodist minister from Ontario, had been singing professionally for only three years. Griffey, a North Carolinian living in New York, was a member of the Metropolitan Opera's young artist development program and had already appeared in three Met productions. One of the Balstrodes was Stephen Salters, a twenty-six-year-old Bostonian who only a month before had won the $50,000 first prize in the Queen Elisabeth International Competition for singers in Brussels.

In 1946 there had been three performances by two alternating casts and orchestras. For the anniversary each cast gave one open dress rehearsal and one performance, using the same orchestra. There were conspicuous differences in emphasis between performances, particularly in the Grimeses. The more experienced Griffey had the stage presence and vocal heft to embody both Grimes's vulnerability and the anger that boils beneath it. Doherty had more of a struggle with the vocal demands and played on Grimes's loneliness and hurt.

In front of the stage, the Theater-Concert Hall looked like the same rustic 1940s building, with exposed rafters and beams, that it had been for year upon year. The seats, though now fitted with cushions, were the same metal backbreakers that had tormented earlier audiences. But the pit had been reopened, the upstage acoustical shell removed, and the back wall painted a mottled and streaked gray-blue, suggesting sea and air. In this somewhat cramped space the design team installed a two-level acting area bisected by a trestle, with a bleak, rock-littered seashore on the lower level. Wheeled on and off behind a hand-drawn curtain, grittily realistic sets showed the courtroom, the tavern, the street, and Grimes's hut. Though an overturned boat, the hut ominously suggested the skeleton of a beached whale seen from inside. The costumes were realistic nineteenth-century frock coats, top hats, long skirts, bonnets, and fishermen's garb.

The production betrayed its student origins in the unevenness of some of the singing. Yet it was a remarkable achievement, not just as a first step toward an ambitious educational goal but as an immersion in a cauldron of hatred and pity. Within the limits imposed by the small stage and young cast, Kneuss, the stage director, created character, drama, and an overarching sense of doom. One of the most striking moments occurred when

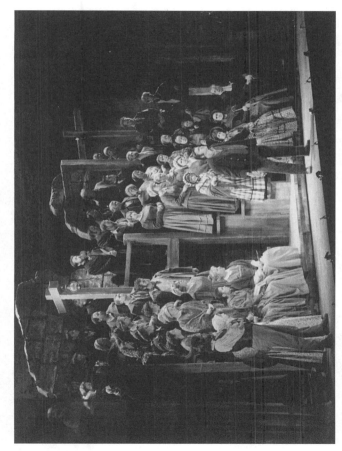

The inquest scene in Peter Grimes. *Thomas Doherty is on trial. (Walter H. Scott)*

Grimes burst into the Boar tavern at the height of the storm and sang his great aria, "Now the Great Bear and Pleiades." The villagers froze around him in a dark tableau that suggested a Rembrandt night scene.

Ozawa and his players brought a savage force to the storm music, and the Tanglewood Festival Chorus chillingly portrayed the villagers' mounting frenzy. Rather than a black-and-white tale of good and evil, the singing, acting, and playing set up a web of ambiguity in Grimes's quest for love and respectability in a society that denies them to outsiders. At the same time the emphasis remained educational. The two casts received equal treatment and equal rehearsal time, including time with Ozawa, who, as a result, conducted two sets of rehearsals, each with a different synergy because of the singers' different personalities. Three student pianists served as rehearsal accompanists, learning opera house skills along with the pit players. Throughout the rehearsal period the singers, at their own insistence, continued to attend Curtin's classes and prepare songs for performance in student recitals. The orchestra players continued to learn and play chamber music as well as works for the Festival of Contemporary Music, which would follow a week later.

Ozawa also took part in the stage rehearsals, familiarizing himself with, and making suggestions for, details of gesture and movement. Helmrich saw the conductor "getting the work in his bones that way, so that he knows where everybody is onstage all the time. He knows all the timings. He really has the work circulating in his brain." Whatever Ozawa's failings as a musician or administrator, he was the Ozawa of total commitment and emotional identification in this project. Once again opera provided one of his finest moments.

So OPERA WAS an octopus. Looking back at the end of the season, Richard Ortner said *Grimes* had taught a number of useful lessons:

> *We learned, first off, that we have a viable opera theater. We also learned that when you get Seiji involved in training singers and an orchestra for an opera, there's really an incomparable educational benefit. We also learned that it is possible to incorporate opera into Tanglewood without completely turning the place upside-down.*

The project, including the repairs to the theater, cost $400,000 (out of a 1996 Tanglewood budget of $12.6 million and total BSO budget of $49 million). It was able to attract qualified students despite the competition of other training programs. Taking these experiences into consideration, a BSO-Music Center committee resumed its study of the direction and form an opera program might take. A decision was still several years off. But Poulenc's *Les Mamelles de Tirésias*, which Ozawa had conducted at the 1996 Saito Kinen Festival, was scheduled as the school's 1997 opera.[9]

A surrealist French farce in one act, *Les Mamelles* is shorter than the three-act *Grimes* and requires a cast of eight and only a small chorus. As a result of the first year's experience, a number of refinements were made in the preparation process. These chiefly involved a return to the 1946 practice of a separate student orchestra for each of the two student casts and a shorter stage rehearsal period, made possible by a shorter opera. The separate orchestras resulted from comments made by student instrumentalists who had not played in *Grimes*. They felt left out of a valuable experience.

Kneuss, Deegan, and Conly were back as the staging and design team, and Ozawa again conducted. The sets and costumes were borrowed from the 1996 Saito Kinen production, which Kneuss also directed. This not only saved Tanglewood $200,000 but gave it a lavish, colorful seaside setting in Poulenc's "Zanzibar" (actually the French Riviera, circa 1910). The 1947 opera is based on a play by Apollinaire. The moral is a call for the public to "make babies"—in Poulenc's treatment, not quite as outrageous as it sounds in the light of the recent depletion of Europe's manhood by two world wars. Both the heroine, Tirésias (previously known as Thérèse), and her husband (known only as the husband) undergo sex reversals, and in response to the story's imperative, he produces 40,050 babies in a day. Of the opera Poulenc writes: "If my music succeeds in producing laughter, while still allowing to be felt through it some moments of tenderness, and real lyricism, my aim will have been fully attained."

In the staging Kneuss took ample advantage of the opportunities for Busby Berkeley–like burlesque (Papa, meet Dada), but a candlelit ball scene at the end was rich in nostalgia and romance behind its mockery of those very qualities. Again, there were differences in synergy between the casts. One cast brought out more of the slapstick, the other more of the tender, lyrical qualities. Ozawa, with his comic flair, was a master of madcap. When Thérèse underwent her sex change and her liberated breasts flew up into the air as balloons, Ozawa stepped out of the pit to puncture them with his baton. Even the curtain calls were choreographed as split-second comic turns. Again, the production, including both orchestras' playing, was a success as both theater and training.

Taking a longer view of opera, Tanglewood opened the 1997 season with two performances of Luigi Rossi's 1647 *L'Orfeo* in a 350th-anniversary production from the Boston Early Music Festival. The four-hour baroque spectacle, enriched by costumes from the Drottningholm Court Theater in Stockholm, extensive use of dance, and a period-instrument orchestra, revived a virtually unknown but musically vital work that had played a part in history: it introduced opera into France when Cardinal Mazarin had it performed in Louis XIV's Paris. Although the Theater–Concert Hall stage was somewhat cramped for the large company of dancers and singers—about thirty in all—Tanglewood had taken another step into the operatic future. The way was open for other productions by visiting troupes.

Yet major questions remained, not least of which was funding. Largely because of the school Tanglewood runs an annual deficit of about $750,000, and the $400,000 for *Grimes* had to be raised through special events, which included a New York evening of song in honor of Curtin, and an extra solicitation of patrons. If opera was to become a habit, something would also have to be done about the Theater–Concert Hall's seats, and probably the backstage storage and dressing facilities as well. Modernization of the seating would not only be an additional expense but cost money at the box office; under state building codes the new seats would have to be wider and therefore fewer. With two years' experience, moreover, it became clear that

Ozawa's fervent commitment to student opera carried a price. He could give three or four weeks to the project only by taking time away from the BSO and other Music Center activities, including the conducting program.

In terms of repertory Tanglewood would have to choose between standard works like *Carmen* and *Bohème* or a more adventurous repertory as in *Grimes* and *Les Mamelles*. The final decision would be Ozawa's, and since he would probably conduct, he would be influenced by which operas were fresh in his mind from recent performances with other companies or at the Saito Kinen Festival. But tradition and educational goals suggested an adventurous course. Goldovsky's program had enjoyed its success not just because it was unique at the time but also because it took the less-traveled road and emphasized ensemble values rather than the spotlighting or making of stars. There are ample opportunities for young singers to do *Carmens* and *Bohèmes* in conservatory productions or professional companies' training programs. Tanglewood could recreate the strengths of the Goldovsky years but now link them with training in the song literature and contemporary music, which had become key features of the studies program since Goldovsky's day. *Grimes* and *Les Mamelles* showed that the balancing act was possible.

But why opera in the first place? Despite its golden age of opera under Goldovsky, Tanglewood had achieved international renown as a mecca for symphonic music. At most student opera could provide a handful of performances for audiences of twelve hundred. Opera was not going to make much difference in terms of audience appeal or box office figures.

One reason for opera, obviously, was that Ozawa wanted it. Another was given by Phyllis Curtin in a reminiscence in the *Grimes* program book:

Boris Goldovsky began the training of performers who are musically secure, theatrically skilled, and always aware that the musical score is the primary director in the realization of the character, of the scene. While Boris Goldovsky did not direct Grimes, along with others we [singers] were under his guidance in scenes and class, taking his work with us to every Britten rehearsal. Like many others I returned to his opera program in two ensuing summers. For me, and I daresay most of his students, the fundamental techniques and philosophy of operatic acting were instilled in us by him here at Tanglewood.

A new opera program could revive the Goldovsky glories and make Tanglewood a leader in vocal as well as instrumental training. But there was an underlying significance in opera's visual—and often visceral—appeal. In a visually oriented age, opera, probably more than any other art-music form, could speak to the emerging audience. It was no accident that while symphony orchestras and chamber music societies scrambled to hold on to audiences, opera houses continued to fill seats. Even such contemporary works as John Corigliano's *Ghosts of Versailles* and Philip Glass's *Voyage*, two 1990s Met commissions in vernacular styles, managed to gain toeholds in the repertory. If Tanglewood was going to be the complete music festival that Ozawa said he wanted—if it was going to march fully armed into the twenty-first century—it needed *Grimes*es to fit the age.

Along with *Wozzeck*, *Grimes* is the quintessential twentieth-century opera. Both works deal with the struggle of the individual against society, and in both the hero, a common man who cannot fathom the crushing forces arrayed against him, must die. In *Grimes* the musical language is at once traditional in its use of form and melody yet unmistakably modern in its transformation of those devices through dissonance, compression, angularity, and ambiguity. At the end of his "Great Bear and Pleiades" aria Grimes, contemplating "the clouds of human grief," asks: "Who can turn skies back and begin again?" The villagers arrayed around him in the tavern mutter, "He's mad or drunk. Why's that man here?" and the two "nieces" chime in, "His song alone would sour the beer." In both words and music the issue is joined. Rather than the savior that Bernstein envisioned, the dreamer, the visionary, the man of feeling—however right or wrong his actions may be—has no place in this society.

In the late twentieth century it was not only the individual who had to struggle against the pressures for conformity brought about by the entertainment industry, the media, marketing techniques, and an economy based on acquisition. Music itself faced the same struggle for identity. The star system, fed on the one side by audience demand and television and on the other by clever management and promotion techniques, was one symptom. Another was the rise of postmodern styles that, unlike the yearning for the old verities in *Grimes* and *Les Mamelles*, reduce human experience to cartoon versions of itself. With its new concert hall opening the doors for new music and new audiences along with opera, Tanglewood became a battleground—albeit one where the tranquillity of the lawn appeared to reign—for the soul of music.

7

The
Selling
of a
Festival

Serge koussevitzky, who could barely abide the Boston Pops because of its light repertory and players' pranks, would be astonished if he could see the sometimes casual attitude toward music at his festival today. Opera may be returning, and the original campus may look as it did in his era. But gone are the times when concertgoers dressed up in suits and evening dresses—when, in the early 1950s, management handed out wraparound skirts to women brazen enough to show up in shorts (The experiment in propriety lasted only a few seasons. Recipients kept making off with the skirts as souvenirs.) As fashion today just about anything goes, especially on the lawn, where on a warm day shorts and T-shirts look like required dress. Applause between movements is so common that purists in the audience and conductors no longer try to quell it. (It is hardly the capital offense that purists think it is, in any case.) The standing ovation has become a meaningless habit. Socialites regularly overstay intermissions and return to their seats in the Shed, often trampling feet en route, after the music has resumed. Rattling papers, jangling bracelets, beeping watches, talking during the performance, snoring: although most concertgoers sit quietly, the distractions pose a constant hazard to listening. The dangers mount on Sunday afternoons, when tour buses disgorge crowds of passengers doing the circuit of New England tourist shrines and shopping malls.

This is de Tocqueville's democracy, with its fear of a tyranny by the majority, carried over into the arts. Yet change did not come entirely on the audience's side. Tanglewood, and arts presenters generally in America, invited some of it in their quest for new audiences. Amid the inroads wrought by television, film, and rock, they borrowed some of the enemy's weapons. The

153

most common, and most likely to backfire, is television itself. As Itzhak Perlman, Luciano Pavarotti, and other idols have shown, it brings music to many who would never go near an opera house or concert hall. It may even entice some of the many to take the fateful step. But it brings a whole new set of values into the musical equation. Show takes precedence over substance.

Tanglewood landed on the national and international television map in 1988 with the four-day party for Leonard Bernstein's seventieth birthday, Japanese and European television were there, sending back live coverage; American networks taped the scene. Since then Tanglewood has regularly caught television's eye with special events such as opening nights, celebrity artists, and the Ozawa Hall opening. As in other aspects of popular and celebrity culture, exposure breeds more exposure. As in other cultural institutions do it. Tanglewood, with its allure of lawn, lake, and hills plus celebrities, just has extra appeal. Since the Bernstein party, in fact, it has acquired something of a mystique with the media.

A press office of six full-time staff members and various part-timers cultivates media attention not only among critics, who favor unplebeian events like the Festival of Contemporary Music, but also by regional and network television, which come for the tinsel of glamour and personalities. Sometimes, especially when the cameras are from Europe, the coverage is unobtrusive. At other times it invites artistic disaster.

In 1989 Jessye Norman, accompanied by NBC and Japanese television crews, swept into the Shed for what had been billed as a concert performance of *Carmen*—her first public appearance in the title role. Audience expectations and ticket sales ran high. But though Norman had recently recorded the opera in France with Ozawa, she had second thoughts about performing it in front of an audience. The reason was not hard to imagine: her regal bulk made her an unlikely gypsy temptress. Taking a more prudent course, she dropped *Carmen* and joined Ozawa and the BSO in a mixed program of French orchestral music and operatic excerpts.

Many listeners, having paid premium ticket prices (Norman always commands top dollar at Tanglewood), were already unhappy about the program change. Their disappointment turned to outrage over what followed. When Norman made her entrance and began singing Berlioz's *La Mort de Cléopâtre*, a loud electrical buzz emanating from the rafters wiped out the performance. The noise was worst for concertgoers in the highest-priced seats in the center, who were directly beneath the source: equipment running the specially installed spotlights that flooded the stage (and the audience's eyes) for the cameras' benefit. At intermission listeners vented their anger on ushers, passing BSO officials, and cameramen stationed in the aisles.

In a sensible world the extra spots would have been shut down and television would have had to do without. But in the video world things don't happen that way. The consort of Caesar and Anthony died with an electronic asp at her throat. The home audience enjoyed what the paying audience couldn't.

The buzz was reduced to a hum when Norman returned after intermission (and a change of gowns) to sing excerpts from *Les Contes d'Hoffmann*, *La Périchole*, and *Carmen*. Now, apparently playing to the cameras, she sang at half-voice and turned coy. In the habanera from *Carmen*, the only remnant of the canceled opera, she crooned and swayed through the music; it sounded and looked like a lullaby. The made-for-television evening became a parody of a concert.

In 1994 jazz trumpeter Wynton Marsalis arrived with a Sony television crew and a caravan of equipment trailers for a two-week stay. The occasion was not a concert, though he occasionally takes part in Tanglewood's Labor Day weekend jazz festival, but the filming of a four-part music appreciation series for public television, videocassette, audiocassette, book, and CD-ROM distribution by Sony. Before the shooting was over, it disrupted the Music Center schedule, left students disgruntled, and led to a fateful fight between Ozawa, who had pushed for the project, and Music Center leaders, who objected to its commercial and intrusive aspects.

The idea was that Marsalis, a 1979 Tanglewood graduate, and his jazz band would team with Ozawa and the Music Center Orchestra in a 1990s sequel to Leonard Bernstein's televised "Young People's Concerts" from the 1950s to the 1970s. The Sony crews transformed a ramshackle barn across the road from the Shed into a high-tech television studio with blacked-out windows and air conditioning blown in from trucks. A back wall was torn out and replaced with a giant blue screen for projections. The set was a shiny glass platform like a basketball court. Under multicolored spotlights larger-than-life Plexiglas cutouts of jazz players bobbed and danced around the jazz band. Grade schoolers from Tanglewood's Days in the Arts program for inner-city children were pressed into service as an audience. Draped with legs dangling from a stairway and balcony, they provided child appeal, applause, and answers to Marsalis's occasional schoolteacherish questions.

The four programs were titled "Why Toes Tap," "Listening for Clues,"

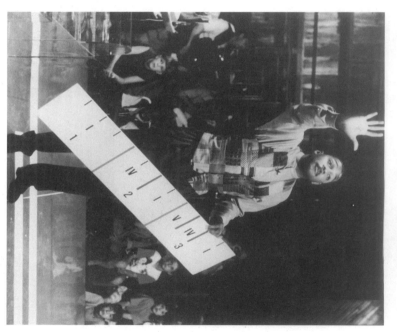

Wynton Marsalis uses a visual aid as he lectures in his "Marsalis on Music" video project. (Frank Stewart. Copyright 1995 by Sony Music)

"Sousa to Satchmo," and "Tackling the Monster." In each Marsalis and Ozawa led performances—sometimes separately, sometimes in tandem—to demonstrate some of the ABCs of classical music and jazz and the connections between the genres. Marsalis, a thirty-two-year-old Grammy winner who also plays classical trumpet, wrote his own scripts in collaboration with a team of Sony producers and directors. He said his goal was "just to inspire people to participate in music—young people and old people." They can participate on any level. "You sing it, you play the kazoo. That's what we say in the series. We don't really care what level of participation it is. We inspire an interest in music as music, not just as a commodity."

Although Music Center leaders had approved the project at Ozawa's urging, they were not prepared for the collision with marketplace demands that was to come. For two weeks the Music Center Orchestra was tied up as Marsalis frantically wrote and rewrote the script to meet Sony's specifications. The frequent changes required long hours of takes and retakes on top of the students' other work. Students vented their frustration on faculty members, who had no part in the project, and the orchestra's playing suffered in the annual Leonard Bernstein memorial concert, given in the Shed with Itzhak Perlman as the soloist. Most of the Tanglewood on Parade gala, usually a showcase for the student orchestra, had to be performed by the BSO because the students had little time to rehearse. Although the student players liked Sony's union-scale pay, they complained—in some cases bitterly—that they were shortchanged in chamber music and orchestral studies, Tanglewood's principal attractions for young players. In one of the more moderate reactions to the disruption, Glen Cherry, a violinist then in his first of three Tanglewood summers, said he "didn't mind" the project greatly at first because of the pay. But in looking back, he could "see why other people were so angry, because the artistic rewards were not very high." The experience was of no value to him as he went on to an orchestral career.

Preparations for the Festival of Contemporary Music also suffered. Dissension spread in the faculty ranks and finally spilled over in a row with Ozawa at a senior staff meeting. Normally open to suggestions and even criticism, he accused the objectors of undermining him, when in fact they had tried to quell students' anger. He said the television experience would be good for young musicians going out into the world. Faculty members replied that young musicians could get all of that they wanted any time they needed to earn a buck on the outside. Leon Fleisher, Gilbert Kalish, and Richard Ortner were among the objectors. Three years later all three loyal lieutenants were gone—victims of Ozawa's determination to reinvent the Music Center without opposition.

The finished product, titled "Marsalis on Music," seemed at best a good try at winning over an MTV generation with some of MTV's tricks. Though favorably received by New York and Boston critics, the four one-hour programs delivered no consistent message or viewpoint about music's means or ends. They were also heavy on high-tech imagery such as skyscrapers that pop out of a harbor and instruments that fly through space (motifs for the show) and waltzing roses (for Tchaikovsky's "Waltz of the Flowers").

Marsalis proved knowledgeable and articulate as a host. He was also adept at coming up with metaphors and analogies. (Children shape a story about buying a hamster at a mall with the same basic ABA form—beginning, middle, end—that underlies much classical and jazz music.) But he also came across as rather earnest and even condescending, more concerned with music's techniques than its pleasures. He gave, for example, a detailed formal analysis of the first movement of Prokofiev's *Classical Symphony* without ever mentioning that the genius of the piece—its fun—is its witty reinvention of the eighteenth-century classical form. The most effective segment, the last, dropped the high-tech gimmickry and simply showed Yo-Yo Ma rehearsing with three student cellists and then discussing the hows and whys of practice (the "monster" of the show's title) with the host.

The executive producer for the project was Peter Gelb, who had previously done documentaries on Ozawa and Vladimir Horowitz and overseen the BSO gala in Prague. The former BSO assistant manager, who went on to become president of Sony Classical, is known in musical circles for his packaging and marketing of classical music as a commercial product. He described Ozawa as "the first and only choice" as conductor for the project. Ozawa, who has always had a streak of the showman in him, evidently enjoyed the assignment. He mugged, high-stepped, and threw himself into the performances like a trouper. His players, on the other hand, looked grim, and their performances sounded that way, too. Marsalis said he wanted Tanglewood because it is "one of the greatest places for music for young people in the country." Yet in the final product the barn was so transformed by gadgetry, high-tech visuals, spotlights, and air conditioning that only an occasional moth fluttering by remained to show that it was summer in the Berkshires.

Bernstein, in black and white and standing before fixed cameras, was a more galvanizing teacher in his "Young People's Concerts." Rather than turn schoolmaster to his young charges, he treated music and talk about music as an entry into a world of excitement that they would be eager to visit. He would never, for example, have let his audience miss the jokes in the *Classical Symphony*. But then Bernstein made his series at a time when music was widely taught in schools—parents and teachers can be seen attending his concerts with their children—and classical music had not become so entangled with commerce.

Another television crew was prowling the grounds while the Marsalis series was being filmed. It came from Sandcastle Productions of Andover, Massachusetts, and was shooting a documentary about the Music Center, which would be shown on public television the following summer.

There was unintended irony in the title of the hourlong program: "Perfect Harmony." The action took place at and around the very Tanglewood on Parade program that, because of the Marsalis project, was marked backstage by anything but harmony. Not a hint of this discord wrinkled the happy face that television's Tanglewood turned toward the world. The concert and rehearsal scenes and the interviews with students and faculty members, including Ozawa, painted a sketchy though accurate picture of the teaching process. But the show was so disjointed and begged so many musical questions that it seemed like a tourist's peek at the art and institution.

The dozen or so students chosen for interview represented, in the words of Music Center director Leon Fleisher, "a musical United Nations." They came from Russia, Taiwan, the Netherlands, Canada, Honduras, Korea, and Japan in addition to the United States. These smiling, camera-friendly faces described a supercharged summer that, in the words of Hsing-Chwen Hsin of Taiwan, packed "the experience of a year within two months" —the kind of observation that began with Bernstein in the inaugural season. The teachers presented the longer view of that experience. Faculty chairman Gilbert Kalish, for instance, pointed out that the music the audience saw Hsin practicing was a difficult piece by George Crumb, which she would probably not have touched had she not come to Tanglewood.

But how she came to be working on a piece by Crumb—whether by choice or assignment, for public performance or as an exercise—was not a topic considered fit for discussion. Nor were Beethoven's *Leonore* Overture No. 3 and Tchaikovsky's *1812* Overture, the music performed in the scenes from the gala evening concert, identified for the living room audience. Nor were viewers told that in the *1812* Overture the parent BSO and the student orchestra combine for the only time all season, the goal being to double the firepower for Tchaikovsky's noisemaker. As host, Marvin Hamlisch, the film and Broadway songwriter, lobbed creampuff questions at all comers. He and the producers seemed so afraid of putting viewers off with questions of substance that they never even identified the concert as Tanglewood on Parade, the year's principal benefit for the Music Center.

The show's most revealing moment came near the beginning, when Ozawa prepared to conduct the *Leonore*. The camera caught him in what looked like a moment of prayer. Later, in his interview, Ozawa hinted at the probable meaning of the gesture when he spoke of his strong emotional attachment to Tanglewood as the place where he got his start in the United States. In fact, he often indulges in a moment of prayerful remembrance, particularly for his mentor, Charles Munch, before beginning a concert recalling his own or Tanglewood's past. Yet in the film there was no suggestion of what he was thinking or doing. A more perceptive interviewer would have thought to ask.

It is still possible to take music seriously in video form. That was proved by a documentary, "A Tale of Tanglewood: *Peter Grimes* Reborn," filmed in connection with the 1996 *Grimes* revival. Produced by Rhombus Media of Toronto, the fifty-five-minute film crosscut scenes from the 1946 and 1996 productions, along with interviews with participants in both. The difficulties of mounting an opera from scratch with a student cast were made clear, as were the dramatic and educational rewards. Although there was some fakery in the filming—the opening-night audience was seen cheering scenes that were actually filmed at private sessions for the cameras—this was essentially *Grimes* as it happened in both history and the present. Perhaps the seriousness of approach accounted for the failure of the documentary to get wide distribution in the United States.

It is perhaps too much to expect that a program designed for a general audience, as "Perfect Harmony" was, will grapple with deeper musical issues. But if Tanglewood is as serious about music as it purports to be, it is a misrepresentation to treat the music and personalities as if they came out of sitcom country. "Perfect Harmony" showed the best side of Tanglewood, and Hamlisch was an affable host. But it seemed symptomatic of the medium and the time that the program opened and closed with him tickling the ivories in his own show tunes, not Mozart, Beethoven, or Chopin, much less George Crumb. In television's blinkered world, art and entertainment are one.

TELEVISION is only one weapon in an up-to-date arts organization's marketing armory. A variety of public relations and fund-raising devices also dangles the enticements of glamour, uplift, and fun.

The selling of Tanglewood begins every February with the press announcement of the coming season and a simultaneous mailing of brochures to donors, who get first crack at tickets—the high-end donors first. A few weeks later comes a general mailing of a more elaborate, full-color brochure to other known concertgoers, with additional copies posted at the Tanglewood gates, libraries, restaurants, inns, and other public places. After this opening salvo the general sale of tickets begins in early April. Full-page ads in the *New York Times*, the *Boston Globe*, and the *Berkshire Eagle* list the complete concert schedule and tell how to order tickets. In the late spring a follow-up ad campaign begins in regional newspapers. Newspaper ads and radio announcements keep up the momentum throughout the summer.

Since ticket sales account for only about 60 percent of the BSO's income, there is a constant push to stimulate giving as well as attendance. A BSO development staff of thirty works with volunteers to arrange solicitations from the individual to the corporate level. Corporate sponsors, such as Lexus and the Red Lion Inn—the latter is the no. 1 hotel destination in the Berkshires—underwrite concerts for a minimum contribution of $25,000.

In return they receive prominent mention in the program book and other publicity; they also earn the privilege of entertaining employees and other concert guests, many of them new to Tanglewood, in a hospitality tent near the Shed. In Lexus's case, the prominent display of a shiny new car during pre- and postconcert receptions was an additional benefit.

High-end individual givers gain membership in the supper clubs at Highwood and Seranak, where they may dine in casual elegance amid views of the lake and hills. The annual appeal to the general public also offers perquisites, ranging from free admission to Music Center concerts up to parking and hospitality privileges. A network of "friends" among smaller, mostly regional businesses receives similar courtesies. Among the other giving opportunities offered the public are endowment of a chair in the Shed ($5,000) or of an existing or freshly planted tree on the grounds ($10,000).

Other programs specifically target new audiences. Through support from TDK, the Japanese electronics manufacturer, children under twelve receive free admission to the lawn if they are accompanied by a parent or other guardian; sometimes young and old together are initiated into the pleasures of classical music. For parents inclined toward more serious listening, a child entertainment service is available at a nearby private school. An annual family concert, instituted in 1995, offers a nice twist on an old rule: an adult may attend only if accompanied by a child. The Music Center Orchestra, with a narrator, plays a program tailored for the grade school set. At the annual Berkshire Night any county resident may attend a Music Center Orchestra concert without charge. BSO broadcasts reach thousands of other potential concertgoers in the Boston, Albany, and Berkshire areas.

Caroline Smedvig, the BSO's director of public relations and marketing, said the goal in the advertising and promotional materials, all of which use the enticing Tanglewood logo of trees, is to keep the tone low-key, the demographics "fairly upscale." The ads seek a dignified look and "a sense of elegance, budget permitting." The brochure has "a seriousness of purpose, and at the same time isn't off-putting by being pretentious. It's a tricky balance." The description fits all aspects of the image that Tanglewood seeks to project.

Dignified or not, the push for money and audiences by arts institutions intensified in the 1990s. After the nationwide boom in symphony orchestras, cultural centers, and other monuments to the arts in the 1960s through 1980s, when a symphony orchestra became a badge of civic pride and the Ford Foundation assisted with a massive infusion of funds, a severe contraction set in with the 1990 recession. A number of second-rank and third-rank orchestras, such as those in Denver, New Orleans, and San Diego, went under, and others had to cut back seasons and musicians' pay. Strikes often followed. Performance standards were endangered as full-time symphony players became part-time and had to find other work.

Well-endowed, and blessed with a tradition of public support and labor relations that in recent years had gone to the brink of a strike but not beyond, the BSO successfully weathered most of the shocks. The chief effect at Tanglewood was the end of the BSO's semistaged operas after 1991. But, in common with the other "big five" American orchestras—New York, Philadelphia, Chicago, and Cleveland—the BSO lost radio and recording contracts as costs soared and corporate sponsorship dwindled. Although Ozawa recorded the Berlioz and Fauré *Requiems* with the BSO and continued his recording work with European orchestras, whose fees are lower than those of their American counterparts, the BSO's principal recording activity during the mid-1990s consisted of the Brahms and Ravel cycles conducted by Bernard Haitink. When the orchestra's national broadcasts on public radio ceased for lack of a sponsor, a network of public and commercial stations was cobbled together to provide regional coverage.

The causes of these dislocations were only partly economic. Old money—the wealthy family or circle of families that had quietly written checks to cover an orchestra's deficits—had gradually dried up after World War II. Corporations, the new sugar daddies, were either cutting back their support or channeling it into other areas, often having more to do with education or social needs than the arts. (A corporation, for example, might support youth concerts but no longer contribute heavily to an orchestra's general fund.) The National Endowment for the Arts, meanwhile, was undergoing heavy pruning by Republican-dominated Congresses in Washington. NEA grants to the BSO declined from $370,000 in 1990 to $236,000 (out of total individual, corporate, foundation, and governmental giving of $10,480,000) in 1996. State arts councils underwent similar cutbacks, with Massachusetts Cultural Council support for the BSO shrinking from $150,000 in 1990 to $73,000 in 1995 (but rising to $91,000 in 1996 as the state's economy improved).[1] Many state councils also redirected their funding more toward educational needs and grassroots causes. The impact of these cuts was greater than the dollar amounts would suggest. To corporations and foundations, NEA approval, based on thorough artistic and administrative scrutiny, certifies an organization as worthy of support. Reductions in NEA funding become a signal that others may also scale back their giving.

Through all the difficulties the BSO retained a Midas touch in fundraising, as that $10,480,000 total for 1996 (and the orchestra's location in a culturally enlightened city) would suggest. But as much as economics, a shift in public attitudes underlay the turmoil. By the 1990s two generations of television and rock, along with the social upheavals that produced a drug culture, devastated inner cities, and made people afraid to go out of their homes at night, had tilted the balance so far away from high art that symphony orchestras and their music no longer seemed a cultural necessity. Indeed, they had come to seem a playground of the elite, that old bugaboo of the common good.

In the earlier postwar decades there had been enough money and interest, especially among older concertgoers, to sustain a nineteenth-century tradition. Now the older culture, like the funding, was dying out, and new sources with other interests—often more pressing than music—had to replace them. Even the $2 million naming gift for Ozawa Hall, which would confer rare prestige on the donor, had taken several years to negotiate and had to come from a Japanese source. The assaults on the NEA were a symptom not just of a declining interest in the arts but of politicians' belief that there was hay to be made with an indifferent public by stomping the hated elitists. Attacked on all sides, the symphony orchestra indeed was in danger of becoming the "museum" that Bernstein had warned against.

Audiences continued to flock to Tanglewood—ever-bigger audiences, culminating in the record gate count of 376,500 for classical and popular concerts in 1997. In Boston the BSO was blessed with another popular attraction, often imitated by other symphony orchestras through never equaled, the Pops. But the Pops was a moneymaker. At Tanglewood the crowds were an economic as much as artistic necessity. Partly because it supports a summer academy that awards 150 full-tuition fellowships each year, Tanglewood runs up an annual deficit of about $750,000. It counts on the lawn audience, which can go as high as 14,000, to supplement the income from the 5,000 higher-priced (up to $76 in 1997) seats in the Shed. A rainy night for an Itzhak Perlman or Jessye Norman concert (lawn admission $14) can cost the BSO $100,000 or more in lost lawn-ticket sales.

Although Tanglewood no longer indulges in rock concerts, it offers a limited menu of popular attractions. There is an all-day July Fourth celebration culminating in a gala concert by a popular star or group—Arlo Guthrie or Peter, Paul, and Mary, for example—with fireworks afterward. Two or three times a summer a Popular Artists series presents oldies like Bob Dylan and James Taylor. The two Boston Pops concerts and Tanglewood on Parade (the latter also followed by fireworks) are traditions. Jazz is celebrated in a Labor Day weekend festival that features such well-known performers as pianist Chick Corea, the New Black Eagle Jazz Band, and the Dave Brubeck and Sonny Rollins quartets. Except for the jazz programs, which are attended mostly by aficionados, these concerts regularly draw enthusiastic crowds in the 10,000 to 15,000 range.

Gingerly, Ozawa has also begun to use jazz stars in an attempt to bring new influences to the BSO and Music Center. The Marsalis video project was the opening shot in the campaign. With the BSO in 1995 Keith Jarrett played a Mozart piano concerto; in 1996 pianist Marcus Roberts offered his wildly improvisatory version of Gershwin's *Rhapsody in Blue*. Although well-received by the audience, neither experiment was an artistic success. Seemingly put off by the sea of faces in the Shed, Jarrett played stiffly—a surprise for someone noted for his improvisatory freedom in jazz. Roberts rendered the Gershwin work all but unrecognizable in places and used a detachment of BSO players as sidemen for his own jazz band. The sullen BSO members did not make a pretty sight or sound.

If the standard repertory remains the backbone of Tanglewood programming, it is what most listeners come for, some because they already know and love it, others because they want to give it a chance. Furthermore, the standard repertory is standard precisely because it comes out of a great tradition. That is also why musicians, given an imaginative conductor, want to play it. There is nothing wrong—and much that is right—in this. Yet the courting of media, money, and masses produces a tacit agreement. For some listeners this means a willingness to try high culture if culture can deliver a star, a bit of social status or entertainment, or some combination of those delights. For Tanglewood it means a willingness to admit that music can be only a soothing backdrop to the pleasures of lounging and dining.

There is a long tradition of inattention and snobbery in American operagoing and concertgoing, as any reader of Edith Wharton knows. What is new today is the expectations bred by television and popular culture generally. With their accommodation of short attention spans and confusion of art and show, they suggest that serious music can be enjoyed with no more effort than pop. So the lawn audience sunbathes, picnics, reads newspapers, chatters, and cuddles while Beethoven plays, and pressure builds in concert venues everywhere for more stars, more galas, more glitz, in pursuit of more crowds and money. The audience waxes shallower as it waxes larger: a case of simultaneous anemia and obesity.

And Tanglewood sometimes isn't averse to playing the game by television's rules. In 1992 the press office floated a story that a ghost was wandering about after dark in the Highwood manor house, where Smedvig and her staff have offices on the top floor. The revenant was supposed, among other things, to have gone around brushing up amorously against female employees of the press office and the downstairs supper club. Leonard Bernstein, a fancier of the supernatural, was reported to have felt its presence at one time, and John Williams, it was said, played *eine kleine Nachtmusik* at midnight on a piano to woo it. For years Koussevitzky's ghost was said to have inhabited Seranak, his former mansion across the road, and nobody gave it a second thought. But when the Highlood ghost made its debut in print, reporters and cameramen, along with a squad of ghostbusters, stormed the gates.

Ever savvy where publicity is concerned, Tanglewood did nothing to discourage the circus. To the deep thinkers of the media, Beethoven, Mahler, and Stravinsky were just some old men out there in the woods. But let a poor, lonely ghost show its face, and the world bear a path to Tanglewood's door.

The ghost, of course, never appeared.

Standing at a microphone on the Ozawa Hall stage, Leon Fleisher heaped scorn on what he described as "the music business" and the consumer culture it reflected. Their bottom lines, he said, "are marketability and profitability, and they are quite willing to dilute and adulterate to achieve their twin goals."

The Music Center's normally peaceable artistic director was an angry man as he addressed the students, faculty, and guests at the school's 1995 opening exercises. He recited the doleful litany: the United States spent more on its military bands than on the National Endowment for the Arts. France, though a smaller country, spent $2 billion a year on culture, while the United States allotted only $160 million to the NEA. And Congress wanted to wipe out even that amount.

"That's *B* for billion," Fleisher said as he puzzled over the culture-crazed French. "*B* as in Beethoven and other composers, and in Botticelli. What's the matter with those people? Are they nerds? Are they wimps? We have our own *B*'s—Beavis and Butthead."

The audience roared with laughter.

The warning followed in a long opening-exercises tradition. Koussevitzky had hurled similar thunderbolts in his day, and Bernstein had added some potent ones of his making in his 1970 "Principle of Hope" address. In 1979 Gunther Schuller, Fleisher's predecessor at the Music Center, had gone further, using the ceremonies to mount a scathing attack on American symphony orchestras for mediocrity, cynicism, a "corporate mentality," and "absentee" music directors. Schuller's speech, which he later carried to other forums around the country, became a cause célèbre. With evangelical

Leon Fleisher addresses the Music Center's opening exercises. (Walter H. Scott)

fervor he declared that "the ills of the modern symphony orchestra" were not entirely financial, as orchestra leaders complained:

Not so, my friends. The problems of the symphony orchestra are by now mostly within. In fact, orchestras have become in some ways too much successful businesses; their techniques of survival are now those of the American corporation, including the full panoply of managerial and public relations accoutrements, as well as absentee music directors, and orchestras run not by artists, but by committees.[2]

Schuller named no names. But five years later he resigned from the Music Center, angrily accusing the BSO of making his position at the school untenable through commercial pressures, as in the choice of guest conductors from the BSO roster for the student orchestra.

Schuller claimed he was upholding the grail of Koussevitzky's vision. But since the founder's day orchestras have become unionized—the BSO, in 1942, was the last major one in the country to take the step—and the jet age has given birth to a new breed of peripatetic music director, in one city one night, another city the next. Management, meanwhile, has indeed taken on corporate stripes and colors. Typically for a symphony orchestra, the BSO's chain of command shows a board and officers at the top, a president as chief executive officer, a managing director as chief administrative officer, and various division heads beneath them.[3] Budgets grow year by year; there is constant pressure for expansion and new products, including special concerts and social events to bring in new audiences and bigger givers. The public relations accoutrements are boldly displayed in promotional and fund-raising efforts. Yet if there is a corporate analogy here, there is also a major difference: an orchestra's product is an intangible, music; the stockholders are the concertgoers, and the organization is not out to show a profit.

The offenses Schuller cited are audible and visible at Tanglewood, as at other orchestral showplaces across the country. Some BSO performances are indeed routine or mediocre (but others are electric). Though Ozawa gives more time to his orchestra than any other director of a major American symphony, he is out of the country more than half the year (but regularly in touch). Fleisher's complaints could likewise have been turned against the institution that gave him a rostrum. A few days after his speech, on the BSO's opening night, Ozawa led his rafter-rattling performance of Orff's *Carmina burana* with Kathleen Battle as a starry soloist. It was clearly a rallying cry for a gala occasion, complete with a preconcert dinner for patrons and benefactors; the music business and consumer culture, regaled in black tie and evening dress, were king and queen for a night. A year later the "Three Birthdays" celebration for Ozawa, Perlman, and Ma not only attracted the largest audience ever for a classical music event at Tanglewood but also offered patrons and benefactors an opportunity afterward to party in private with the stars. Meanwhile, ticket prices rose year after year, putting Tanglewood (except perhaps on the lawn) beyond some concertgoers' reach, and Fleisher himself felt compelled by marketplace pressures to resign, just as Schuller had. The name inscribed on Music Center headquarters, Leon Fleisher Carriage House, would carry a strange ring in the years ahead.

The 1990s, in other words, were not the 1930s and 1940s, when Koussevitzky could announce a season—take it or leave it—and put tickets up for sale, and listeners would come year after year, even with liberal amounts of new music. The Koussevitzky way undoubtedly had its advantages. (Its disadvantages, too: even under unionization the orchestra lived in terror of his temper and dictatorial ways.) But Koussevitzky did not have to deal with the fragmenting and leveling of culture in the age of the sitcom, the mall, and the electric guitar. Even amid the Great Depression the nation had a commonality of purpose, and "classical" music commanded general respect. In the 1990s orchestras were fighting for survival with whatever weapons they had at their disposal—often, as it happened, the weapons of popular culture. Galas, glitz, celebrity artists, warhorse programming, free admission for kids, television, even ghosts: all were fair game in the push to get people inside the doors.

The Marsalis project was a good idea gone wrong; educational goals were subverted by marketplace demands, misuse of a student program, and possibly Marsalis's own limitations as a television personality. At the Music Center students may still, as they did in Koussevitzky's time, get advanced training in their art without the financial or commercial pressures that will weigh upon them when they take jobs in the outside world.

While the BSO may reflect those outside pressures and operate along corporate lines, most of the players—this must also be true to a large extent in other orchestras—are serious musicians who have devoted their lives to their art and want to play well. Their concern is evident in both performance and conversation. The breakdowns, when they occur, are due less to cynicism, union greed, or laziness than to such factors as fatigue, boredom (especially a hazard for string players), rehearsal problems, and lack of rapport with conductors. These become a major consideration at a place like Tanglewood, where the BSO must prepare its three programs each week (compared with one a week in Symphony Hall) and face a revolving door of guest conductors, some excellent, a few bad, but most somewhere in a gray middle. Inescapably routine sets in. Yet in every BSO summer there will be a few first-rate concerts, electric both on the stage and in the audience. The average may not be as good as in Symphony Hall, but it is creditable, given the time pressures. There is a fairly high standard of quality below which Tanglewood does not willingly drop.

"We live in difficult times," Fleisher told his Ozawa Hall audience, "and I fear for the world we are bequeathing to you young people." He named no names, but he was clearly referring to House Speaker Newt Gingrich and the Republican majorities in Congress as he went on: "When our political leaders decry our need for maintenance and support of culture with slightly snide sneers and label us 'cultural elite,' I'm certainly not embarrassed or ashamed of that title. I don't think any of you should be, either."

In 1970 Bernstein had delivered his fiery charge to the students: "It's the artists of the world, the feelers and thinkers, who will ultimately save us." Now, in an echo of those words, Fleisher said, "Yes, indeed, we are our brothers' and our sisters' keepers." Tanglewood, he said, wanted to "inject the twin viruses of idealism and commitment" into its students, "so that you will go out and redefine and ultimately transform the world."

The music business is guilty of many transgressions—perhaps most seriously the promotion, at sometimes outrageous fees ($100,000 per concert for Luciano Pavarotti, $45,000 for Itzhak Perlman), of audience idols over serious but less popular performers, and kitsch over serious music.[4] In this environment packaging and marketing, of both repertory and musicians, can determine programming as much as quality does. Fleisher did not mention the Marsalis project, which had tied the Music Center in knots just a year before, but as an art-based commercial product it was emblematic of the corruption that both Fleisher and Schuller decried. Yet denunciations, for all their Jeremiahlike satisfaction, fail to address the underlying question: how to save a great musical tradition in an era when people, left to their own devices, don't listen. The music business bears much of the blame, but it is also a handy scapegoat. The trouble begins not in an attempt to preserve the symphony orchestra through corporate stratagems, but in a consumer culture that wants to remake everything, including the orchestra, along the lines of a Disneyland and television show.

ℱAR FROM the camera's eye, serious study and performance of music, even by celebrity artists, goes on.

Bobby McFerrin first landed on Tanglewood's doorstep in 1988. He couldn't remember how it happened, but somebody—he thought it might have been Leonard Bernstein's children—invited him to take part in the Bernstein birthday celebration. He sang "Somewhere" from *West Side Story*, embellishing it with his body-drumming scat style. He had never before met Bernstein, much less performed for him, and was "more nervous singing those four minutes than anything I'd ever done in my life."

Hanging out with Seiji Ozawa, Bernstein, and other conductors, the dreadlocks-topped master of improvisation got a bad case of the conducting bug himself. He had already made about twenty-five podium appearances, usually of the pops or light-classics variety, and the winter after Tanglewood, on his fortieth birthday, he would make his debut with the San Francisco Symphony, his hometown orchestra. So he wrote to Bernstein, saying he was thinking about taking up conducting seriously and what did Bernstein think of the idea?

Bernstein thought it might work. He invited McFerrin to Tanglewood for a lesson the next summer. Ozawa also provided a lesson, and McFerrin began studies with Gustav Meier, head of the student conducting program. He also got to know Tanglewood personages like Phyllis Curtin.

"My wife and I just fell in love with the place," he recalled, echoing John Williams and countless others. "We thought it was magical and wonderful, and decided to come the following year for the entire summer, just to see what that was like." Taking advantage of McFerrin's presence, the Boston University Tanglewood Institute, which runs vocal and instrumental programs for students of high school age, asked him to give master classes for its vocal students. From 1989 until 1992, when he became preoccupied with composing an opera as well as conducting, he taught for periods as long as two weeks. The classes, which took place in a barn next to the one where Wynton Marsalis held forth, were more like a jazz riff than a Curtin seminar.

Sporting a "Crabby Bill's" T-shirt with the motto "Don't worry—be crabby," McFerrin faced a semicircle of about twenty-five excited teenagers in the musty barn. He started the basses singing a doo-doo-dah-doo scat rhythm and moved on to the tenors, starting them in a melody. Then he got the altos and sopranos going in the harmony. Bodies began swaying and fingers snapping, and two of the bassists improvised a dance to the rhythm. For fifteen minutes McFerrin went from section to section, improvising new rhythms, melodies, and harmonies and leaving student leaders to keep them going. When finally he wound the whole thing down, applause broke out and the class ended, but the beat went on as happy students leaving the barn kept on doo-doo-dah-dooing.

Describing his method, McFerrin said:

It's taking the elements of music—rhythm and harmony and melody and whatever—and playing with them. What I basically do is come in with a simple idea without really a conclusion. I just come up with sort of a premise and then I ask the group how they can change it somehow to make it more complicated or more simple—but usually complicated. I don't want to fill in all the blanks, so the students can have a chance to take control over the project and the idea.

Despite his jazz and pop renown, the multiple-Grammy winner and "Don't Worry, Be Happy" songwriter—he resented George Bush's appropriation of the tune in the 1988 presidential campaign—began life as a classical musician. Both of his parents were classical singers. His father, Robert McFerrin Sr., studied with Goldovsky at Tanglewood and went on to sing at the Met; he was, the son proudly recalled, the first black man ever under Met contract. Bobby's jazz career took off after an appearance in the 1981 Kool Jazz Festival in New York, and in 1990 he formed his Voicestra, a scat-style, a cappella vocal group. By the mid-1990s he was making the rounds of the country's major orchestras, conducting the classics straight and sometimes embellishing them with scat accompaniments. He was also composing an opera, *Gethsemane*, in collaboration with librettist Ishmael Reed and director Peter Sellars on a commission from the San Francisco Opera.

Bobby McFerrin works with Boston University Tanglewood Institute students during one of his workshops on improvisation. (Walter H. Scott)

The Bernstein celebration was responsible for another fateful encounter in McFerrin's life. He met Yo-Yo Ma.

Hitting it off right away, he and the cellist struck up a friendship. Ma appeared as a soloist with him when he made his San Francisco Symphony debut, and they collaborated on *Hush*, a top-of-the-charts compact disc of classical and pop numbers done in improvisatory style. In the liner notes for the album, Ma described his baptism into improvisation as "a terrifying as well as exhilarating experience." "We had a ball doing that," McFerrin said in the Tanglewood barn.

The father of three children, McFerrin said that if he could do only one kind of music, it would be classical music. But he really wanted to settle down into a career in composing:

I love singing and I love performing, but I feel like I'm entering a period when I want to spend more time with my family and really write a lot of the kind of choral music I like to write. My dad was one of the best baritones ever. So classical music was the first music that I heard when I was a kid. But still I was exposed to Joe Williams, to Count Basie and Billie Holliday. And then I grew up in the sixties, so I got to know Janis Joplin, Jimi Hendrix, and James Brown and all those people. And all this music was in my house. So I never really thought of myself as one kind of musician.

If McFerrin hung out in a barn away from the cameras, Ma played music unlikely to attract them. Though he has also come in for ample television attention, nearly every year at Tanglewood he performs one or more difficult contemporary works, many written for him and some in premieres. Besides making him a musical brother to McFerrin, the willingness to venture into new and sometimes strange realms is what distinguishes him from figures like Perlman. Understanding of new styles gives insights into old ones. Both kinds of music thereby gain in comprehension and feeling, and composers gain a champion.

In 1992 Ma held the Theater–Concert Hall stage alone for an entire evening, playing all six of Bach's suites for unaccompanied cello. The cycle makes a long night of music, demanding the utmost in concentration from the performer and audience. (On the Theater–Concert Hall's unyielding metal chairs it also demanded an ascetic's indifference to discomfort.) With Ma as the soloist the program was part marathon, part spiritual quest.

The six suites, composed around 1720, become progressively more complex, both technically and emotionally. Ma said the evolution enables a performer to trace the growth of a composer's mind as he tries new ways of writing.

What you sense is a development from One to Six both in terms of instrumental experimentation—by the Sixth Suite he's actually writing for a five-stringed instrument—and in a journey of celebration. On the one hand Suites One, Three, and Six are celebratory. And then in the minor-key suites, Two and Five, you get a sense of grief and resignation, or defiance.

For Ma a complete performance was "a spiritual journey with an audience, with Bach, and with yourself."

And such a journey it became as, solitary in a summer tux, he played from memory, keeping his eyes shut for concentration. The performance style was beyond categorization as early music, romantic, modern, or anything else. The music unfurled like miles of golden rope. Bach gives few instructions to the performer beyond the bare notes, yet for four hours under a full moon, with two intermissions, Ma clothed the notes in tonal warmth and an unerring sense of musical destinations.

Ma came to this rarefied music early. Born in Paris in 1955 to Chinese parents, he received his first cello lessons and introduction to Bach from his father, a violinist. By the age of four he was playing the suites; by five he had learned three of them. His father had him memorize two bars a day, leading him not only to the music but also to a sense of structure. In a 1989 *New Yorker* profile Ma said of the process:

During the German occupation of Paris, my father lived by himself in a garret. He would memorize violin pieces by Bach and play them in the dark. He eventually advised me to follow his example and play through a Bach suite from memory every night before going to bed. This isn't "practicing"; it's contemplating. You're alone with your soul. It was a strong image—total concentration, total dedication. Although I can't actually do this now at bedtime, because I give so many concerts, the image remains with me. This helped me understand the continuity of feeling within all music—how all the movements are related and shouldn't be disturbed by tuning or other distractions. I know my greatest joy as a musician when I am playing a concert dedicated exclusively to Bach. Then for a whole evening I'm living in one man's mind—and a great man's mind. That's how I can justify being a performer. One is involved in a process that is larger than oneself.

Again, the idea of spirit: of music as something larger than concerts, star performers, and picnics with friends. It goes to the essence of music, and it is what audiences sense and respond to in Ma's playing, apart from his flings with television and pop. The questing is intellectual as well as musical. Before his performance of the suites, Ma took part in a weekend conference called "The Spiritual Beauty of Bach." The lectures, performances, and discussions were sponsored by the Berkshire Institute for Theology and the Arts, of which Ma and his wife, Jill Hornor Ma, were directors. He appeared on a panel with Jaroslav Pelikan of Yale University, the author of *Bach among the Theologians*. Ma said afterward that the discussions had crystallized his thoughts, feelings, and knowledge about music he thought he knew well. He realized Bach's music was "actually more incredible than I thought it was." It was indeed "a process that is larger than oneself."

N OBODY KNEW where music was going as it approached the twenty-first century, but it seemed fairly clear that changes in the audience and corporate marketing techniques to meet those changes were taking it in directions away from its traditions. McFerrin and Ma, with their voyaging between classical and popular styles, offered one paradigm for the future. But McFerrin and Ma are classically trained musicians who understand subtleties of effect and respect differences in styles, even in a lighter repertory. Televised spectacles like "The Three Tenors" offered a cruder paradigm, presenting operatic and classical hits in a pop format with an interlarding of pop tunes. The justification, which Pavarotti has used many times, is that such blockbusters not only provide entertainment but attract new listeners to serious music.

"Three Tenors"–like circuses might be good for ratings; they might be good for the singers' and promoters' lifestyles; they might even be good as entertainment and initiate people into the Met. But are they good for music?

Without an up-to-date market survey there is no way of knowing how many people television draws to Tanglewood—or, more significantly, how many return after the initiation. But there seems little doubt that the increased television exposure beginning with the 1988 Bernstein celebration has attracted some concertgoers. The audiences have continued to grow, reaching the 1997 record of 376,500, and the lapses in concert etiquette point to a new, less sophisticated clientele. Just as the 1980s hit movie *Amadeus*, with its cartoonish portrait of Mozart, attracted listeners to Mozart's music, some of these newcomers must have discovered Tanglewood on the flickering screen, smelled glamour or excitement, and driven to the Berkshires to see and hear for themselves.

Yet television is a visual medium, and except to a limited extent in dramatic works like operas, it cannot capture the musical experience. Indeed, in telecasts of symphonic concerts the constant shifting of camera angles becomes an outright distraction from the music. After two generations of television and rock, the more complex, slowly unfolding forms and styles have become more and more a foreign language. The decline of music performance in the home and music education in the schools has further widened the gulf between the public and its heritage. Hence the concern in musical circles about the "graying" of audiences, with their numbers declining as the grave approaches. The real issue, however, is not aging audiences or even the music business, but whether audiences and music can again meet on a common ground that satisfies Matthew Arnold's definition of culture: "the acquainting ourselves with the best that has been known and said in the world, and thus with the history of the human spirit."

Without change, symphonic music—"classical" music generally—does indeed become a museum, as lifeless as a stuffed moose. Change can come as a McFerrin-Ma willingness to explore new areas and cross boundaries, building upon music's traditions. Or it can come as the kind of revolution proclaimed by television, rock, and rock's stepchild, postmodernism, which decree that there is no tradition or spiritual quest—only an endless succession of desires and pleasures, all taking place now. The battle being fought on the tranquil greensward at Tanglewood, above the lake and hills, was, in fact, one that was being fought in many areas of American life, from churches and schools to businesses and the halls of government. Would the values that Koussevitzky stood for endure, or would they be swept aside by the juggernaut of commerce and pop culture that was rolling across the land?

8

Be
Embraced,
Ye
Millions!

*I*N 1993 the American Symphony Orchestra League shocked the music world with a call for the orchestra to lower itself to the level of a public that had not been educated up to it.

In a 203-page report, *Americanizing the Symphony Orchestra*, a task force of league members found the old way of doing things was not good enough for survival in an increasingly multicultural society. To fit the orchestra to the age, the study recommended arena-style video screens, pop and ethnic music, use of local performers such as rap and gospel choirs, child-care facilities, talks from the stage by the conductor, and preconcert and postconcert receptions for the audience, with the conductor, musicians, and board members available to chat. While orchestras may pick and choose among these tactics to suit their needs, the report warned, failure to adopt such reforms will send the American orchestra to its grave.

Some of the ideas—socials and talks from the podium, for instance—were already in use, usually in smaller cities, where orchestras have closer tics with the community and American-born conductors are comfortable with informality. But, coming from the orchestras' own service and coordinating organization, the call for a wholesale transformation of mission and methods seemed to many music professionals a stab in the back. It was, in effect, a summons to undermine the very heritage that they had set out to foster. Kenneth Haas, the BSO's former managing director, was one of 150 league members who took part in the discussions leading up to the report, yet he termed the findings "very much one-sided." The study, he said, raised "good and valid questions," but "was something of a shock to a lot of us":

Among other things, the report tended to suggest that something we were doing was really very wrong, and we needed to change it in order to be able to continue to draw audiences. Many of us don't feel that way. Many of us feel that what we do is right and very satisfying to people, and our job is to try and get them to come and hear it, rather than change it around and dilute it in some way.

While the league's bugle call was still reverberating, the National Endowment for the Arts in 1996 issued another alarm. Its report was titled, innocuously, *Age and Arts Participation*.[1] The contents were anything but innocuous. From comparative studies made in 1982 and 1992, the study showed that audiences for classical music and opera were declining to dangerous levels among the nearly 80 million baby boomers born between 1945 and 1965 and the later grouping labeled Generation X. In fact, the report said, of the seven art forms surveyed—classical music, opera, ballet, musicals, jazz, plays, and art museums—only museums, jazz, and to a lesser extent ballet showed gains in attendance over the ten-year period. For classical music the decline in attendance, ranging as high as 7 percent per age group, occurred in every grouping except those thirty-seven to forty-six and sixty-seven to seventy-six.

Even the gains (both less than 2 percent) were deceptive because Generation X was smaller and less interested in the arts than the boomers, and attendance would drop off more precipitously as the younger cohort came up. To make matters worse, the survey defined jazz loosely as a variety of popular styles that could appeal to a wider audience than mainstream jazz alone would. The gains at art museums raised the question whether these visitors were committed art lovers or only browsers attracted by moderate admission fees, freedom of movement and conversation, gift shops, and cafeterias.

The NEA findings confirmed what the eye could see. But there were some surprises. For one thing, the old belief that the better educated people are, the more they patronize arts events, no longer held true. As a group the boomers had stayed in school longer than their parents, but arts participation, in both numbers and percentages, was higher for the older generation. Yet the study also found a fairly strong level of interest in classical music on radio and in compact-disc and video formats among younger listeners. The authors, four university sociologists, speculated that high ticket prices and a lack of leisure time amid family and work demands lay behind the preference for canned music. And while opera made the poorest showing of the opera companies were actually reporting.² There were simply fewer opera companies to draw listeners than there were orchestras, chamber music societies, and other concert presenters.

The authors found the usual villains behind the sagging attendance: stagnant or falling incomes, two-jobholder families, increased vocational emphasis in college studies, television, rock, rejection of parents' values, and a pervasive cynicism toward the established social order. The report warned of serious consequences for the arts, in terms of both earned income and public and private giving, if the downward trend persisted: "In an increasingly hostile environment for cultural endeavors, if the largest segment of the adult population—the baby boomers—turns away from providing support and from participating actively in core art forms, the future of the arts is indeed grim."³

Where the orchestra league study had provoked cries of foul, the NEA findings, which largely documented the obvious, did little more than raise eyebrows. Contrasting the thriving popular culture with the struggling high arts, cultural critic Edward Rothstein wrote in the *New York Times*: "Now the very notion of high artistic achievement is often regarded as a chimera and the products of these long and sophisticated Western traditions are often treated as if they have no greater claim on America's attention than the latest music video." Such attitudes in themselves "already prove that the arts can no longer assume stability."⁴

No one seemed prepared to argue the point.

Change was under way in the music world even before the two reports were out. Many orchestras, such as the New York Philharmonic and Baltimore and Houston Symphonies, were trying "casual" or "rush-hour" concerts—abbreviated versions of subscription programs given late in the afternoon or on Saturday morning in informal dress, often with the conductor providing a spoken introduction. The Pittsburgh Symphony experimented with video screens and went to the public, asking what listeners wanted and hoping to provide it. Many orchestras took programs of performance and instruction into the schools, parks, and other institutions.

The Saint Louis Symphony went further, taking over a community music school in addition to dispatching orchestra members to other sites to perform and teach. The San Francisco Symphony brought in pop musicians, including members of the Grateful Dead, to perform with it and its youth orchestra in postseason festivals of American and other thematically programmed music. Other orchestras performed works designed specifically to attract a popular audience. The Symphony Orchestra League study, for instance, commended a piece commissioned by the Minnesota Orchestra that called for an improvised solo violin part, a large percussion section, a rap choir, the work of a graffiti artist, and a light show. Other stratagems included use of magicians and lasers in concerts, promotional tie-ins with businesses, and in-house ensembles to perform cutting-edge classical and rock music.

Perhaps the most innovative effort took place in Detroit, where the orchestra turned entrepreneur in a downtown redevelopment project in a blighted area around Orchestra Hall. In addition to expansion of the concert hall itself, the $80 million project involved construction of a high school for the performing arts, an office building that would become the headquarters of the Detroit Medical Center, a 250-seat restaurant, and a 1,000-car parking garage. Scheduled for completion in late 1999 or 2000, the project quickly attracted interest among other developers for construction nearby, including a baseball-football stadium complex. Because the city is predominantly African-American, the orchestra also offered an unusual number of opportunities for black musicians, such as a training program for orchestral players and a composers' residency and symposium.

These initiatives took on special relevance for the BSO in July 1997, when Mark Volpe, the Detroit Symphony's executive director, was named the BSO's new managing director. He succeeded Kenneth Haas, who had been incapacitated the previous October by a massive heart attack. The BSO had no immediate problems of neighborhood blight, but Volpe would bring valuable experience in dealing with changing demographics and audiences. His accomplishments in Detroit also included rescuing the orchestra from the brink of insolvency and increasing its radio, recording, and touring activity. But inner-city problems were the key to the orchestra's survival. Volpe said: "We really needed to rethink our position in the community and take a much more defined role. We needed an urban approach to an urban set of challenges—and frankly, to secure investment from sources that traditionally haven't supported the orchestra." In essence it was the problem of orchestras everywhere.

Boston, with a stronger university presence and cultural tradition than other cities, could afford to say no to the more radical programming changes. But even the BSO recognized the risk of standing pat. In 1990, at the behest of then-President George H. Kidder—the same George Kidder who was a driving force behind construction of Ozawa Hall—the BSO launched a diversity program to reach new segments of the community. Kidder recalled telling the board that "we were behind the times in addressing the changing demographics of the city where we performed our winter season. "Rather than the piecemeal efforts undertaken in the past, he "wanted to begin a serious effort, . . . with sustained intentions of maintaining it over a longer period of time."

Already the BSO was running a Days in the Arts program at Tanglewood, bringing in four hundred mostly inner-city schoolchildren yearly for a week each to acquaint them with the music, theater, dance, and other arts displayed at the Berkshires' summer festivals. (The cost to the BSO was $155,000 a year.) There were also a regular series of BSO youth concerts in Boston, now conducted with considerable ingenuity by Keith Lockhart, and a Boston concert-with-reception series aimed at young professionals. Individual BSO members took part in Project STEP, an innovative Boston program of instruction in string playing to introduce minority-group children to serious music at an early age. Among the initiatives begun by Kidder was a training program in music, at Tanglewood, for Boston elementary school teachers. In Boston the new efforts also included open houses and receptions, a review of hiring and auditioning practices, sensitivity training for ushers, ticket takers, and other "front house" personnel, and recruitment of additional minority-group members for the boards of trustees and overseers. Some of these programs, both old and new, were offered in conjunction with other Boston institutions, such as the public schools, museums, and music conservatories.

In terms of repertory and artists, little changed at the BSO. The only projects specifically tailored to appeal to an ethnic or minority group were a Gospel Night at the Pops, sometimes conducted by Isaiah Jackson, an African American, and a BSO concert in memory of Roland Hayes, a black tenor from Boston who enjoyed a national career in the first half of the century. On a commission from the BSO, George Walker, an African American, composed *Lilacs*, a vocal-orchestral work that won the 1996 Pulitzer Prize in music after its BSO premiere. His, however, was one of only a handful of pieces by black composers on the programs over the years. Black artists like Jessye Norman, Kathleen Battle, and André Watts continued to find favor, but they were popular not because of their color but because they were stars. And while the BSO as of the mid-1990s had a sizable sprinkling of Asians and numerous women in its ranks, there were only two black members. Similarly, few black conductors had come along to share the podium superintended by Ozawa, an Asian. (James DePriest, who returned in 1997, was a rare exception.) While discrimination had undoubtedly existed in earlier decades, the problem in the 1980s and 1990s, it was generally agreed, was a lack of classically trained black musicians. By contrast, Asians and Asian-Americans, especially string players, were pouring into the conservatories and orchestras in large numbers.

Unlike many orchestras, however, the BSO had the Pops. Under John Williams as under Arthur Fiedler, the BSO reached out to a broad spectrum of listeners with its mix of symphonic works, show tunes, jazz, swing, film music, and pop, all performed to an accompaniment of drinks at tables set up in Symphony Hall. It could attract audiences in the tens—sometimes hundreds—of thousands to outdoor concerts on Boston's Esplanade. It gave the BSO a financially and artistically successful arm into the community that other orchestras could only envy, and nobody (except some BSO members who disdained the Pops repertory) complained.

To whatever extent orchestras' programming devices put people in seats, they performed a useful service. Twentieth-century Americans are not bewigged aristocrats listening to string quartets in the Esterháza palace for which Haydn composed them—nor are they Viennese listening to the half-deaf, eccentric Beethoven conduct premieres of his Fifth and Sixth Symphonies, Fourth Piano Concerto, and other of his works in an exhausting, badly rehearsed four-hour marathon. Such initiatives as casual concerts, educational programs, and even an occasional collaboration with the Grateful Dead clearly offered a way of reaching those unreachable by other means. The question was whether Pops fans would turn into BSO fans—whether those new listeners attracted by pop stars, ethnic music, chat sessions, and light shows would return for Beethoven and Stravinsky. The choice was defined by Evans Mirageas, the BSO's former artistic administrator, who said it would be absurd to create a *Mona Lisa* with altered facial features to make the painting more acceptable to Asians. For the same reason, Mirageas said, bringing cultural diversity into a symphony concert "is bound to fail, because you will alienate all the audiences. The audiences that don't know much about classical music will be turned off by the music that they don't understand, and the audiences that do know something about classical music will say, 'What is this sort of music doing in here?'"

So, at any rate, spoke the BSO.

Some critics drew opposite conclusions, proclaiming traditional concertgoing and concert giving dead. Bernard Holland, senior music critic of the *New York Times*, periodically declared current developments in pop music more interesting than those in classical forms, his own field. Joseph Horowitz wrote a series of books debunking a "great music" and "great performances" syndrome, which he termed products of a music-appreciation and star-worshiping system poisonous to a healthy musical life. As an alternative, in *The Post-Classical Predicament* he propounded a "diversified 'post-classical' music," which he described as "an integration of concert music and society unknown since the turn of the century, when Dvořák studied African-American spirituals, American Indian chants, and Stephen Foster songs, and Anton Seidl led the *New World Symphony* for a public eager to participate in the quest for an American music." Unsurprisingly from the executive director of the Brooklyn Philharmonic, he held up the Philharmonic's programs as a model for the future:

[They] embrace Virgil Thomson, Charles Ives, Kurt Weill (in both his Berlin and Broadway modes), Duke Ellington, Colin McPhee, and Philip Glass. They debunk the distinction between high art and popular culture. Rather than elevating Great Music and Great Performances, they leaven Mozart and Stravinsky with large helpings of folk music and jazz. And this assault on "classical music" is not a premediated strategy, but a natural direction dictated by the orchestra's venue, its audience, its time and place.[5]

One inescapable fact was that classical music has always been a minority taste and probably always will be. The recording industry has found that in an average year classical music and opera account for only 4–5 percent of total American sales. Concert and opera attendance among the population as a whole is somewhat higher in the NEA study, but still a small minority: about 10 percent for classical music, though only about 3.5 percent for opera. It is also true—it only became more so in the 1990s—that the audience for serious music over the years has been predominantly gray-haired, largely because such listeners are more likely to have the leisure, income, and perspective that this music requires. Meanwhile, the dismantling of music education in the schools by a society that regards the arts as frills has lessened young people's chances for an introduction to serious music, and rock and other popular forms have increasingly become the sounds heard in the home, where many children first acquire a feeling for music. Bringing the masses to Beethoven (or Beethoven to the masses) might be the old story of leading the horse to water but not being able to make it drink.

Renewing the audience might, as Horowitz suggested, mean breaking down the walls between Beethoven and Ellington, Glass and Stravinsky. But if a postclassical model was to replace the classical tradition, it ran up against an apparent contradiction set on five hundred scenic acres in western Massachusetts: Why did audiences come in growing numbers for the standard repertory at Tanglewood? Was it only for stars, picnics on the lawn, and scenic beauty? Was it only because they had seen the action on television or read the glossy brochure? Was Tanglewood an anachronism, a museum, a special case—in other words, an exception in a society drugged on an entertainment culture? Or did the music tell us something about ourselves that the postclassicists and postmodernists had overlooked in their rush to break down walls and topple old masters from pedestals? And if so, what was that message?

AARON COPLAND'S *Fanfare for the Common Man*, performed by a brass-and-percussion ensemble from the Music Center, rings in the climactic evening concert at Tanglewood on Parade. A daylong musical bazaar and benefit for the Music Center, Tanglewood on Parade has been a fixture of each season since 1940, when Koussevitzky initiated the celebration to raise relief money for the blitz-battered people of England. Today it features everything from bagpipers and balloon rides to a round-robin of student concerts, all culminating in the joint program in the Shed by the BSO and Music Center Orchestra, with fireworks afterward. A party-going audience of families, picnickers, tourists, and business groups, many of whom would not go near an ordinary symphonic concert, overflows the lawn and Shed. The weather always seems to smile.

Tanglewood on Parade and the *Fanfare for the Common Man*: in their shared affirmation of democracy, they seem to have been born in the same crib. The heroic proclamations by a member of the Tanglewood pantheon recall a time, back in Copland's 1930s and 1940s, when a broad spectrum of Americans was united in seeking a better world. The common man was the embodiment of those strivings. He built a nation and, in league with intellectuals, would work to make it greater. Composers, writers, and painters created art—sometimes bad but sometimes good, like Copland's—celebrating this symbol of democracy. The faith may have been naïve, but it was genuine. Today the common man is little more than an object to be manipulated by advertising and politicians. Even the term "common man" is obsolete. Americans today are defined and divided by other labels: white male, black militant, feminist, welfare mother, right-to-lifer, senior citizen, suburbanite, gay, straight, and the rest of the dreary assortment.

Tanglewood had its beginnings, with Copland as the faculty chairman, in the populist 1930s and 1940s. In the polarized 1990s it still celebrates the common man, by whatever name he or she may be called. On the spacious grounds, in the informal atmosphere, the untutored and literate listener alike may find respite from the hustle beyond the gates. The democratic ideal was proclaimed by Koussevitzky himself. In a 1940 "statement" on the opening of the Music Center, for example, he said Tanglewood "will be a place for those who wish to refresh mind and personality by the experience of the best in music and the related arts, and who long for a creative rest in the summer."

The next year, in his opening address at the Music Center, Koussevitzky elaborated on the theme. "In what," he asked his audience, "does the active drawing of the wide masses nearer to music consist?" It consisted, he said, "in breaking down artificial barriers between the 'initiated' and the 'noninitiated'" and "in making the musical language as accessible to the general understanding and emotion as is the spoken language." He also put forth such educational goals as an understanding of musical forms and participation in ensembles. But the keystone, he said, "is to introduce into the consciousness of listeners the truly spiritual essence of music, which stands high above the level of vulgar amusement and musical diversions." He concluded:

The undying glory of Beethoven and Bach is based not on their technique and skill, which the public neither knows nor understands, but on the great and inexhaustible love for these men. But for such love to be able to arise it is necessary, first of all, that we ourselves do not smoulder like dying embers, but are aflame with sacred love for that which we serve and those whom we serve—that is to say, for living art and living men.

The language may be old-fashioned, but the message holds true at Tanglewood today. "The best in music and the related arts" is a welcoming embrace, not a closed door or an embossed invitation to the elite. *Seid umschlungen, Millionen! Be embraced, ye millions!* Beethoven exults in his Ninth Symphony: *Be embraced, ye millions!* Along with Copland's fanfare it is the perfect theme music for Tanglewood, repeated on ceremonial occasions year after year.

For six decades, despite flirtations with commerce and glitz, Tanglewood has hewed to the Koussevitzky ideal. The bulk of the season—probably 90 percent of it—remains devoted to Beethoven, Bach, and their brethren, both past and present, in performances that are rarely less than professional and sometimes of considerable distinction. (Less Bach now than in Koussevitzky's day, however: modern orchestras have largely ceded that territory to early-music groups.) Even the more popular programs, such as Tanglewood on Parade and an occasional evening of American song by the husband-wife team of soprano Joan Morris and pianist William Bolcom, stand safely "above the level of vulgar amusement." In 1996, during his first Tanglewood residency as the BSO's principal guest conductor, Bernard Haitink unconsciously echoed Koussevitzky, saying that "one should not be too snooty about audiences who applaud between movements. You never know how you will reach them." Though Tanglewood's kind of music requires a certain amount of "introvert feeling" that not everyone has, Haitink said, it "is there for everybody."

Yet the pressures were unrelenting for change, as the orchestra league and NEA studies attested. Pushing on the one side were the new audience, with its expectations of being entertained, and the music industry, with its creation and promotion of stars. Pulling from the other side was a small but vocal assortment of reform forces, including patrons who demanded more audience education programs, especially for children, and critics who yawned at yet another Beethoven Fifth and clamored for more contemporary music. The emergence of a youth brigade of soloists like violinists Midori, Sarah Chang, and Gil Shaham heightened the effect, offering the appearance of change amid a largely unchanging repertory. Meanwhile, the galas and television coverage went on, and every now and then a voice would arise calling for more use of giant video screens such as those that figured in the Bernstein birthday gala and a 1992 showing of the Sergei Eisenstein film *Alexander Nevsky* with the BSO, live, playing Prokofiev's music. Already, the argument ran, there was amplification of music on the lawn (but not in the Shed). Why not video, too? Enhancement of music or sop to the rock generation ("vulgar amusement")? The debate went on.

Not the least of the voices in the debate were the BSO players themselves, who have a direct line—however effective or ineffective—to management through their Players Committee. Most, having spent their lives with the masters, love the classics and resist change in either repertory or concert formats. Most, too, were agreed that jazz stars, now being touted by Seiji Ozawa as a way to bring new blood to the festival, were not the avenue to the future. In an article in the newsletter put out by dissident players, double bassist James Orleans criticized the BSO's 1990s collaborations with jazz pianists Keith Jarrett (in a Mozart concerto) and Marcus Roberts (in *Rhapsody in Blue*) as "plugging celebrity talent from a more popular medium into the same old repertoire." (In the same sentence he was equally critical of "plugging classical celebrities into popular music.") Let the jazzmen do what they do best, he wrote, probably speaking for a BSO majority, and we'll do what we do best—and we'll do it without them.

Orleans probably spoke for a minority, however, when he called for more contemporary music as a way of revitalizing the repertory, audience, and orchestra. Recalling the missionary work done for living composers by Koussevitzky and Munch, who would repeat their works year after year until audiences understood and accepted them, he said that under Ozawa performances of recent works were a "token" gesture, seldom repeated. The criticism reflected the realities of the celebrity milieu in which Ozawa, along with other orchestra directors, moved:

This disposable music syndrome has reached epidemic proportions in the music world. It is a sickness not confined to the BSO, however. It is nationwide. No, worldwide. It is a result of fundamental changes in music directorship that have occurred over the past few decades. Conducting schedules that put the needs of international careers before those of home orchestras (where music directors spend fewer weeks of the season than their predecessors) conspire against building the repertoire. Conductors' dismissive attitude toward what they should be viewing as the repertoire of the future is what is at the root of audience inacceptance of new music.[6]

Any attempt to reform the BSO's summer programming butts up against the rehearsal schedule. It is impossible to adequately prepare more than a handful of new or stylistically unusual works when each program gets only two rehearsals of two and a half hours each. That is also the problem with adding programs for children to the mix. There is no rehearsal or performance time without cutting into the existing schedule at either the BSO or the Music Center, as the Marsalis video project showed. Much of the BSO summer season, in fact, consists of repeats of works performed in Boston during the winter and "reheated" for Tanglewood purposes. The other major barrier to change is the audience. By his own admission Anthony Fogg, the BSO's artistic administrator, faced

a very difficult balance at Tanglewood, because the demands of box office are enormous. There is a large portion of our audience for whom name recognition [of star performers] is a really very significant factor. Let's be honest: to keep this mighty institution going, we do have to draw audiences. It would be foolish of us to think that we could head off and do idealized programming that is going to be attractive only to a select few.

An Australian (and pianist) then in his late thirties, Fogg came on board in 1994 as the eyes-and-ears assistant to the music director in the choice of artists and repertory. Caught in the crosswinds of change, he began introducing gradual programming reforms of his own devising at Tanglewood. These involved a certain amount of new or at least less shopworn repertory, including a modest increase in American music (in both BSO and chamber programs) and a toe in the waters of thematic programming. Fogg also continued a policy of introducing a select group of debut artists and bringing back others, like Robert Shaw, who had not been heard for many years. The

Anthony Fogg. (Walter H. Scott)

celebrated choral conductor's 1996 concert, one of the great moments of the season, paired Stravinsky's *Symphony of Psalms* and Mozart's *Requiem*, the works he had conducted in his only previous Tanglewood program (and BSO debut), forty-eight years earlier. He returned in 1997 to end the season with the Beethoven Ninth.

Fogg had not expected to leave Sydney, where he had a satisfying career as artistic administrator for six symphony orchestras under the umbrella of the Australian Broadcasting Corporation. But when Haas, then the BSO's managing director, phoned in 1994 and asked whether he would be interested in the BSO position, Fogg thought that "if the Boston Symphony actually makes the approach, I've got to take this seriously." He took it seriously enough to pull up his roots and come.

Because planning for a Tanglewood season begins eighteen months in advance, 1996 was the first complete season that Fogg planned in consultation with Ozawa. Fogg's thumbprint showed in a number of thematically designed programs: one of Scandinavian music (conducted by the Estonian

Neeme Järvi), one devoted to music about night, another devoted to works based on Shakespeare, and a weekend exploring late romanticism (Brahms's *German Requiem* and Dvořák's Symphony No. 5) and American and English responses to it (works by Edward MacDowell, Leon Kirchner, Ralph Vaughan Williams, and Edward Elgar). In addition, some warhorse symphonies were replaced by less familiar works by the same composers. These included Brahms's *Serenade No. 1*, Tchaikovsky's *Manfred*, and the Dvořák Fifth.

New ensembles made debuts: the Kirov Orchestra and Chorus from Saint Petersburg (under their director, Valery Gergiev), the gagaku ensemble Reigakusha from Japan, the Tafelmusik Baroque Orchestra from Montreal, and the male chorus Chanticleer from San Francisco. (The Kirov and Reigakusha were shared with the Lincoln Center Festival, which was in its inaugural season in New York.) Notable solo debuts were made by soprano Mitsuko Shirai and the young Norwegian pianist Leif Ove Andsnes. Most of the American works played by the BSO were by figures from the past—MacDowell, Barber, Copland, Gershwin, and Bernstein—but Fogg planned to tip the balance further in future seasons. "This is an American festival," he said, "and I think there should be a greater presence of American music."

The 1997 season was an eleven-week affair that opened with an additional opera, Luigi Rossi's *L'Orfeo*, in the production from the Boston Early Music Festival, and also featured the Handel and Haydn Society Orchestra, a period-instrument ensemble from Boston. Both early-music events brought luster to the season. Yet the overall programming seemed a retreat from the experiments of 1996. The BSO season lacked any attractions like a visiting symphony orchestra or thematically provocative programs. Rather, the programming was built around the two operas (*L'Orfeo* and *Les Mamelles de Tirésias*), Brahms's four symphonies (for the centennial of his death), American music (still in a minority on the programs), and two blockbuster-style popular events via Hollywood and television. In one of these, John Williams conducted the Pops in his music from the *Star Wars* trilogy and other sci-fi films, capitalizing on the twentieth-anniversary rerelease of *Star Wars*. In the other, Itzhak Perlman was featured in an evening of klezmer music with four klezmer bands, capitalizing on his public television show, tour, and compact disc with the same groups.

The *Star Wars* program brought back video screens, deployed both inside and outside the Shed to show montages from the films as Williams conducted the music. At the same time the debate over the propriety of the rock-concert devices in a classical music setting moved forward a step with their first trial at a BSO concert of the classics. The night before *Star Wars* two screens were in place on the outside of the Shed for the lawn audience's viewing at an all-Brahms program. Audience response in questionnaires handed out at the two concerts ran strongly in favor of the screens, but the expense ($40,000 for the two nights) and artistic considerations returned the issue to a BSO study committee. In a year when Tanglewood was moving further into opera and early music, however, it was also thinking about a video-age attraction.

Jessye Norman and Barbara Bonney were back as featured singers, Norman opening the season. Soprano Renée Fleming gave a Tanglewood debut recital, and pianist Ignat Solzhenitsyn, son of former Soviet dissident Alexandr Solzhenitsyn, made an impressive BSO debut. The BSO played two programs of American music—one conducted by Williams, the other by André Previn—but again the emphasis was on composers from the past. Lukas Foss was back to conduct and play the piano for his seventy-fifth birthday, and Yo-Yo Ma repeated his performance of the Bach suites for unaccompanied cello, now spread over two programs.

Along with Berlioz's familiar *Roman Carnival* Overture there was his rarely performed *Te Deum*. Along with the four Brahms symphonies there was the Cello Concerto by composer-in-residence Christopher Rouse, with the always adventurous Yo-Yo Ma as soloist. The Festival of Contemporary Music featured works by Rouse and Sofia Gubaidulina, who spent two weeks in residence. The BSO's Brahms cycle, the nearest thing to thematic programming in the season, dissipated its energy by spreading the symphonies over three weekends and omitting most of the choral and other orchestral works. A series of chamber works in the Friday Prelude Concerts provided stronger continuity.

Thematic programming was nothing new at Tanglewood. Erich Leinsdorf had used it in the 1960s during his years as BSO music director, devoting seasons to surveys of the romantic concerto and the music of Prokofiev and Richard Strauss. More recently Ozawa had built seasons around the works of Stravinsky, Copland (in 1989, in connection with the Music Center's jubilee), and Mozart (for the 1991 Mozart bicentennial). In 1995 there was Ozawa's World War II commemorative weekend, pairing Mahler's *Resurrection* Symphony and the Berlioz *Requiem*. But the season-long surveys, like the Brahms observance, had tended to lose focus by spreading out performances rather than presenting works in clusters. Fogg was trying a different tack, binding together programs or groups of programs through unifying strands in 1996, moving out more into opera and early music in 1997.

This was hardly an assault on the barricades, even by Tanglewood standards. In New York and other musical capitals, thematic programming more typically consists of programs that range off the beaten track to explore the newest styles, forgotten composers, links among composers, or music with literary, graphic arts, or historical associations. With the American Symphony Orchestra in New York City and at his fortnight-long festivals at Bard College in New York state, conductor-educator Leon Botstein was a leading proponent of this marriage of the classroom and concert hall.[7] The Bard Music Festival, held in August, devotes concerts, lectures, and panel discussions each year to a single composer—Brahms, Schumann, Bartók, Ives—and other music defining his place in history.

The BSO would never be the Brooklyn Philharmonic or American Symphony, with their younger, urban audiences, much less a Bard Festival with its mating of scholars with performers. Even if the BSO had wanted or been able to play more new music, concerts in the country and a conservative audience were not fertile grounds for revolution. Thematic links and a gradual increase in American and early music (the early music performed mostly by visiting ensembles) could provide a sense of adventure that more contemporary music couldn't. They might also attract new listeners along with Tanglewood's core over-fifty following. But even with Fogg's changes the bulk of the programming would probably remain a mix-and-match affair drawing on standard works from the eighteenth, nineteenth, and early twentieth centuries.

Much depended on Ozawa. He had done important service for the BSO and Tanglewood in the return of student opera, performances like the Mahler Second, and the attraction of crowds and money. But the upheaval at the Music Center, the Lowe-Eskin letter criticizing him as concerned with trivia during rehearsals, and the Orleans article accusing him of indifference to new music were straws in the wind. Many players saw him as more interested in advancing his own career than improving the orchestra's performances and national standing.

His enthusiasm for jazz brought back Wynton Marsalis and Marcus Roberts in a 1997 black-tie fund-raising gala with the Tanglewood Music Center Orchestra, which Ozawa conducted. (The "Evening of Stars" concert and dinner-dance was part of a campaign to raise $130 million for the BSO by the year 2000. Already $60 million had come in.) The danger was not that jazz or pop would take over Tanglewood. Nobody wanted that, and jazz is an art form with a niche of its own to fill. But wedging jazz into places where it wouldn't fit seemed of a piece with alienating your concertmaster, principal cellist, and faculty, pressurizing your conducting, and hop-scotching to other podiums in Europe and Japan. In expanding his horizons to other orchestras and musical styles, Ozawa appeared to lose touch with some of the strengths of his own orchestra and festival. In this sense jazz became a "vulgar amusement" such as Koussevitzky had warned against.

Yet for all the emphasis on stars and the cultivation of money, the opportunities remained great. The return of opera seemed an example of the festival's Januslike ability to renew itself by looking to the best in its past. With the Pops to handle the lighter repertory and the Boston outreach programs to work toward diversity, Tanglewood could remain within the mainstream charted for it by Koussevitzky, where its greatest strength lay. The audiences were coming, and as the economy improved, corporate money was again plentiful ($60 million toward a $130 million goal is not pennies from the piggy bank). The BSO stood ready to perform well for any conductor who fired its interest, and the contemporary festival provided a forum for new styles and ideas. All Tanglewood and Ozawa had to do—and it was a big order—was to remember Koussevitzky's injunction: to be "aflame with sacred love for that which we serve and those whom we serve—that is to say, for living art and living men."

WHEN THE BSO bought the 120-acre Highwood property, town officials in Stockbridge fretted that the out-of-towners were scheming to turn the prime real estate into a condominium colony.8 When the BSO disclosed plans for a concert hall that would reach sixty-six feet into the Berkshire heavens, the town fathers sounded the alarm over a skyscraper.

Both fears proved misplaced—comically so. Even if the BSO had wanted to get in on the condo boom then engulfing the Berkshires, the condo bust was just around the corner. And though a sixty-six-foot building was a monster for a town that prides itself on its Norman Rockwell heritage, the height was an acoustical necessity, and in any case the building would be far enough inside the grounds to be all but invisible to anyone outside.

Still, the town's concerns were not wholly unreasonable. With many of the region's textile, electrical, and paper mills having fled to low-wage areas in the South and Asia, the Berkshires' manufacturing base had shrunk, and a tourist economy was replacing it. The voice of the bulldozer was heard in the land. In the rolling countryside visible from the Tanglewood lawn, the signs of change were few, thanks partly to the BSO's protective land acquisitions, including Highwood. But within a few miles in nearly every direction, discount outlets, malls, fast-food joints, and home building were on the march. And the houses were not modest Cape or ranch types built for working or merchant Berkshire families. They were the second-home palaces of newcomers, principally from the New York metropolitan area. Like camp followers, entrepreneurs rolled into town behind them, opening upscale shops, inns, and restaurants. Garden-variety tourists swelled the demand for goods and services. The Berkshires were not yet a New England shopper's paradise like Manchester, Vermont, two hours' drive up crowded U.S. Route 7. But in the area's burgeoning malls visitors flocked to buy the same brand-name goods they could buy at the same prices anywhere else in America.

On the verge of the twenty-first century, America had become a society more concerned with comforts, purchases, and pleasures than with the "introvert feeling" in music that Haitink had spoken of. The problem for Tanglewood—for any arts presenter—became how to fit in.

In some respects it was easier in the cities. There young, college-educated audiences, bred on rock but open to new experiences, would give classical music a chance if it somehow connected to the music they already knew or could be seen as part of broad historical or intellectual currents. Nor were all of the young as indifferent to Beethoven's charms as the NEA's attendance figures suggested. Hundreds of passionate seekers clamored to get into the Tanglewood Music Center each summer. The figure could be duplicated at other music festivals and conservatories. Interest also ran high at the better liberal arts colleges, and record, radio, and video listening by the young, as documented in the NEA study, showed a continuing interest. (Also a possible danger: live performances could never match the glossy perfection of a symphony orchestra as captured on a shiny compact disc.)

But Tanglewood, an oasis for young and old alike (even a meeting place for singles) in the early years, now depended primarily on a graying, vacation-oriented audience to keep it in business. Some of the hardcore following of music lovers, wearying of familiar concert fare and traffic jams, had fallen away as season after season presented the standard repertory for ever-larger crowds. Into the breach, in addition to other music lovers, rushed the new listeners drawn by marketing, the Tanglewood mystique, and the Berkshire allure of scenery plus culture: those to whom name recognition was important, those drawn by television, those who wanted concerts with their golf, dining, or shopping, those who were following the crowd, those on tour buses, those seeking something beyond the thrills of rock.

Whatever drew them, wherever they came from, these audiences came to hear the old masters.

Audiences are music's final arbiters. They determine what will live and

Picnics and music: the crowd gathers outside the Shed for a BSO concert. (Walter H. Scott)

what, after a brief flowering, will die. In an impassioned plea for the best of musical culture—jazz and bluegrass as well as symphonies and opera—to be available to the millions beyond the community of music lovers, Gunther Schuller writes in *Musings:*

> *What we need now—in the field of music, at least—is not more artists, more musicians, but an audience that can support our musical institutions, performers, and creative artists and, over the years, cause our musical culture to flourish and to become a part of all Americans' lives, not just a lucky few.*[9]

Underlying the plea was a cruel paradox. Tanglewood and the other schools were turning out more musicians and better-trained musicians than the job market could absorb.

It is not only in the public schools and the home where serious music has been neglected or abandoned. Schuller rightly blames commercial radio and television, the primary teachers of the day, for fostering and exploiting "the public's self-perpetuating cultural illiteracy." He suggests that "even a modest amount of arts programming" by the networks could substantially raise the level of understanding and enjoyment. Since such a scenario is as unlikely as the public's rising up and demanding more arts programming, Schuller urges that musicians get involved, teaching and doing missionary work in the community.

That is a start, and most orchestras, including the BSO, are doing it. But there is only so much lifting by the bootstraps that musicians can do. In the end change is going to have to come from a society that values "the best that has been known and said in the world" (to quote Arnold again). A first step would be a stronger moral force in Washington for the arts and a healthy NEA. Despite Jimmy Carter's love of classical music and Bill Clinton's call for adequate NEA funding in his 1997 budget message, not since John F. Kennedy's administration has the nation had a government that made poetry, symphonies, and paintings a measure of a nation's greatness. As long as politicians see profit in making artists and the arts scapegoats for such genuine problems as racial divisions, poverty, and an overreliance on arms, cultural illiteracy will find encouragement. Campaign reform might be one of the best friends music could have. Beyond that the solutions will be the same as for society's other moral and cultural ailments. They will come—if they come at all—in a pendulum swing away from the tin gods of consumerism and popular culture and back toward the humane values embodied in the school, the church, and the concert hall.

The masterworks of the past live because they speak to people in a profound and enduring way. They have what Koussevitzky, Louis Krasner, Yo-Yo Ma, and many other musicians have described as—and most listeners sense as—a spiritual dimension. The newer works championed by such groups as Bang on a Can have the jangle of the city street, the hum of the computer, the buzz of the mall, the howl of the rock coliseum. There is no reason why a new Mozart could not come along and turn these raw materials into art; John Adams seems perpetually on the verge of doing it in his operas and other postminimalist works. But except among new-music audiences these works do not speak to the public as the old masters do, nor does it seem likely that they will. When the BSO plays a challenging contemporary work at Tanglewood, it is careful to put it on the first half of the program and follow it in the second half with an audience pleaser. The alternative is to risk an exodus at intermission, if not a failure at the box office. In 1988, for example, Henze's apocalyptic Seventh Symphony was followed by Yo-Yo Ma in the Dvořák Cello Concerto—despite all of Dvořák's charms and Ma's skills, one of the great anticlimaxes in the annals of orchestral programming. The audience swallowed the new work like a dose of medicine and grumbled during intermission.

Instead of more contemporary music, the Ozawa era has brought a steady expansion in other areas: more concerts, more visiting artists and ensembles, more cars, more amenities, more crowds. Ozawa's wish for an American Salzburg with an international ambiance and roster of artists has largely come to pass. (Paradoxically, post-Karajan Salzburg was becoming more adventurous in programming just as Tanglewood was acquiring more of a Salzburg veneer.) Camera-laden Japanese tourists stroll the grounds singly and in tour groups, and European languages can be heard on all sides. These and other visitors come because at Tanglewood they can hear the core repertory played by a leading orchestra. For many listeners the old standbys are still virgin or largely unexplored territory. For others they are the heart and soul of music, which means the heart and soul of life itself.

The hunger for the older values is real. It can be seen in the appeal of fundamentalist religion, the pieties of such lay prophets as William Bennett, and an underlying dissatisfaction with pop culture even as that culture grips the public imagination. The orchestra league's urgings of a more popular (or at least populist) repertory miss the point. New listeners may indeed come for a night to hear a rock band or gospel choir with their hometown orchestra, but the only thing that will bring those listeners back night after night is a responsiveness to serious music and the values it embodies. As Evans Mirageas suggested, you can paint almond eyes on the *Mona Lisa* to give her an Asian look—but then you no longer have the *Mona Lisa*. That is not to say that changes to make the concert hall a more welcoming place are a waste of time. Philip Glass and jazz at the Brooklyn Academy will do as nicely as the Pops at Tanglewood. But it is impossible to strengthen and cheapen the arts at the same time. There comes a point at which a line must be drawn.

All the horror stories of Tanglewood—the galas, the television, the traffic jams, the money, the glitz—can also be read as signs of hope. Whatever brings people to Tanglewood, they experience great music in a setting of great natural beauty and can go home feeling cleansed by the "creative rest" that Koussevitzky envisioned at the founding. The old masters, Tanglewood's stock in trade, satisfy a human need expressed in earlier times in cave drawings and medieval cathedrals. Perhaps in time the new masters like Henze, Harbison, and Dutilleux will be understood to express similar yearnings. The music of all these composers, from Bach through Dutilleux, engages the mind and heart at the highest level, and the BSO and Tanglewood management understands this fundamental truth even if Washington doesn't.

Tanglewood, then, embodies both the worst and the best aspects of American musical life at the end of the twentieth century: the commerce, the celebrity hunting, and the confusion between art and entertainment, yet also the humane tradition, the search for values, the preservation of the best of the past. In that, Tanglewood mirrors the larger dichotomies in the American soul: the yearnings for the old verities of beauty, permanence, and—to use Bernstein's word—nobility amid the junk and clutter perpetuated in everyday life. For thousands of people, some of whom may not even know what they are seeking, Tanglewood offers a place where the glories of music and nature combine to evoke timeless values rather than the day's fads and sensations.

To end the 1994 inaugural for Seiji Ozawa Hall, the conductor for whom it had been named led the audience and musicians in singing Randall Thompson's *Alleluia*. The five-minute a cappella anthem provided a fitting closure for a three-hour program celebrating not just a $9.7 million concert facility but also the Tanglewood experience. Ever since the founding of the Music Center in 1940, the student body has sung the *Alleluia* to conclude the school's opening exercises, those ceremonies at which Koussevitzky, Bernstein, Schuller, and Fleisher have stood up in turn and spoken for the highest ideals of their art.

The route to the end of the concert had sometimes been torturous. The weather was like a hot breath from the tropics, with thunder racketing through architect Rawn's room for music. The performances, though never less than celebratory, were variable in quality, and the music, nearly all of it with Tanglewood associations, added up to the kind of hodgepodge deemed appropriate for such institutional housewarmings. But when Ozawa threw himself into the *Alleluia* with a passion, it became more than a Music Center signature piece. It evoked a half-century of dedication to music by performers, teachers, students, volunteers, and patrons, who had paid for the hall and filled most of its seats. Whatever had divided these disparate groups before—whether wealth, age, professions, musical skills, or social status— was forgotten for the moment in the rededication to a shared art.

Tanglewood would never be the same afterward. That everyone knew. The Theater-Concert Hall—scene of Koussevitzky's speeches, the *Peter Grimes* premiere, other notable first performances, Bernstein's sessions with students, Yo-Yo Ma's Bach marathon, Ozawa's beginnings, and those of innumerable other musicians, famous and obscure—was dark: closed for an indefinite time. The new hall looked and sounded a hundred times better, but Koussevitzky's school had left his campus and concert hall to take up residence in what was, in Koussevitzky's day, uncharted territory. A link with the past was broken. Yet, strangely, it was not broken at all. Instead, a new link, one to be consummated with the rebirth of opera, was forged around it.

Tanglewood had changed, but it remained itself, rooted in the rocky New England soil that had also been home to Emerson, Thoreau, Melville, and—

just across the road—Hawthorne. In the cities fads would come and go. In the countryside malls would bring the latest goods. People streamed to Tanglewood to see the miracle of the new concert hall. But they also streamed to experience the enduring miracle of Tanglewood, the symbol of permanence in a throwaway world.

Notes

U NLESS OTHERWISE IDENTIFIED, all quotations in this book are from interviews or reporting by the author. Notes on other sources follow.

Chapter 1. A Shot Fired across the Bow

1. Katharine Whittemore, "Bill Rawn's Room for Music," *Boston Globe Magazine*, July 10, 1994.

2. Ibid.

3. Eliel Saarinen also provided the original design for the Shed, but when the cost came in too high for the Berkshire committee of festival sponsors, it called in a local engineer, Joseph Franz, to modify the plans. The principal change was the use of steel columns inside to support the roof.

4. The following account of the planning and construction of the hall is adapted from "In Search of a 'Perfect' Concert Hall," an essay by the author appearing in *Seiji Ozawa Hall: A Room for Music*, an unpaged book published in 1994 by the Boston Symphony Orchestra to commemorate the opening of the hall.

5. Robert Campbell, "Creating a 'New' Tanglewood," in *Seiji Ozawa Hall: A Room for Music*.

6. Edward Rothstein, "Tanglewood, Changed but the Same," *New York Times*, July 9, 1994.

7. Peter G. Davis, "Splendor in the Grass," *New York*, July 25, 1994.

Chapter 2. The Complete Music Director

1. Rock concerts, since discontinued because of problems of crowd control, went over the 20,000 mark during the Woodstock era of the 1960s and 1970s.

2. A damning picture of Wilford's use of Ozawa, and of Wilford's imperial ways with musicians and concert presenters in general, appears in Norman Lebrecht's book *Who Killed Classical Music?* (New York: Carol, 1997).

3. *Counterpoint*, a newsletter published by "musicians of the Boston Symphony Orchestra," July 31, 1995.

4. Bernard Holland, "The Decline and Fall of the Classical Empire," *New York Times*, November 10, 1996.

5. Philip Hart, *Conductors: A New Generation* (New York: Scribner, 1979), p. 165.

6. Charles A. Radin and Mugi Hanao, "Ozawa Conducts Japan's Best," *Boston Sunday Globe*, January 22, 1995.

7. Ibid.
8. The Wilford-Gelb nexus is scathingly described in Lebrecht's *Who Killed Classi-cal Music?*

Chapter 3. The Riderless Horse

1. Leonard Bernstein, *Findings* (New York: Simon and Schuster, 1982), p. 320.
2. The letter is quoted in Burton Bernstein's *Family Matters* (New York: Summit Books, 1982), p. 137.
3. Bernstein, "Of Tanglewood, Koussevitzky, and Hope," in *Findings*, pp. 273–84; the description of Koussevitzky appears on pp. 273–74.
4. James Orleans, "Brahms: Breaking the Fetters," in *Sennets & Tuckets*, a Bern-stein *Festschrift* (Boston: Boston Symphony Orchestra, 1988), p. 176.
5. Alsop's description of her concert first appeared in *New York Newsday* on Octo-ber 17, 1990. It was reprinted in *Prelude, Fugue, & Riffs*, a newsletter of the Leonard Bernstein Society, autumn 1991.
6. At his 1988 Tanglewood press conference Bernstein said, "I know that to do a really good performance, I have to feel I wrote the piece." He made up the music onstage "as if it had never been heard of before."
7. The account of Bernstein's concerts and physical collapse in Japan is taken from Humphrey Burton's *Leonard Bernstein* (New York: Doubleday, 1994), pp. 516–20.
8. Burton recounts a comical scene at the concert's end, when the royal couple did not recognize their cue to leave ahead of the rest of the audience and Bern-stein had to wave good-bye to them to move them out.
9. Ibid., p. 519.
10. Richard Dyer, "Bernstein Comes Home to Tanglewood," *Boston Globe*, August 14, 1990.
11. Burton, *Leonard Bernstein*, p. 521.
12. Bernstein, *Findings*, p. 274.
13. Ibid., p. 276.

Chapter 4. Bearers of the Torch

1. Richard Dyer, "Spirit of Christmas Pops May Be Past," *Boston Globe*, December 18, 1996.
2. Geraldine Fabrikant, "A Virtuoso Who Plays It Safe," *New York Times*, October 22, 1996.
3. K. Robert Schwarz, "How to Succeed at Success," *New York Times*, October 2, 1988.
4. Alfred Brendel, *Music Sounded Out* (New York: Farrar, Straus & Giroux, 1990), p. 206.

5. Ibid., p. 207.
6. Krasner recounted his European career and association with Berg in "The Origins of Berg's Violin Concerto," *Keynote*, October 1983, pp. 18–23. The quotation about twelve-tone music appears on p. 20.

Chapter 5. Intruders in the Temple

1. Gunther Schuller, "Toward a New Classicism?" in *Musings* (New York: Oxford University Press, 1986), p. 181.
2. Lloyd Schwartz, "Hard-won Directness," *Atlantic*, March 1984, p. 118.
3. Andrew L. Pincus, "For Henze Now, a Life in Harmony," *New York Times*, July 31, 1988.
4. Ibid.
5. K. Robert Schwarz, "Pop Goes the Music—Classical, Too," *New York Times*, January 20, 1991.

Chapter 6. Grasping an Octopus

1. Arturo Toscanini had conducted the American radio premiere with the NBC Symphony in July 1942. The Tanglewood performance attracted Russian ambassador Maxim Litvinoff and Crown Princess Juliana of the Netherlands as well as widespread public attention.
2. Boris Goldovsky, *My Road to Opera* (Boston: Houghton Mifflin, 1979), p. 347.
3. Humphrey Carpenter, *Benjamin Britten* (New York: Scribner, 1991), p. 240.
4. Olin Downes, "Britten's 'Grimes' Unveiled at Lenox," *New York Times*, August 7, 1946.
5. John Briggs, "Britten's 'Peter Grimes' Hits You between the Eyes," *New York Post*, August 7, 1946.
6. In Herbert Kupferberg's history *Tanglewood* (New York: McGraw-Hill, 1976), Goldovsky remembers Price's arrival this way: "She impressed us all right off. She was skeptical of her chances, but I pushed her into the opera. Tanglewood always was the haven of the black singer. They acted, sang, and worked alongside the whites from the very start" (p. 151).
7. Erich Leinsdorf, *Cadenza: A Musical Career* (Boston: Houghton Mifflin, 1976), p. 217.
8. Andrew L. Pincus, *Scenes from Tanglewood* (Boston: Northeastern University Press, 1989), p. 215.
9. Another sign of Ozawa's infatuation with stars occurred when he wanted to use the professionals from the Saito Kinen cast, including Barbara Bonney in the role of Anne Trulove, as the principals in the student production. The faculty talked him out of it.

Chapter 7. The Selling of a Festival

1. The BSO received an additional $1 million per year in 1996 and 1997 from the Massachusetts Office of Travel and Tourism in support of the "Evening at Pops" concerts and telecasts.

2. Pincus, *Scenes from Tanglewood*, p. 128.

3. To give players a greater role in running the orchestra and thus improve morale, the Milwaukee Symphony Orchestra in 1994 allotted them two ex-officio positions on the board and one each on the executive committee and other standing committees, as well as places on search committees for music and executive directors.

4. There is a distinction to be drawn between artist managers, who are in the business of promoting their clients, and symphony orchestra managers, who must hire guest conductors and soloists from those rosters. The former have an interest in selling at the highest possible fees (from which they take commissions). The latter will bargain for a musician at fees they can afford.

5. David Blum, "A Process Larger Than Oneself," *New Yorker*, May 1, 1989, p. 64.

Chapter 8. Be Embraced, Ye Millions!

1. National Endowment for the Arts, *Age and Arts Participation* (Santa Ana, Calif.: Seven Locks Press, 1996).

2. Opera America, the national service organization for opera companies, reported a 10 percent increase in attendance from the 1993–94 season to 1994–95, the latest year for which figures were available; attendance totaled 7.1 million in the later year (*Quick Opera Facts*, a newsletter published in December 1996). Citing NEA figures, Opera America also reported a 25 percent increase in attendance between 1982 and 1992.

3. NEA, *Age and Arts Participation*, p. 5.

4. Edward Rothstein, "The Tribulations of the Not-So-Living Arts," *New York Times*, February 18, 1996.

5. Joseph Horowitz, *The Post-Classical Predicament* (Boston: Northeastern University Press, 1995), pp. 201–2.

6. James Orleans, "Revitalizing the Art," *Counterpoint*, January 28, 1997.

7. Yet Botstein did not despair of the orchestra's survival. In the summer 1996 edition of the *Musical Quarterly*, which he edits, he wrote that the orchestra's potential "as a primary instrument of education directed at adults and young people has been wildly underestimated and underutilized. . . . The first step is for management and conductors to abandon their siege mentality and desperate search for a quick fix" (p. 193).

8. Although Tanglewood uses a Lenox mailing address, most of the land is actually in the adjoining town of Stockbridge.

9. Schuller, *Musings*, p. 271.

Index